Oscar Wilde
The Importance of Being Irish

Oscar Wilde
The Importance of Being Irish

DAVIS COAKLEY

Town House, Dublin

Published in 1994 by
Town House and Country House
Trinity House
Charleston Road
Ranelagh
Dublin 6
Ireland

A CIP catalogue record for this book is available from the British Library

ISBN: 0-948524-97-9

Cover: *Photograph of Oscar Wilde from an album that once belonged to Lady Augusta Gregory (Courtesy of Colin Smythe)*

Cover design: Bill Murphy
Printed in Ireland by Betaprint

For my sons
Peter, Stephen, John Davis and James

Acknowledgements

I am most grateful to Merlin Holland, Oscar Wilde's grandson, for the interest he has shown in my work and for agreeing to write a foreword to the book. Professor Jim Malone and Professor Denis Weaire both read the text and made very constructive suggestions. I am particularly grateful to Mary O'Doherty, archivist, Royal College of Surgeons in Ireland; Robert Mills, librarian, Royal College of Physicians of Ireland; Stuart O'Seanóir and Áine Keegan, librarians, Trinity College Dublin; Noel Kissane, librarian, National Library of Ireland; Michael Bott, archivist, Reading University, and John Bidwell, archivist, The William Andrew Clark Memorial Library, Los Angeles. Robert Bennett, headmaster, Portora Royal School, made helpful suggestions which improved my chapter on his school. David Smyth, Department of Medical Illustrations, St James's Hospital, Dublin, patiently responded to my requests. I also wish to thank Seamus Heaney, Maurice O'Connell, Olga Rowe, Peter Walsh, Walter Nelson, Keith Schuchard, Bobby Fong, Joy Melville, Brian Kennedy, Adrian Le Harivel, Marcella Senior, Marie de Montfort Supple, Colin Smythe and Bridie Graham.

I am grateful to the following institutions for permission to reproduce extracts from manuscript material in their possession: William Andrews Clark Library (Lady Wilde's letters, Oscar Wilde's Trinity College notebooks and L C Purser's letters to A J A Symons); Oxford University Press and John Murray Ltd (extracts from Oscar and Lady Wilde's letters, © the Estate of Oscar Wilde; the University of Reading (Lady Wilde's letters), and The National Library of Ireland (letters of Lady Wilde and of William Rowan Hamilton).

I am particularly indebted to Gay Williams, my secretary, who patiently worked with me through various drafts of the book. Finally, I thank my wife Mary, my most exacting critic, who read the manuscript several times and improved it in many ways.

Contents

List of Illustrations

Foreword

UNTIL ABOUT FIFTEEN YEARS AGO there seemed to be a very real danger that Oscar Wilde's reputation was ossifying. The public appeared quite happy with its view of him as a clever writer of comedies, some children's stories, a poem or two and a Gothic novel. He was the undisputed master of the witty one-liner and the king of paradox. Add to this an endlessly fascinating, flamboyant lifestyle as well as a newly imposed role as first martyr to the gay cause and the picture was complete. Or was it becoming a caricature? A sympathetic one, certainly, but without any great depth. He was not really a subject for serious study. He lacked the necessary gravitas.

This did not, however, deter a growing number of academics from probing beneath Wilde's superficial brilliance in an attempt to reassess him. Letters, previously regarded as being of marginal interest both to biographer and literary critic, assumed new significance when used to interpret his life as a working journalist. Notebooks kept by Wilde at Oxford threw much new light on his intellectual development and his early reading. Yet there is one area of study that has been almost entirely neglected — the lifelong effect on Wilde of his Irish background.

My grandfather spent the first twenty years of his life in his native country. Even after he had gone up to Oxford he returned regularly to Dublin and to the two family properties in the west. By the time he had reached his formative years his mother's nationalist energies had been channelled into hosting a salon at 1 Merrion Square for some of the keenest minds in Dublin, which did nothing if not prepare him for his conquest of London Society in the 1880s. Nor could he have remained uninfluenced by both his parents' remarkable knowledge of the customs, traditions, antiquities and history of Ireland.

But Wilde's Irishness does not manifest itself in his work in the same overt way as a writer like Joyce. It comes more subtly in nuances of style, or in the elements of an Irish oral tradition, or in people and events half-remembered from an Irish childhood. As a result he has been more frequently classified, particularly on the Continent, as an English writer. It is a mistake which Davis Coakley argues eloquently to correct, showing just how deeply the Irish element pervades nearly every aspect of Wilde's life as well as his work.

Once you are alerted to the fact it becomes an addictive game of detection, as I discovered this summer in Connemara. On an afternoon scrubbed crystal clear by the morning's rain I climbed to the top of Mweelrea. You could see to the edge of the world in the watercolour light unique to the Atlantic coasts of Scotland and Ireland. Lough Fee, with Wilde's old fishing lodge, reflected polished silver from the grey clouds and the Benna Beola rose behind, neither blue nor purple yet both. 'How could I get to you? The purple of the mountains and the silver of the rivers divide us', wrote Wilde sadly, excusing himself to an old friend who had invited him to stay in 1899, and suddenly it was at my feet, no longer a contrived piece of prose but an image probably dredged up from memories of youth in County Mayo.

This book by Davis Coakley is part of the vital process of keeping Wilde's reputation on the move. It is a view of his creative genius that has not been attempted before and, erudite and eminently readable at the same time, it is bound to encourage lovers of Wilde's work to start their reassessment of him as one of the nineteenth century's most charismatic writers.

Merlin Holland

Introduction

. . . it must not be forgotten that though by culture Wilde was a citizen of all civilised capitals, he was at root a very Irish Irishman, and as such, a foreigner everywhere but in Ireland.[1]

George Bernard Shaw

ALTHOUGH IT IS A HUNDRED years since his works were first published, Oscar Wilde remains one of the most widely read Irish writers. He has been classified as an Anglo-Irish writer by literary scholars, placed at the 'Anglo' end of the spectrum, and is often only grudgingly included in anthologies of Anglo-Irish literature. This is ironical, as Wilde always described himself as either Irish or Celtic. This neglect of Wilde by academia was not confined to Ireland. It is only in fairly recent times that literary historians have given Wilde the scholarly attention he deserves, and as a result there has been a significant revaluation of the playwright's importance. It is now appreciated that Wilde was 'thoroughly engaged with some of the most important social, cultural, political and intellectual issues of his age'.[2]

I first became interested in Oscar Wilde's Irish years through my research on his father.[3] William Wilde was one of a group of remarkable physicians and surgeons who put Dublin medicine on the centre stage of international medicine in the last century. Most of these men lived in stately Georgian homes on Merrion Square, and they formed the nucleus of a unique cultural environment. They were familiar with contemporary English literature and their visitors would have included such notable figures as Walter Scott and Thomas Carlyle. It was taken for granted that they all had a good classical education. They had regular contact with continental Europe, and many of them had spent time studying there. A number of them, including Oscar's father, were pioneers of the Celtic Revival, a movement that revitalised interest in Gaelic literature and

1

art. They entertained regularly, and wit and paradox were particularly highly prized in a society that valued good conversation. This was the environment in which Oscar Wilde grew up, and its importance in the life and work of the playwright has been underestimated and poorly understood.

The fact that Wilde left Ireland in his early twenties and returned only on two occasions has been used to argue that the writer rejected his native country. Wilde's exile, however, unlike that of James Joyce, was not designed to be symbolic. Wilde rarely returned to Ireland for the simple reason that his father had died and his mother had moved to London, and as a consequence the family base was no longer in Dublin. Wilde has been accused of not drawing on traditional Irish themes for his inspiration, but this was in part due to his desire to distance himself from the 'stage Irish' plays that were very popular at the time. It is generally believed that Wilde took little interest in Irish affairs, and one of his first biographers wrote that 'although Oscar Wilde never denied his nationality, he took particular care not to let it transpire'.[4] Yet letters and contemporary records of his conversations show that he was a consistent supporter of Home Rule for Ireland, and of the movement's leader, Charles Stewart Parnell. Wilde also admired the Land League leader Michael Davitt, who spent many years in prison for his campaign on behalf of tenant rights; Wilde's essay *The Soul of Man under Socialism* outlines a philosophy that Davitt would not have faulted. When Anglo-Irish tensions increased during the 1880s, Wilde openly supported Parnell, and he criticised English policies on Ireland in a number of reviews. When the Irish writer Shane Leslie suggested in the New York *Evening Post* in 1917 that Oscar Wilde neglected Ireland for England, he provoked a sharp response from the Irish-American novelist Vincent O'Sullivan, who had known Wilde in Paris. 'If he is speaking for Ireland when he says that England can keep Wilde's prose,' O'Sullivan wrote, 'then he is speaking for Ireland grown very smug and foolish . . . . Oscar Wilde's genius was essentially and ineradicably Irish.'[5]

The early chapters of this book describe the influence that Wilde's parents and their associates had on him. Sir William and Lady Wilde shared a love of learning, and their son inherited this trait from them. Wilde was particularly influenced by his mother, and he shared many of her characteristics and eccentricities – her love of conversation and of flamboyant clothes and her horror of old age. It was from her that he developed his lifelong interest in Roman Catholicism. A considerable part of the book is devoted to Wilde's early years in Dublin and the west of Ireland, where the foundation for his future brilliance was formed. Through the scholarship of his parents and his holidays in the west of Ireland, Wilde became familiar with the oral tradition of the Celts. He was also steeped in the literary traditions of his native city, which had produced such great Irish writers as Jonathan Swift, Richard Brinsley Sheridan and Charles Robert Maturin. From both these traditions and from his wide reading in European and classical literature, Wilde constructed his own literary synthesis.

I have drawn on previously unpublished material to present a new picture of Wilde's school years at Portora Royal School in Enniskillen, County Fermanagh. From Portora, Oscar went to Trinity College Dublin, where he came under the influence of John Pentland Mahaffy and where he began to develop his interest in aestheticism. When Oscar left Trinity for Oxford, he already had most of the characteristics that would later distinguish him in London. Throughout his subsequent career, Wilde maintained a far greater interest in Irish literary and political affairs than has generally been assumed. His own literary achievements gave confidence to other Irish writers, and he had a direct influence on Irish playwrights and poets such as W B Yeats and J M Synge.

This book demonstrates unequivocally that Wilde's formative years in Ireland left a significant imprint on his writing. I hope it will increase the enjoyment of those reading or listening to Wilde's works by giving them a deeper understanding of the early influences that shaped the man and his work.

CHAPTER 1

Sir William and Lady Wilde

I should like so much to have the privilege of introducing you to my mother – all brilliant people should cross each other's cycles, like some of the nicest planets.[1]

Oscar Wilde

Wilde's father was certainly a knight; but heaven alone knows who his grandfather was.[2]

Alfred Douglas

OSCAR WILDE'S PARENTS, William and Jane Francesca Wilde, were remarkable people. In the nineteenth century, when men of ability often excelled in a number of fields, William Wilde's achievements were regarded as exceptional, and in an age not noted for its opportunities for women, Jane Francesca Wilde played a prominent role in the political and cultural life of Ireland. Yet their reputations suffered greatly after their deaths. Their eccentricities were highlighted and their faults exaggerated by biographers in an attempt to explain or to mitigate their son's behaviour. Oscar Wilde wrote in *De Profundis* that his parents had bequeathed him a name 'they had made noble and honoured' and that he had 'disgraced that name eternally'.[3] He was wrong, as in recent years more considered and scholarly judgements are helping to restore them to their rightful place in history.

JANE FRANCESCA WILDE – REVOLUTIONARY AND POET

Oscar Wilde's mother was better known by her pseudonym 'Speranza'. She was the daughter of Charles Elgee, an attorney who was based originally at 8 Essex Bridge and later at 6 Leeson Street, Dublin. She liked to infer that the Elgee family was a branch of a noble Italian family whose name derived from the Alighieri family, and in this way she established family ties with the famous Italian poet Dante Alighieri. One suspects that she did not expect her audience to take these stories too literally, and the truth was much more prosaic. Her great-grandfather, Charles Elgee, born at Staindrop, County Durham, in 1714, was a bricklayer by trade, and his family had been living in the area for years.

Charles Elgee moved with his brother William to Dundalk, County Louth, around 1730, where they prospered as builders. William was commissioned to build the court-house in Dundalk and Charles built a residence in the town, known as Cumberland Castle, later number 1 Francis Street. As a consequence of this new affluence, Charles and his wife Alice were able to send their son John, the sixth of their eight children, to Trinity College Dublin. John, Jane's grandfather, became a clergyman, and he was eventually appointed rector of Wexford and archdeacon of Leighlin. In 1782 he married a daughter of Cadwallader Waddy of Wexford, and they had seven children. Their eldest child, Charles, who was an attorney in Dublin, was born in Wexford in 1783.[4] In 1809 Charles married Sarah Kingsbury. Their eldest child, Emily Thomasine, married an army officer, Captain Samuel Warren, and they lived in England. Their second son, John, followed a successful legal career in Louisiana and he played a prominent part in the American Civil War on the Confederate side. The third child died in infancy. The fourth and youngest, Jane Francesca, was Oscar Wilde's mother.

Although Speranza invented a few extra flourishes for her Elgee ancestry, this expedient was not necessary on the Kingsbury side, as they were a well-established Dublin family. Speranza's great-grandfather Thomas Kingsbury was a leading Dublin physician, a friend of Jonathan Swift and president of the Royal College of Physicians of Ireland in 1736 and 1744. Her grandfather Thomas was a commissioner of bankruptcy. One of Speranza's aunts, Elizabeth Kingsbury, married a baronet, Sir Charles Montagu Ormsby. Another aunt, Henrietta Kingsbury, married the writer Charles

Maturin. Speranza and Oscar were always very proud of this literary connection. Speranza was very young when her famous uncle died yet she was well aware of his literary achievements and of the unusual lifestyle that he and her aunt led.

Charles Maturin was born in Dublin in 1780 of Huguenot stock. After studies at Trinity College he was ordained a clergyman in 1803, and the following year he married Henrietta Kingsbury. He served as curate to St Peter's Parish in Dublin. Maturin wrote several books and plays and he became one of the leading exponents of the horror-fantasy tale. 'If I possess any talent,' he once said, 'it is that of darkening the gloomy, and of developing the sad; of painting life in extremes, and representing those struggles of passion when the soul trembles on the verge of the unlawful and the unhallowed.'[5]

Maturin had a passion for dancing and he spent a considerable part of most days practising. A contemporary wrote: 'He was the first in the quadrille – the last to depart. The ballroom was his temple of inspiration and worship.'[6] One day he would dress as a dandy in the height of fashion with pantaloons and a tight, well-fitting coat, the next day he might be seen dressed as a preacher in worn, shabby clothes. When they entertained guests, the window shutters were closed and candles were lit, even on bright sunny days, a practice that Speranza would emulate in later years. Maturin made some money from his literary work, but he never became a rich man. Yet he and Henrietta could be very extravagant, a quality that Oscar Wilde also displayed. After the success of one of Maturin's plays, he redecorated his house in York Street and invited friends to a series of lavish parties. On another occasion when he received £50 from a friend during a period of financial hardship, he and Henrietta spent all the money on a magnificent party, at which Henrietta welcomed the guests while seated upon a throne.[7]

The Gothic novel *Melmoth the Wanderer*, which was published in 1820, was Maturin's masterpiece. It was admired by Scott, Rossetti, Baudelaire and Thackeray and it was seen as a rival to Mary Shelley's *Frankenstein*, which had appeared in 1818. It tells the story of a man named Melmoth who was born in the seventeenth century and who purchased 150 years of life without ageing in exchange for his immortal soul. Maturin describes Melmoth's search for someone to share his fate in a hopeless bid to cancel his contract. In the autumn of 1816 Melmoth's time was drawing to a close, so he returned to his ancestral home in Wicklow, where he found his brother's descendant, a young student of Trinity College Dublin named John Melmoth. Melmoth the Wanderer felt his doom approaching, and shortly before his death his youthful features disappeared: 'the lines of extreme age were visible in every feature. His hairs were as white as snow, his mouth had fallen in, the muscles of his face were relaxed and withered – he was the very image of hoary decrepit debility.'[8] Maturin describes how John Melmoth found a sinister portrait of his mysterious ancestor in a locked closet:

> There was a great deal of decayed and useless lumber, such as might be supposed to be heaped up to rot in a miser's closet; but John's eyes were in a moment, and as if by magic, rivetted on a portrait that hung on the wall, and appeared, even to his untaught eye, far superior to the tribe of family pictures that are left to moulder on the walls of family mansions. It represented a man of middle age. There was nothing remarkable in the costume, or in the countenance, but *the eyes*, John felt were such as one feels they wish they had never seen, and feels they can never forget.[9]

The young Melmoth visited the closet again, and each time he was convinced that the eyes of the portrait were following him, so he resolved to destroy it:

> After a few moments, he raised himself with an involuntary start, and saw the picture gazing at him from its canvas . . . . He seized it; – his hand shook at first, but the mouldering canvas appeared to assist him in the effort. He tore it from the frame with a cry half terrific, half triumphant; – it fell at his feet, and he shuddered as it fell. He expected to hear some fearful sounds, some unimaginable breathings of prophetic horror, follow this act of sacrilege, for such he felt it, to tear the portrait of his ancestor from his native walls.[10]

This dramatic scene finds an echo in the climax of Oscar Wilde's only novel, *The Picture of Dorian Gray,* when Dorian stabs the portrait and a cry is heard 'so horrible in its agony that the frightened servants woke, and crept out of their rooms'.[11] Wilde was greatly influenced by Maturin's work, and he reveals his own fascination with the dark side of life throughout this novel. There are many similarities between Dorian and Melmoth – they both have their youth prolonged, and they are both in the relentless grip of sinister and evil forces. Wilde's preoccupation with the supernatural and macabre is also apparent in other works, such as *Salomé* and 'The Sphinx', and in his short stories *The Canterville Ghost, Lord Arthur Savile's Crime* and *The Fisherman and His Soul.*

The Elgee and Kingsbury families had unionist leanings, and like many of their class they felt threatened by the mass movement for Catholic Emancipation led by Daniel O'Connell, which was taking place around the time of Speranza's birth. Following the granting of Catholic Emancipation in 1829, O'Connell concentrated his efforts on repealing the union between the parliaments of Great Britain and Ireland. Here his progress was less spectacular, and in 1842 a new movement, Young Ireland, emerged on the political scene, led by idealists like Thomas Osborne Davis, Charles Gavan Duffy and John Blake Dillon. They founded a paper entitled *The Nation* which was edited by Gavan Duffy. Their nationalism developed from the liberal philosophy of eighteenth-century Irish republicans such as Wolfe Tone and from the romantic nationalism of contemporary Europe. They wished to create a nation where all Irish men and women could live in mutual harmony, irrespective of creed or class, and they gave their ideology a particularly Irish flavour by steeping it in the myths and traditions of the country's Gaelic past. The Young Ireland movement, by fostering Irish genius and ability, attracted many middle-class Protestants and Catholics into its ranks. Davis, a Protestant who had been educated in Trinity College Dublin, was the central figure in the movement. He wrote some stirring nationalistic poems and articles which were published in *The Nation.*

Jane Elgee was influenced by this idealism, and she soon became an enthusiastic supporter of the Young Irelanders. As with many other episodes in her life, there are several versions of her 'conversion' to the nationalist cause. Oscar Wilde, as might be expected, gave a highly embellished account:

> The other poetess of this movement was a young girl who had been brought up in an atmosphere of alien English thought, among people high in bench and senate and far removed from any love or knowledge of those wrongs of the people to which she afterwards gave such passionate expression. And one day in 1845, standing at the window of her lordly home, she saw a great funeral pass in its solemn trappings of sorrow down the street and followed by a crowd of men and women in bitter and unrestrained grief. Wondering much what man had died whom the people so loved, she asked who it was they were burying and learned it was the funeral of one Thomas Davis, a poet of whom till then she had never heard. That evening she bought and read his poems and knew for the first time the meaning of the word country.[12]

At the time of this moving account Speranza was living with her mother in rented rooms on Lower Leeson Street, in a house that could not be described as lordly, and the street was not on the route of Davis's funeral procession – Wilde never allowed facts or details to compromise a good story. The poet W B Yeats gave a slightly different version of the same story when he recalled that Lady Wilde had told him of how she came upon the funeral of Thomas Davis unexpectedly when walking through a Dublin street: 'She was so struck to find so many people honouring a poet and one she had never heard of, that she turned Nationalist and wrote those energetic rhymes my generation read in its youth.'[13] Speranza told a reporter that she first became interested in the Young Ireland movement when she read a book of nationalist poetry called *The Spirit of the Nation*. First published in 1843, it contained the most popular songs and ballads that had appeared in *The Nation*, and was edited by Thomas Davis. A more ambitious second edition appeared in 1845. Speranza appears to have been greatly influenced by the book and within a short time she found that 'all the literature of Irish songs and sufferings had an enthralling interest for me. Then it was that I discovered that I could write poetry'.[14]

Speranza's father died when she was very young, but her mother ensured that she received a good education. She was familiar with Greek and the classics, and she also mastered German, Italian and French. This erudition is reflected in her contributions to *The Nation*, which began to appear early in 1846. She submitted poetry translated from a number of languages, as well as original verse. Many of her own compositions were rousing and patriotic, as was most of the poetry of the other Young Ireland poets. John Boyle O'Reilly in his *Poetry and Songs of Ireland* wrote: 'In the stormy days of "Young Ireland", from 1846 to 48, the poems of Speranza, next to those of Thomas Davis, were the inspiration of the National movement.'[15]

These poets were caught up in the revolutionary spirit that was sweeping through Europe at this time. They were also writing during the Great Famine, when thousands of Irish people were dying from starvation. Speranza expressed her anger in her poetry, which became increasingly strident and militant. She wrote an emotional poem about the execution of the brothers John and Henry Sheares, who had played prominent roles in the rebellion of the United Irishmen in 1798. Oscar Wilde admired the ballad for its strength and simplicity, and years later he would compose one of the world's most famous poems on a similar theme, 'The Ballad of Reading Gaol'.

The death of Thomas Davis, the horrors of the Famine and the collapse of Daniel O'Connell's movement for reform through parliamentary methods, led to the emergence of an extreme element in the Young Ireland movement, under the leadership of John Mitchell, which began to advocate armed rebellion. Speranza's poetry and prose left little doubt where her sympathies lay. Around the time of the abortive Young Ireland rebellion in 1848, Speranza wrote an article for *The Nation* entitled 'Alea Jacta Est' (The Die is Cast). It was an inflammatory article which called on the masses to rise up in arms and fight for liberty. The article was found by the police when they raided the offices of the newspaper, and they used it as evidence when the editor, Charles Gavan Duffy, was tried for high treason, in spite of the fact that he was in prison at the time of its publication. Speranza wrote a letter during the subsequent court proceedings in which she courageously acknowledged authorship of the article. It was the first of a number of dramatic trials to involve members of the Wilde family. Speranza's fearless advocacy of a free Irish nation lived for many years in the memory of the people. She once wrote: 'I express the soul of a great nation. Nothing less would satisfy me, who am the acknowledged voice in poetry of all the people of Ireland.'[16] Speranza was indeed a great favourite with the citizens of Dublin and she was cheered whenever her carriage was recognised on the streets. As a small child, Oscar Wilde was a regular witness of this adulation and public acclaim.

Apart from revolutionary verse, Speranza wrote poems of a more personal nature. One of these poems, entitled 'Death's Wishes', had a sadly prophetic note when one considers her lonely death in London as her son languished in Reading Gaol, having been refused permission to visit her:

> Oh! might I pass as the evening ray
> Melts in the deep'ning twilight away;
> Calmly and gently thus would I die,
> Untainted by ills of mortality.

> Thou wilt pass, but not till thy beauty is withered,
> Not till thy powers and hopes lie shivered:
> Silence and beauty are Nature's death-token;
> But the poor human heart, ere it die, must be broken.[17]

Oscar Wilde was proud of his mother's poetry, although he admitted that 'criticism is disarmed before love'.[12] He was very familiar with the work of the Young Ireland poets, and their influence on him can be discerned in a lecture he gave on Irish poets and poetry in San Francisco on 5 April 1882. In the course of the lecture he spoke of the poetry and music of Ireland, of the country's ancient ruins, and of Celtic myths and their impact on European literature. He criticised Goldsmith for his lack of national feeling and he praised the poets and writers of the 1848 rebellion. He quoted from the works of several of the poets, including Gavan Duffy, James Clarence Mangan,

Richard D'Alton Williams and Denis Florence McCarthy. He finished the lecture on a high note:

> Indeed the poetic genius of the Celtic race never flags or wearies. It is as sweet by the groves of California as by the groves of Ireland, as strong in foreign lands as in the land which gave it birth. And indeed I do not know anything more wonderful, or more characteristic of the Celtic genius, than the quick artistic spirit in which we adapted ourselves to the English tongue. The Saxon took our lands from us and left them desolate. We took their language and added new beauty to it.[12]

WILLIAM WILDE – SURGEON, WRITER AND ANTIQUARY

Oscar's father, William Wilde, was the son of a general practitioner, Dr Thomas Wilde, and the grandson of Ralph Wilde, who is described in various documents as a dealer, a farmer and a gentleman.[18] Ralph Wilde acquired property in and around Castlereagh, County Roscommon, and he married Margaret O'Flynn, a member of a distinguished Connacht family. They had a son, also named Ralph, who entered Trinity College Dublin in 1779 to prepare for a career as a clergyman. He was a brilliant student and he won the Berkeley Medal for Greek, an achievement that would be repeated by his grandnephew Oscar Wilde nearly a century later. Thomas Wilde studied medicine and established a practice in Castlereagh. He married Amelia Fynn, daughter of John Fynn, who was originally from County Mayo but who had settled in Lucan, County Dublin. Thomas and Amelia had three sons, Ralph, John and William, and two daughters, Margaret and Emily. The two eldest sons, Ralph who was born in 1798 and John who was born in 1807, became clergymen. The youngest son, William Robert Wills, was born in 1815.

William Wilde spent much of his childhood in the company of the local countrypeople in the west of Ireland, and from them he imbibed a love of folklore and history that would remain with him throughout his life. He went to the grammar school at Elphin, County Roscommon, where Oliver Goldsmith had studied in the previous century. When he was seventeen he was sent to Dublin to study surgery. He was apprenticed to Abraham Colles, the most distinguished Irish surgeon of the nineteenth century, whose name is still remembered in the eponym, Colles' fracture of the wrist. Colles worked at Dr Steevens' Hospital, one of the oldest voluntary hospitals in Ireland and Great Britain. It had strong literary associations: Jonathan Swift was a member of the first Board of Governors and Esther Johnson (Stella) was a benefactor. The hospital also possessed a remarkable library which had been bequeathed to it by a physician named Edward Worth. The books covered a wide range of subjects and the library reflected the interests of a cultured eighteenth-century gentleman. The novelist Charles Lever was a fellow medical student with William Wilde at Dr Steevens' Hospital and they developed a friendship that lasted throughout their lives. Lever later abandoned medicine to devote himself entirely to literature. His best-known novels are *Charles O'Malley, the Irish Dragoon* and *The Confessions of Harry Lorrequer*.

William Wilde also studied at the Park Street Medical School, which was one of the leading private medical schools of the period. Park Street, at the back of Trinity College Dublin, was a red-light district; the Victorians changed the name to Lincoln Place later in the century in an effort to create a new image. Here Wilde came under the influence of the distinguished Irish physicians Robert Graves and William Stokes. He also studied at 'The Rotunda', the famous Dublin maternity hospital, during his undergraduate years. Wilde developed a fever in his final year and it was thought that he would not survive. Robert Graves was consulted and he prescribed a glass of strong ale to be taken every hour. The student recovered and the following morning Graves found him sleeping comfortably! Soon after this, Graves required a doctor to travel with a patient on a health-seeking cruise to the Holy Land, and he approached Wilde.

It has been suggested that Wilde agreed to the proposition because the change of climate would benefit his health. There was another consideration, however, which may have dictated the expediency of a prolonged absence abroad: a young woman had become pregnant and William Wilde was the father. Wilde left Ireland in September

1837 to begin a series of adventures which he later described in detail in his first book *The Narrative of a Voyage to Madeira, Teneriffe and Along the Shores of the Mediterranean*. The journey lasted over eight months and took Wilde and his patient to Madeira, Teneriffe, Algiers, Sicily, Egypt, Rhodes, Cyprus, Syria, Palestine and Greece. Wilde made detailed observations on the customs, dress, health, natural history, geography, archaeology and history of each area visited. He revelled in the antiquities of Egypt and Greece and he compared modern Greeks most unfavourably with their ancient forebears who had listened to 'the strains of Sophocles and Euripides', and who had witnessed 'the performances of Aeschylus and Aristophanes'.[19]

William Wilde's obsessiveness in collecting and recording facts is apparent in the book but the work also contains some quite rhetorical passages, usually dramatising the historical and cultural significance of a particular place. He was for instance very moved when he visited the ancient city of Tyre:

> I asked myself, was this, indeed, the joyous city, whose antiquity was of ancient days; the mart of nations; the strong city of Tyre; . . . . Where every precious stone was a covering: the sardius, the topaz, and the diamond; the beryl, the onyx, and the jasper; the sapphire, the emerald, and the carbuncle. Whose ships were constructed of the fir-trees of Senir, the cedars of Lebanon, and the oaks of Bashan; . . . . Whose merchandise consisted in silver, iron, tin, lead, and vessels of brass; and whose wares were emeralds, purple, and broidered-work, and fine linen, and agate, and blue cloth, and chests of rich apparel, and the persons of men. At whose fairs . . . Dedan purchased the precious cloths for chariots, in exchange for ivory and ebony.[20]

Oscar Wilde would use similar biblical imagery when writing many of his short stories and poems, but particularly in his play *Salomé* and in his narrative poem 'The Sphinx'. Jokanaan, according to Salomé, had a mouth that was redder than the 'pomegranate-flowers that blossom in the garden of Tyre', he had eyes 'like black holes burned by torches in a Tyrian tapestry', and his hair was like 'the cedars of

Lebanon'. The Syrian wears a ring of agate and Herod calls for 'the ivory tables and the tables of jasper'. When Herod makes his appeal to Salomé to spare the life of Jokanaan, he offers her 'the largest emerald in the world', and when she remains unmoved he offers her topazes (yellow as are the eyes of tigers), onyxes (like the eyeballs of a dead woman), sapphires (as blue as blue flowers), beryl, sardonyxx, turquoise and carbuncle.

Dorian Gray was also enthralled by beautiful jewels and he would:

> . . . often spend a whole day settling and resetting in their cases the various stones that he had collected, . . . rose-pink and wine-yellow topazes, carbuncles of fiery scarlet with tremulous four-rayed stars, flame-red cinnamon stones, orange and violet spinels, and amethysts with their alternate layers of ruby and sapphire.[21]

Oscar Wilde, according to his son Vyvyan Holland, viewed words as beautiful baubles with which to experiment, just as a child plays and builds with coloured bricks. His use of mythical birds and beasts and of the names of precious stones is particularly apparent in 'The Sphinx'. Throughout his life he was fascinated by Egypt, and he wore an emerald scarab ring on the little finger of each hand. A scarab ring has a gem cut in the shape of a beetle and is engraved with symbols on the reverse side. Oscar's father wrote in great detail on the scarabaeus or sacred beetle, describing it as: 'The emblem of creative power, of the earth, and of the sun . . . .'[22] Several of Oscar Wilde's contemporaries have mentioned these rings in their memories of the writer, including Gedeon Spilett who knew him in Dieppe:

> These precious stones are engraved with cabbalistic symbols, and come from an Egyptian pyramid. He claims that the emerald on his left hand is the real cause of all his happiness, and that the one on his right hand is the cause of all his unhappiness. To my observation – which was logical enough, I think – that he should have taken off the evil ring, he replied with a changed voice: 'To live in happiness, you must know some unhappiness in life.[23]

When William Wilde returned to Dublin after his travels in the

Middle East, he did not marry, but arrangements were made for the care of his child, who was given the name Henry Wilson. The name was almost certainly derived from 'William's son', as this would be in accordance with the common practice of the period. Henry Wilson studied medicine with his father's support and he eventually became an eye surgeon. At that time there was a pragmatic approach among the upper classes to children born outside wedlock, and it was expected that the father or his family would be responsible for the upbringing and education of such children.[24] It was considered a much more serious matter to betray one's class through an ill-advised marriage than to have a mistress and illegitimate children. Hence the consternation of Dorian Gray's friend Basil Hallward when he heard of Dorian's plans to marry the actress Sibyl Vane: 'But think of Dorian's birth, and position, and wealth. It would be absurd for him to marry so much beneath him.'[25]

William Wilde also had two daughters before he married, and they were both accepted by his eldest brother, Ralph, as wards. This enlightened approach towards natural children would be replaced as the century advanced by the hypocrisy and intolerance of the Victorian period. In later years, when he was married, William Wilde sometimes took all his children, natural and legitimate, with him on holidays. This probably explains Oscar Wilde's fascination, so evident in his plays, with women who had hidden pasts and with children who were born outside wedlock. William Wilde would eventually employ his son Henry as his assistant surgeon. In *A Woman of No Importance*, Lord Illingworth planned to employ his natural son Gerald as his private secretary:

Lord Illingworth:	So that is our son, Rachel! Well, I am very proud of him. He is a Harford, every inch of him. By the way, why Arbuthnot, Rachel?
Mrs Arbuthnot:	One name is as good as another, when one has no right to any name.
Lord Illingworth:	I suppose so – but why Gerald?
Mrs Arbuthnot:	After a man whose heart I broke – after my father.

Lord Illingworth: Well, Rachel, what is over is over. All I
                     have got to say now is that I am very, very
                     much pleased with our boy. The world will
                     know him merely as my private secretary,
                     but to me he will be something very near,
                     and very dear.[26]

Oscar Wilde also explored the same theme in his novel *The Picture of
Dorian Gray*. James Vane, Sibyl's brother, has doubts about the
legitimacy of his birth. The matter comes to a head when he finally
confronts his mother:

> 'Mother, I have something to ask you', he said. Her eyes
> wandered vaguely about the room. She made no answer. 'Tell
> me the truth. I have a right to know. Were you married to my
> father?'
>
> She heaved a deep sigh. It was a sigh of relief. The terrible
> moment, the moment that night and day, for weeks and
> months, she had dreaded, had come at last, and yet she felt no
> terror. Indeed in some measure it was a disappointment to her.
> The vulgar directness of the question called for a direct answer.
> The situation had not been gradually led up to. It was crude. It
> reminded her of a bad rehearsal.
>
> 'No,' she answered, wondering at the harsh simplicity of life.
>
> 'My father was a scoundrel then!' cried the lad, clenching his
> fists.
>
> She shook her head. 'I knew he was not free. We loved each
> other very much. If he had lived, he would have made provision
> for us. Don't speak against him, my son. He was your father, and
> a gentleman. Indeed he was highly connected.'[27]

In 1839 William Wilde went to London to study eye surgery at
Moorfield's Hospital. He formed a friendship with the celebrated
court physician Sir James Clark, who introduced him to fashionable
London society. Wilde soon made an impact as a talented and quick-
witted young Irishman, and rapidly established a reputation for
himself in both literature and science. From London he travelled to
Vienna, where he spent six months studying eye and ear surgery. He

then moved to Berlin to work with Johann Friedrich Dieffenbach, one of the pioneers of plastic surgery. With the help of an introduction from the Irish novelist Maria Edgeworth he quickly gained access to the intellectual circles in Berlin.

On his return to Dublin he set up practice as an eye and ear surgeon and lived at 15 Westland Row with his mother and his sister Margaret. He also established a small eye and ear hospital at his own expense, and he invited Robert Graves to become consultant physician and Sir Philip Crampton to become consultant surgeon. His own reputation as an eye and ear surgeon soared, and his practice grew in tandem. Like all doctors, he had his failures, and George Bernard Shaw claimed that he operated on his father so effectively for a squint, that he squinted in the opposite direction ever after. When he treated the daughter of the Young Irelander John Blake Dillon, the child's father was not impressed by the consultation: 'To tell you the truth I am afraid Wilde is just as anxious to produce an impression on the *spectators* as to cure the *patient* . . . .'[28]

Inspired by his experience in Egypt, William Wilde began to explore the antiquities of the Irish countryside. He co-operated initially with the artist and antiquary George Petrie in these studies. Petrie was several years older than Wilde and he had invited the young surgeon to assist him with an excavation at Lagore in County Meath. The excavation turned out to be of major importance, as it was the first lake-dwelling to be scientifically investigated in Ireland. Wilde gained considerably from his association with Petrie. The latter was primarily interested in the Early Christian era, whereas Wilde concentrated most of his work on a much earlier period. Wilde spent many hours exploring prehistoric remains and he was particularly fascinated by the megalithic tombs of the Boyne Valley. He was largely responsible for building up the collection of antiquities of the Royal Irish Academy, now housed in the National Museum of Ireland, and he also prepared a detailed catalogue of the collection. This catalogue was far more than a list of acquisitions, as it also described the history and uses of the objects enumerated. He gained a reputation throughout Europe for this work, which enhanced his position as a leading expert on the Celtic world.

William Wilde also found time to pursue other interests. He wrote a book on Austria which was based on his own observations during his period of study in the country. Published in 1843, it is a mine of information, and it has recently been republished in a German translation. Wilde was appointed medical adviser for the Irish census of 1841 and assistant commissioner for the 1851, 1861 and 1871 censuses. In these he collected and collated social and biological data that was not being collected in any other country at the time. His work on the 1851 census has been described as one of the greatest demographic studies ever conducted and has become a standard work of reference on the Great Famine, which devastated Ireland during the years 1845 and 1849.[29] Wilde became editor of the leading Irish medical journal, *The Dublin Quarterly Journal of Medical Science*, in 1845 and held the post until 1850. As editor, he published a series of articles that described the ravages of the epidemic diseases then sweeping through the deprived and starving population, and he was openly critical of the inadequate measures adopted by government agencies. Despite these pressures he found time to research and write a book on Jonathan Swift, entitled *The Closing Years of Dean Swift's Life; with Remarks on Stella*, which was published in 1849. This book contains some passages of very fine prose, including one which describes Stella's beauty.

In 1853 Wilde published his textbook *Practical Observations on Aural Surgery and the Nature and Treatment of Diseases of the Ear*. This was the first textbook of importance on the subject and it is now regarded as a classic in its field. It was translated into German and it remained a standard textbook for many years on both sides of the Atlantic. His output was phenomenal both in range and quantity, and apart from his books he wrote for many periodicals on medical and other subjects. According to Speranza: 'Whatever his hand found to do he did it with all his might, and this energy, that nothing could weary or exhaust, was the secret of his success in all he undertook.'[30]

In 1850 Wilde purchased his former medical school in Park Street and transformed it, at his own expense, into St Mark's Ophthalmic Hospital, the most advanced eye and ear hospital in the country.[31] The new hospital attracted many postgraduate visitors from abroad, especially from America. Henry Wilson became an assistant to his father at St Mark's and he also made his own substantial contribution to medical science.[32] In 1862 William Wilde handed over the management of the hospital to a Board of Trustees for the use and advantage of the afflicted poor of Ireland. In doing this, he joined the distinguished ranks of founders of Dublin Voluntary Hospitals, such as Jonathan Swift, Bartholomew Mosse, Richard Steevens, Mary Mercer and Sir Patrick Dun.

Oscar Wilde was proud of his father's hospital and as a young student he wrote to a friend: 'I know you will take interest in the report I sent you of my father's hospital which he built when he was only twenty-nine and not a rich man. It is a great memorial of his name and a movement is being set on foot to enlarge it and make it still greater.'[33]

CHAPTER 2

A name of high distinction

I inherited from my father and my mother a name of high distinction in literature and art.[1]

Oscar Wilde

One could not know him, even slightly, without realising that he had brilliant gifts, inherited from a father of exceptional mental powers, and a mother . . . not less remarkable in a quite different way.[2]

David Hunter Blair

WILLIAM WILDE ADMIRED THE romanticism and idealism of the Young Irelanders but, unlike Speranza, he did not become involved in their revolutionary aims. His ability was respected by the organisation, and his lectures and papers always received favourable attention in the pages of *The Nation*. He was very distressed by the ravages of the Great Famine and he watched with dismay the devastation of his native province of Connacht through starvation and emigration:

> Such is the desolation which whole districts, of Connaught at least, at this moment present; entire villages being levelled to the ground, the fences broken, the land untilled and often unstocked, and miles of the country lying idle and unproductive, without the face of a human being to be seen upon it. The hare has made its form on the hearth, and the lapwing wheels over the ruined cabin.[3]

Wilde was on the council of the Celtic Society, whose object was 'to publish original documents illustrative of the history, literature, and antiquities of Ireland'.[4] Other members of the council included the poet Samuel Ferguson, the historian John T Gilbert and the Young Irelanders William Smith O'Brien, Charles Gavan Duffy and John Mitchell. Wilde walked behind the funeral cortège of Thomas Davis as a member of the Royal Irish Academy, and he later headed a committee to commemorate the poet and patriot. It was Wilde who commissioned the neo-classical sculptor John Hogan, who had just returned from Rome, to execute the marble figure of Davis that now stands in the City Hall in Dublin. Speranza also wished to promote Hogan's genius and she wrote an article about him in the *Dublin University Magazine* based on notes from a conversation she had had with the sculptor in his studio. It was probably through these shared interests that she first met William Wilde. In 1849 Wilde published a book on his archaeological and historical research, entitled *The Beauties of the Boyne*, in the first chapter of which he included a verse on druidism by Speranza.

The marriage announcement appeared in *Saunder's News-Letter* of 13 November 1851:

> Married on the 12th inst., at St Peter's Church by the Reverend John M Wilde, A M, Incumbent of Trinity Church, Northwich, William R Wilde, Esq, FRCS, to Jane Francesca, youngest daughter of the late Charles Elgee, Esq, and grand-daughter of the late Archdeacon Elgee, of Wexford.[5]

It was a marriage of two mature individuals – Speranza was thirty at the time and William Wilde was six years older. In a letter to a friend, Speranza described her husband as 'a Celebrity – a man eminent in his profession, of acute intellect and much learning, the best conversationalist in the metropolis, and author of many books, literary and scientific'.[6] Wilde, according to contemporaries, was slight in figure, constantly alert and active, with inquisitive and searching eyes. Speranza, in contrast, was a tall, beautiful woman with fine features and flashing brown eyes, and she moved in a slow and stately manner. With typical idealism, Speranza was determined to be everything for the man she loved: 'I would not let him love midnight or the moon, nor seem conscious they existed. I must be his Universe, terrestial and celestial.'[7]

Before his marriage to Speranza, Wilde moved from 15 to 21 Westland Row. The latter was a medium-sized Georgian residence which, although situated on a busy street, had the advantage of overlooking the park of Trinity College at the rear. Number 21 forms part of a large terrace and it conforms to the standard plan of terraced houses of the period, with a basement and four floors above. The kitchen was situated in the basement and there were two reception rooms on both the ground floor and first floor. The front reception room on the ground floor was almost certainly William Wilde's surgery, and the diningroom would have been behind this. The front room on the first floor would have served as the drawingroom, and the back room as the family sittingroom. The bedrooms were on the upper two floors.[8]

Their first child, William Charles Kingsbury Wilde, was born in 1852. Oscar was born two years later, on 16 October 1854, at 21 Westland Row. He was baptised at the neighbouring St Mark's Church on 26 April 1855, more than six months after his birth, and was given the names Oscar Fingal O'fflahertie Wilde, reflecting his parents' interest in Irish mythology and history. The publication of *Ossian* by the Scotsman James MacPherson in 1762 had stimulated interest in ancient Ireland and was one of the factors that led to the Celtic Revival. MacPherson's work purported to be a translation of the poems of the Celtic hero Ossian, but it appears to have been the 'translator's' own composition, based on Highland folklore. However, his work prompted scholars to study ancient Irish manuscripts, which told of the deeds of Fionn, leader of the Fianna, Oisín his son, and Oscar his grandson. In the year of Oscar Wilde's birth, the Ossianic Society was established in Dublin to facilitate the publication of the mythology, folklore, history and poetry contained in the old Irish manuscripts. The bilingual texts produced by the society, many of them the work of the scholars Eugene O'Curry and John O'Donovan, brought to life the romances of ancient Gaelic Ireland, such as the stories of the Children of Lir, the Sons of Usna, and the ill-fated love of Diarmuid and Gráinne. These new insights into Ireland's Celtic past fired the imagination of the intellectual leaders of Irish society, and as a result of this enthusiasm, a number of names with Gaelic associations,

'Oscar' among them, became popular in Ireland in the middle of the last century.

Oscar, an Irish Hector, was described as Oscar of the Lion Heart in one of the stories that Speranza wrote about the Fianna.[9] The poet Samuel Ferguson was a regular visitor to the house at Westland Row. He had composed a poem entitled 'The Cromlech on Howth', which told the love story of Aideen and Oscar. Aideen was the daughter of Aongus of Binn Eadair, the ancient Irish name for Howth, a beautiful headland north of Dublin. Oscar fell in love with Aideen as he watched her fetching water from a well. They married, but shortly afterwards Oscar was slain at the battle of Gavra in County Meath. Aideen was grief-stricken and, remaining unconsolable, she died and was buried by the Fianna in a cairn on the Hill of Howth. In Ferguson's poem, Oisín, Oscar's father, tells the sad story of the doomed lovers:

> In sweet remembrance of the days
> When, duteous in the lowly vale,
> Unconscious of my Oscar's gaze,
> She filled the fragrant pail.[10]

Speranza was impressed by the heroic and tragic qualities of the poem. Years later she wrote to Ferguson telling him that of all his poems, the 'Cromlech on Howth' was her favourite.

Some of Oscar Wilde's biographers claim that Oscar was named after King Oscar of Sweden, who was said to have had a cataract operation performed by William Wilde. There is no record of such an operation, and William Wilde visited Stockholm for the first time with Speranza when Oscar was four years old. It was Oscar's first biographer, Robert Sherard, who initially suggested that the playwright owed his name to the King of Sweden, but in a later book Sherard withdrew this claim and accepted the Ossianic origin of the name.[11, 12]

'Fingal', Oscar's second name, is the Gaelic for 'blonde or fair-haired stranger'. Ferguson used this name in his legendary poems and MacPherson used it instead of Fionn in his Ossianic tales. It is a common placename in areas where there were Viking settlements and it is the name of the region that stretches along the coast between the Liffey and the Boyne rivers, an area rich in archaeological artefacts. Oscar was given the name 'O'fflahertie' to mark his links through his paternal grandmother with some of the leading Celtic families of the west of Ireland. O'Flahertie was one of the principal chieftains of Connemara and the O'Flahertie clan was the subject of one of the famous precatory mottoes that hung outside the four gates of the old city of Galway. The notice on the north gate read:

From the ferocious O'Flaherties
Good Lord, deliver us![13]

William Wilde wrote enthusiastically about the O'Flahertie clan in his book on Lough Corrib. Later Oscar added the name 'Wills' to his Christian names, in recognition of a family connection with the Wills family, who were substantial landowners in County Roscommon. James Wills the poet and W G Wills the dramatist were members of this family.

According to Lord Henry Wotton, names are everything, and the man who 'could call a spade a spade should be compelled to use one'.[14] In the early years of his literary career, Wilde signed his work with his full initials, but in later years he signed himself Oscar Wilde. At the height of his career, a novelist suggested to him that he ought to have been christened 'plain Oscar':

'How ridiculous of you to suppose that anyone, least of all my dear mother, would christen me "plain Oscar",' was the reply. 'My name has two O's, two F's and two W's. A name which is destined to be in everybody's mouth must not be too long. It comes so expensive in the advertisements. When one is unknown, a number of Christian names are useful, perhaps needful. As one becomes famous, one sheds some of them, just as a balloonist, when rising higher, sheds unnecessary ballast, or as you will shed your Christian name when raised to the peerage. I started as Oscar Fingal O'Flahertie Wills Wilde. All but two of the five names have already been thrown overboard. Soon I shall discard another and be known simply as "The Wilde" or "The Oscar".'[15]

CHAPTER 3

21 Westland Row

Genius should never wed. You cannot serve two masters.

Speranza[1]

IN THE EARLY YEARS OF HER marriage, Speranza adjusted to her new role as a Victorian wife and mother. 'My great soul', she wrote, 'is prisoned within a woman's destiny.'[2] She saw herself as a romantic or heroic figure, and it was difficult to realise this self-image within her domestic circumstances. She expressed similar ideas in a letter she wrote shortly after Oscar's birth:

> A Joan of Arc was never meant for marriage, and so here I am, bound heart and soul to the home hearth . . . behold me – me Speranza, also rocking a cradle at this present writing in which lies my second son – a babe of one month old the 16th of this month and as large and fine and handsome and healthy as if he were three months. He is to be called Oscar Fingal Wilde. Is not that grand, misty, and Ossianic?[3]

Speranza was delighted with her two young sons: 'Oscar is a great stout creature who minds nothing but growing fat. Willie is slight, tall and spirituelle looking, with large beautiful eyes full of expression. He is twined round all the fibres of my heart'.[4]

It would be a mistake to conclude that Speranza's life was dominated by domestic drudgery. There were servants to relieve her of such duties and nurses to care for the children. But there were other factors that weighed heavily upon her in the early years of her marriage, not least William Wilde's susceptibility to dark moods. She confided to a friend in 1852 that her husband had a 'strange, nervous, hypochondriacal home nature which the world never sees . . . . My husband so brilliant to the world envelopes himself . . . in a black pall and is grave, stern, mournful and silent . . . . His whole existence is one of unceasing mental activity, and this has made the peculiarities of his nature – for myself I died long ago . . . nothing interests me beyond the desire to make him happy.'[2] It was an aspect of Wilde's character that was unknown to most of their wide circle of friends and with which his wife had to cope alone.

The Wildes had a busy social life and they were involved in a number of societies. One such society was known as 'The Mystics'. This society, which placed considerable emphasis on social activities, was considered too frivolous by the more serious-minded, such as John Edward Pigot who was the treasurer of the Celtic Society. In a letter to the young historian John T Gilbert, he warned him about the Mystic Society and advised him not to be too influenced by 'the Jupiter-Esculapius and the Juno-Minerva of Westland Row'.[5] Gilbert ignored the advice and he became a close friend of the Wildes. He presented the first copy of his *History of the City of Dublin* to Speranza when it was published in 1854. He also had a good relationship with the children, particularly Oscar, as can be seen from the following note, which he received from William Wilde: 'Tomorrow is Oscar's birthday, and you are such a favourite of his you must be sure to come and dine.'[6]

The marriage of two high-profile people naturally attracted considerable attention, and the predictable gossip. Speranza was even suspected of writing a critical review of one of William Wilde's works in the *Irish Quarterly Review*. The poet Denis Florence McCarthy wrote to Gilbert:

> You have, of course, seen the announcement (in *Saunder's News-Letter*) that the *Irish Quarterly Review* is the property of Dr Wilde, that he is also the editor, and that the leading articles *are all written by him and his gifted wife, Speranza!* Now, as I suppose that even doctors perform painful operations on themselves but very rarely, I must conclude that the critical scalpel was in this instance wielded by the editor's gifted partner, Speranza . . . terrible and beautiful as an Amazon.[7]

Wilde was neither the editor nor the owner of the *Quarterly Review*. The competing demands of William Wilde's social life, his professional career and his historical research and writing must have placed him under considerable pressure, but it may have been that the resultant tension contributed to his creativity. There is some evidence to suggest that at times he made valiant efforts to reduce his social activities. Samuel Lever was editor of the *Dublin University Magazine* at the time and he was famous for his hospitality and conviviality. Wilde found it difficult to resist the invitations of his friend. On one occasion the novelist called at Westland Row with the intention of asking Wilde to dinner, only to be told at the door that the doctor was busy in his surgery. Lever went away, but when he returned later with a bandage over one of his eyes he found no difficulty in getting into Wilde's surgery. Wilde was greatly amused by his friend's strategy and he accepted the invitation.

At Westland Row the Wildes began to attract the leaders of the scientific, literary and artistic world to their home. John Hogan, the Irish neo-classical sculptor, was a frequent visitor. William Wilde was a good friend to Hogan and after the sculptor's death in 1858 Wilde became a trustee for the Hogan family. Another friend, George Petrie, who encouraged William Wilde in his archaeological interests, was a man of many talents. He was a gifted painter, book illustrator and historian, and he supervised the Antiquities Section of the Topographical Survey of Ireland. He wrote a number of books on Irish antiquities and he was also a notable collector of ancient Irish music. An accomplished musician, he played Irish airs on the fiddle for his friends in Dublin. As an artist Petrie is remembered for his watercolours of Irish scenes. Oscar Wilde almost certainly derived 'Georges Petit', the name he gave to the French art connoisseur who was to arrange an exhibition for Basil Hallward in *The Picture of Dorian Gray*, from the name of his father's friend.

Henry O'Neill was another artist whom the Wildes knew at this time. He was originally a portrait painter and he did a chalk drawing of the young Oscar, which is thought to be the one reproduced in Sherard's *Life of Oscar Wilde*.[8, 9] The artist devoted considerable attention to antiquarian interests and he produced some beautifully illustrated books, his most famous being *The Sculptured Crosses of Ancient Ireland*. In 1868 O'Neill wrote a short but controversial book on land reform, entitled *Ireland for the Irish*, in which he advocated the nationalisation of land and stressed that if sweeping reforms were not introduced, then social revolution was inevitable. It has been suggested that this book may have influenced the young Oscar Wilde, introducing him to radical concepts at an early age, which he would later develop in *The Soul of Man under Socialism*.[9]

Speranza admired the work of the novelist William Carleton. The friendship between them began in the years before her marriage to Wilde. Carleton, who was nearly thirty years older than Speranza, is best remembered for his collection of tales, *Traits and Stories of the Irish Peasantry*. Carleton was married, and when a friend of Speranza implied that Carleton's letters to Speranza were too effusive, Speranza responded indignantly, claiming that one should always make allowance for the passionate nature of poets and artists: 'They speak in painted words . . . you must not translate liking – a poet's liking – into Love unless it is as Dante loved Beatrice and Tasso Leonora and Michel Angelo Vittoria Colonna, our language wants a word for this beautiful feeling . . . .'[10] This defence of her letters from Carleton is very similar to the defence her son advanced when confronted by Carson in a London courtroom with an effusive letter that he had written to Lord Alfred Douglas. Wilde told the court that it was a 'prose poem' and that such a 'beautiful letter' could only have been written by an artist.[11] Speranza, unlike her son, could heed advice and, despite her protestations, she wrote to Carleton and asked him to temper his prose.

The poet Samuel Ferguson was one of William Wilde's most loyal friends. He was born in Belfast in 1810 and was educated at Trinity College before being called to the bar in 1837. His beautiful elegy 'Lament for Thomas Davis' is the poem by which he is best remembered. Speranza described him as the historic bard of Ireland and she encouraged him to make posterity his client 'even though Posterity only pays in marble wreaths on marble brows'.[12] Ferguson did make posterity his client, as it was he who introduced to Irish literature that enthusiasm for the country's past, its legends, topography and archaeology, that was to become the cornerstone of the Irish literary revival. Ferguson did not draw his inspiration purely from Irish sources, as his style was greatly influenced by the Greek classics, and particularly by the work of Homer. This fusion of Irish and Greek scholarship appealed to Speranza. When Ferguson published his epic poem 'Congal' in 1872, he sent an inscribed copy to Speranza. Her acknowledgement was gracious: 'I look with wonder on this large and handsome volume evolved out of the dull routine of Dublin life, where so little exists to stimulate the intellect. What thought, what courage, what intellectual fervour, to produce so noble a poem!'[13]

Despite the varied intellectual interests of many of the visitors to 21 Westland Row, Speranza often found their company tedious. 'They deal in facts too much. I can be overwhelmed with knowledge any minute I like on every fact of creation', she wrote in November 1854, 'Everything has been examined and analysed and essays written on it – until I grow sick of too much information, but I long for someone to ascend the mount with me where I can see God face to face or go down into the thought world of my soul . . . .'[3] Within a matter of months of writing this, someone whom she felt would supply this need had entered her life. This was William Rowan Hamilton, the most brilliant Irish intellectual of his time. Hamilton had been such an outstanding undergraduate at Trinity College Dublin that he was appointed professor of astronomy and astronomer royal in 1827, before he had taken his primary degree. He became one of the greatest mathematicians of the nineteenth century and his work had a major influence on modern mathematical thinking. His name is still remembered in the Hamiltonian function, which is central to modern theoretical and quantum physics, but he is probably most famous for his discovery of quaternions. Hamilton also wrote poetry, and William Wordsworth, a close friend, once said that Hamilton was the only man he knew who was as wonderful as Coleridge. Hamilton first met Speranza in April 1855 and he immediately fell under her spell. 'She is almost amusingly fearless and original and *avows* . . . that she likes to make a *sensation*' he told his friend, the poet Aubrey de Vere.[14] When they first met, Speranza was arranging Oscar's baptism:

> When I met her for the first time in my life, she told me of this 'young pagan' as she called him (or *it*, for I did not know the sex. I don't call new born infants in these countries *pagans*); and she asked me to be godfather, perhaps because I was so to a grandson of Wordsworth, . . . and because she is an admirer of Wordsworth. However, I declined. But it seems I have not fallen entirely out of favour thereby, for she paid me, on Saturday last, a visit of three hours and a half, it being my *second* time of seeing her . . . . My visitress told me, as we drank a glass of wine to the health of her child, that he had been christened on the previous day, by a long baptismal name, or string of names, the two first of which are Oscar and Fingal! the third and fourth sounding to me as a tremendous descent, that I daresay she prefers them . . . . She is quite a genius, and thoroughly aware of it.[14]

The visit referred to by Hamilton was a rather unconventional one, when Speranza travelled five miles out of the city without her husband to see the astronomer's observatory and residence at Dunsink. Hamilton conducted her around the observatory and he was both surprised and impressed when she remarked: 'Let a woman be as clever as she may, there is no prize like this for *her*.'[14]

Hamilton's friendship with Speranza continued, and on 23 April 1858 she was among a group of friends, which included the poets Aubrey de Vere and Denis Florence McCarthy, who were invited by Hamilton to the observatory. They had a wonderful day and Hamilton referred to the occasion as a 'Feast of Poets'. He wrote enthusiastically to Speranza:

> I am unable to recall – so much of human music was there in the poetical party at which you were so kind as lately to assist – whether the *birds* were singing at that time. This morning I have unlocked the hall-door, that I might listen more freely to the storm, the tempest, the whirlwind of delight, and of music, with which the birds are now surrounding this house and me.'[14]

31

CHAPTER 4

Life on Merrion Square

*Dublin is a city out of the Eighteenth Century, adorned by beautiful
and spacious squares bordered with lilac, hawthorn and laburnum.*[1]

Oliver St John Gogarty

WHEN OSCAR WAS STILL an infant, his family moved from Westland
Row to Merrion Square. Westland Row, although convenient to
William Wilde's hospital, was not a prestigious address. Several
merchants, a druggist, a dyer, a miniature painter and a dressmaker,
lived on Westland Row and the Wildes' immediate neighbours
included a builder, a coachmaker and a coal merchant. At this time
the Church, the law, medicine and the army were considered the
only professions worthy of a gentleman, and there was a definite
contempt for those associated with trade. Merrion Square was also
convenient to Wilde's hospital but it boasted the residences of the
leading doctors, barristers and bankers of the city, as well as a few
members of the aristocracy.[2]

The luminaries of early–eighteenth-century fashionable Dublin
lived on the north side of the city in streets and squares such as
Marlborough Street, Henrietta Street, Rutland Square and Mountjoy
Square. In 1740 however, the Earl of Kildare announced his intention
to build a mansion on the south side of the city, on undeveloped land
near Trinity College. Friends questioned his wisdom in choosing this
area, but he confidently assured them that Dublin would follow him.
Soon after the mansion was finished, its owner was raised to the
dukedom of Leinster and he was acknowledged as the undisputed
head of the Irish peerage. The house became known as Leinster
House, and the duke had a fine garden laid out on its eastern side

which became known as Leinster Lawn.[3] As he had predicted, fashionable Dublin soon began to move south of the river.

In 1762 Lord Fitzwilliam of Merrion asked the architect John Ensor to design a square which would be bounded on the west by the lawns of Leinster House. It was anticipated that these fine houses with their elegant interiors would serve as town houses for the country's aristocracy. For a time they fulfilled this function, and leaders of the landed gentry had substantial houses on the square. Lord Llandaff and the Earl of Barrymore had houses on the north side of the square; the Marquis of Antrim, Lord Frankfort, Lord Carhampton, Lord Fitzgerald and Sir Capel Molyneux lived on the east side; and the Earls of Wicklow and Limerick, Lords Lifford and De Vere, and the Countess of Massereene lived on the south side. Several members of the Irish House of Commons also had houses there. When the Wildes arrived on the square in June 1855 it already had a fascinating history, and stories abounded about illustrious and eccentric former residents. Viscount Harberton, a great art collector, lived at number 5, a house on the north side which was bought in 1840 by the physician William Stokes. Among Harberton's art collection were landscapes by Salvator Rosa, Both and Wynant as well as paintings by Titian and a San Sebastian by Van Dyck.[4] The most impressive house on the north side of the square was built originally for Lord Llandaff who spent a large fortune entertaining his friends. He told each guest on arrival: 'This is your castle: here you are to command as in your own house; you may breakfast, dine, and sup here whenever you please . . . but from this moment you are never to consider me the master of the house, but only as one of the guests.'[5] Naturally he found many friends who were eager to help dissipate his fortune. One of the finest houses on the east side of the square was built in 1778 by the first Marquis of Antrim and was known as Antrim House. In 1794 the Marchioness of Antrim gave a 'most superb rout, ball and supper'. During the evening a Scots ballet, which was especially composed for the occasion, was performed by a *corps de ballet* that included several titled ladies. The dancers 'were in uniform dresses of white muslin, trimmed with blue ribbons, blue sashes, and petticoats trimmed with silver fringe; head-dresses – white turbans, spangled with silver, and blue feathers . . .'[6] So many guests thronged to the ballroom to see this unusual event that it was necessary to keep the dance floor clear by the use of 'barriers of ribbon held by noblemen'.

The Act of Union between Great Britain and Ireland in 1801 had a dramatic effect on the social scene in Dublin, as the aristocracy began to gravitate to London. Prior to 1800 there were 270 peers and 300 commoners of the Irish parliament residing in the city; just twenty years later, only thirty-four peers and five commoners remained. The leaders of the liberal professions of law and medicine took advantage of the social vacuum created by this exodus and they began to move into the houses on Merrion Square. A visiting doctor from London, John Gamble, writing about the doctors of Merrion Square in 1811 observed: 'the truth is, a physician here is almost at the pinnacle of greatness: there are few resident nobility or gentry since the Union, and the professors of law and medicine may be said to form the aristocracy of the place. They have, therefore, all the advantages of manner, which a lofty sense of superiority, along with much association with mankind, never fail to produce. A London practitioner is little better than a bon bourgeois, whom people of rank call in when they are sick, but have no intercourse with when they are well . . . .'[7]

The Wildes' house was situated on the north side of the square, the oldest and traditionally the most fashionable side.[8] James Whitelaw observed in 1818: 'The footway on the north side is on summer evenings the resort of all that is elegant and fashionable in this vicinity.'[9] Later in the century, promenading was confined to Sunday afternoons, when a regimental band usually attended. Lady Bracknell in *The Importance of Being Earnest* would have approved of 1 Merrion Square as an address, given her reservations about the location of Jack Worthing's house on Belgrave Square:

Lady Bracknell: You have a town house, I hope? A girl with a simple, unspoiled nature, like Gwendolen, could hardly be expected to reside in the country.

Jack: Well, I own a house in Belgrave Square, but it is let by the year to Lady Bloxham.

	Of course, I can get it back whenever I like, at six months' notice.
Lady Bracknell:	Lady Bloxham? I don't know her.
Jack:	Oh, she goes about very little. She is a lady considerably advanced in years.
Lady Bracknell:	Ah, now-a-days that is no guarantee of respectability of character. What number in Belgrave Square?
Jack:	149.
Lady Bracknell:	The unfashionable side. I thought there was something. However, that could easily be altered.
Jack:	Do you mean the fashion or the side?
Lady Bracknell:	Both, if necessary, I presume.[10]

The Wildes' new home was far larger than the house in Westland Row. They had a staff of six servants and the children had a German governess and a French *bonne*. They were taught to speak French and German, and this early tutoring, combined with visits to France, which included a special visit to see the Paris Exposition, gave Oscar Wilde that great command of French which he used to such advantage in *Salomé*. Both children and guests were reminded of the family's most distinguished literary connection by the presence in the house of a fine bust of the novelist Charles Maturin.

Merrion Square was at the heart of fashionable Dublin society and its residents were regarded as snobs by some of their fellow citizens. George Bernard Shaw once described Oscar as 'a snob to the marrow of his being, having been brought up in Merrion Square'.[11] It was a class-conscious society, which was centred largely on the ceremony and ritual of the Viceregal Court at Dublin Castle. Many receptions, dinners, balls and concerts were organised during the 'Castle season', as Lady Ferguson observed: 'Society in Dublin, agreeable at all times, becomes brilliant during winter and early spring, when the hospitalities of the Viceregal Court attract to the city many of the nobility and country gentlemen and their families . . . .'[12] At 1 Merrion Square, the Wildes were in a much better position to entertain, and they soon became celebrated for the number of dinner parties and balls that they hosted and the remarkable people who attended them. Their neighbours also entertained lavishly: 'The great doctors entertained each other and dined out almost every night with judges, lawyers, or eminent government officials. Wit and anecdote circulated with the port.'[13] Oscar's tutor at Trinity College, John Pentland Mahaffy, described wit in Irish society as a kind of social religion, with rules that demanded spontaneity, and anyone suspected of rehearsing beforehand would be ridiculed. 'There is no doubt', wrote the novelist and academic Walter Starkie, 'that the brilliant epigrams in *Intentions*, *Lady Windermere's Fan* and *The Importance of Being Earnest* sprang up naturally in the mind of one who was brought up in the atmosphere of Dublin in the days when Irish Society was unrivalled for its spontaneous wit.'[14]

Giving a dinner party was a significant undertaking at that time, as a dinner could consist of as many as eighteen courses. Lady Ferguson compared them with similar social occasions among the ancient Greeks: 'The resemblance consists chiefly in the animated interchange of ideas, quick and versatile wit and humour being characteristic of both races.'[15] These sentiments are echoed in a remark that Oscar Wilde once made to W B Yeats in London: 'We Irish are too poetical to be poets; we are a nation of brilliant failures, but we are the greatest talkers since the Greeks.'[16, 17] The Greek influence can still be seen at 1 Merrion Square, as Speranza decorated her rooms with motifs from classical and neo-classical sculpture. She was an enthusiastic supporter of the neo-classical revival, which stimulated interest in the world of Greece and Rome. Her own Greek learning is apparent in her poetry. Her love of the heroic may have motivated the disastrous advice that she gave to Oscar before his trial, when friends were advising him to leave England. 'If you stay, even if you go to prison, you will always be my son, it will make no difference to my affection, but if you go, I will never speak to you again.'[18] Oscar promised her that he would stay, but the advice he had received was reminiscent of that given by the Spartan mother to her son, 'Return with your shield or on it'.[19]

Speranza admired the work of the Danish neo-classical sculptor Bertel Thorwaldsen, and when she was in Copenhagen with her husband in 1858 they visited the Thorwaldsen Museum which was itself designed by the sculptor. There she saw about six hundred of Thorwaldsen's works, and she was particularly impressed by the quality and beauty of the *relievi* from Greek subjects. Some of the motifs on the walls of 1 Merrion Square are copies of *relievi* by Thorwaldsen. During the same tour they visited the villa of the Swedish sculptor Bystrom, just outside Stockholm.[20] In her book *Driftwood from Scandinavia*, Speranza described the villa as a marvel of artistic beauty: 'It seems a villa for a Roman Empress, this caprice of genius, this artist's dream realized with such exquisite and lavish expenditure.'[21] In later years Oscar, with the help of the painter James McNeill Whistler and the architect Edward Godwin, would plan his own 'house beautiful' in London.[22]

William Wilde liked to dominate the conversation at his dinner parties. On one occasion when he was outpaced by a guest he hung his head and pretended to doze. The painter John Butler Yeats often dined at 1 Merrion Square with his father, the Reverend William Butler Yeats. During one visit William Wilde was declaiming authoritatively on salmon fishing when John Butler Yeats heard his father mutter under his breath 'He knows nothing about it'.[23] The medical historian Charles Cameron was also a regular guest of the Wilde household. He later recalled: 'There were two well-known 'diners out' at that time who, like myself, were always invited to the Wildes' dinner parties, namely, the Reverend Charles Tisdall, DD, and Dr Thomas Beatty, an obstetrician in large practice . . . . The reverend and medical doctors had excellent voices. Their habit was to meet in Wilde's study and then to ascend the stairs very slowly, singing a duet, to the drawing room.'[24]

William Wilde's medical and scholarly reputation was achieved through constant work and study. He gave his contemporaries the impression of always being in a hurry and preoccupied with the task in hand. His lifestyle contrasted with that of Speranza, who approached life in a much more leisurely fashion. Wilde would already have the best part of a day's work accomplished before his wife would appear down from her bedroom. According to Cameron, William Wilde worked in his study while his wife entertained her guests, and they communicated with each other by sending notes.[24]

Speranza's Swedish friend, Lotten von Kraemer, visited Dublin in 1857 with her father and they called on the Wildes at Merrion Square. Speranza had not yet appeared from her bedroom although it was one o'clock in the afternoon. The butler coped diplomatically with the situation, observing 'There isn't daylight in her room'.[25] William Wilde was out on clinical duties, but he soon returned to greet the visitors. Lotten von Kraemer described him as a noble figure, slightly bent by ceaseless work rather than years. His quick movements gave her the impression that his time was precious: 'He carries a small boy in his arm and holds another by the hand. His eyes rest on them with content. They are soon sent away to play, whereupon he gives us his undivided attention.'[25] The Kraemers had dinner with the Wildes that evening and the children were present. During the meal William Wilde called the three-year-old Oscar and, after giving him a kiss, asked him to find a book that he wanted. A soprano sang some of Moore's melodies after the dinner.

Visitors to 1 Merrion Square listened in amusement as Oscar was encouraged to recite his Christian names in full. It was not an easy task as there were four names to be remembered. Oscar and his brother were allowed to meet distinguished guests and to sit quietly listening to the conversation. The influence of his parents was stressed in the first biographical sketch of Wilde, published in 1888 when he was only twenty-six, which was almost certainly written with his co-operation:

> Mr Wilde was constantly with his father and mother, always among grown up persons, and, at eight years old, had heard every subject discussed and every creed defended and demolished at his father's dinner table, where were to be found not only the brilliant genius of Ireland, but also celebrities of Europe and America that visited Dublin. He considers that the best of his education in boyhood was obtained from this association with his father and mother and their remarkable friends.[26]

These early experiences made a lifelong impression on the young Oscar, who once said: 'If I were all alone, marooned in some desert island and had my things with me, I should dress for dinner every evening.'[27] Speranza was proud of her children's ability and she told one of her guests, George Henry Moore, father of the novelist George Moore, that 'Willie is all right but as for Oscar he will turn out something wonderful'.[28]

It has been said that Speranza was disappointed when her second child was not a girl and that as a consequence she dressed Oscar in girl's clothes. In fact, it was the fashion at that time to dress young children of both sexes in similar clothing. Moreover, Speranza did have a daughter, Isola, who was born in 1857, when Oscar was only two and a half years old. The children's games were boisterous, and Oscar had his arm broken when playing with his brother Willie in the nursery. Years later Oscar would say, 'It was my first introduction to the horrors of pain, the lurking tragedies of life.'[29] On one occasion, when in a generous mood, Oscar gave Willie a present of a toy bear:

> I had a toy bear of which I was very fond indeed, so fond that I used to take it to bed with me, and I thought that nothing could make me more unhappy than to lose my bear. Well, one day Willy asked me for it; and I was so fond of Willy that I gave it to him, I remember, without a pang. Afterwards, however, the enormity of the sacrifice I had made impressed itself upon me. I considered that such an act merited the greatest gratitude and love in return and whenever Willy crossed me in any way I used to say: 'Willy, you don't deserve my bear'. And for years afterwards, after we had grown up, whenever we had a slight quarrel, I used to say the same: 'Willy, you don't deserve my bear. You must give me back my bear.' He used to laugh at this recollection.[30]

William Wilde apparently read beautifully, and we know from a sentimental poem written by Speranza after his death that he read to his family. Speranza also read to the children, and Oscar remembered listening to her reading the poems of Walt Whitman soon after they were first published. The children enjoyed these poetry sessions and they had favourite poems, such as Tennyson's 'Lady Clara Vere de

Vere' and Longfellow's 'Hiawatha'. Speranza also read the poetry of the Young Ireland poets, and Oscar would later admit that these poems made a deep impression on him: 'As regards these men of '48, I look on their work with peculiar reverence and love, for I was trained by my mother to love and reverence them as a Catholic child is the saints of the calendar . . . .'[31] He told the American writer Mary Watson that it was his mother who inspired him to become a poet. He had access to his father's extensive library which contained hundreds of books on a wide variety of subjects including art, poetry, biography, English and continental literature, theatre, classic Greek and Roman authors, Irish history and topography, and many books on religious subjects.[32] Among his mother's books were the novels of Disraeli, and it has been suggested that these influenced the development of Oscar Wilde's paradoxical wit. Disraeli's technique was to reverse well-known axioms. 'He was born of poor but dishonest parents' would be a typical example.[33] Such methods were greatly admired by Speranza. All these childhood experiences in Merrion Square had a major influence on the young Oscar Wilde.

> From his earliest childhood his principal companions were his father and mother and their friends. Now wandering about Ireland with the former in quest of archaeological treasures, now listening in Lady Wilde's salon to the wit and thought of Ireland . . . . He had, of course, tutors, and the run of a library containing the best literature, and went to a Royal school; but it was at his father's dinner table and in his mother's drawing-room that the best of his early education was obtained.[34]

Every afternoon between two and four o'clock during Oscar Wilde's childhood, carriages would jostle for space outside the houses in Merrion Square, as patients alighted to visit their doctors. At this period Dublin possessed a leading international school of medicine, largely due to the efforts of a remarkable group of physicians and surgeons, several of whom lived near each other on the square. William Wilde established himself as one of the great ear specialists of his time and he helped to place the subject on a scientific footing. He introduced many new instruments, including the first dressing forceps and an aural snare known as Wilde's snare. One of the operative approaches he devised for mastoiditis became known as Wilde's incision. Wilde enjoyed surgery, and his enthusiasm impressed the poet William Allingham, who recorded a meeting with Wilde in his diary in 1865:

> Call At Wilde's, and drive with him as far as Hospital, where a patient is waiting for him – 'to have his eyelids chopped off.' There is no doubt but surgeons enjoy operating, and were it otherwise what tortures would not surgeons suffer, and would they be able to do the needful work so well?[35]

Sir Philip Crampton, who was surgeon-general to the army in Ireland, consulted at the Meath Hospital and also worked with Wilde at St Mark's Opthalmic Hospital. He was one of the most distinguished surgeons living on Merrion Square, a Fellow of the Royal Society and a close friend of the novelist Maria Edgeworth. She sent him a pen, which she had been given by Sir Walter Scott, and the gift was accompanied by a poem. The surgeon rose to the occasion and acknowledged the pen with a poem which began:

> Immortal Pen! what destiny is thine
> To pass from Edgeworth's, to a hand like mine![36]

Crampton was a noted conversationalist and he was well read in history and the classics. Sir Walter Scott admired 'the liveliness and range of his talk' when he met him during a visit to Ireland.[37] Like Oscar Wilde in later years, Crampton's love of fine clothes was legendary. On the occasion of George the Fourth's visit to Dublin, Crampton wore such a splendid uniform at the Castle Levée that the king enquired to what corps he belonged. With typical Dublin wit, the chief justice, Sir Charles Kendal Bushe, replied: 'He commands a regiment of Lancers your Majesty!'[36] A contemporary satirical medical writer referred to Crampton as a dandy in a sketch in *The Lancet*, and went on to express amazement that he had recently lectured to his students dressed in a plain but elegant suit of black: 'We never, indeed, saw him look better, nor more like one of his own species; for, on other occasions, he seemed to us half bear, half

41

beaver, so completely had the pelts of these animals concealed his human form.'[38] Several of the other leading doctors on Merrion Square were also noted for their elegance. The term 'dandy' at that time did not imply lack of masculinity, but rather that the person appreciated beautiful things and was elegant in appearance. Oscar Wilde defined dandyism as 'an attempt to assert the absolute modernity of beauty . . . .'[39] Crampton was physically very strong and he was heard to boast one day that he had swum across Lough Bray, ridden into Dublin and amputated a limb before breakfast. Oscar Wilde, who was to develop similar interests to Crampton, including his enthusiasm for furs, was also physically strong and a very able swimmer. According to his son Vyvyan, he ploughed through the water like a shark.

The three leading physicians of the Irish school of medicine – Robert Graves, William Stokes and Dominic Corrigan – lived on Merrion Square. Graves together with Stokes championed the development of bedside clinical teaching in the English-speaking world and their books had considerable influence on the development of medicine in North America. Their names are linked to medical syndromes and are still recalled daily in hospitals throughout the world. They were highly cultured men who did not confine their interests to medicine. Robert Graves painted with Turner on the Continent, Sir Dominic Corrigan wrote a book about his travels in Greece, and William Stokes wrote the biography of his friend, the painter George Petrie.

William Stokes, who was regius professor of medicine at Trinity College, lived at number 5 Merrion Square, just a few doors away from the Wildes. Stokes was described as the most distinguished physician of his time in Europe. He was a leading patron of Celtic studies in all its branches, and on Saturday evenings, scholars, painters, writers and musicians made their way to his house in Merrion Square where they found an environment congenial to their tastes. His son Whitley became a leading Celtic scholar. When Oscar Wilde was still a child, Whitley Stokes was counted among the friends of writers such as Richard Moncton Milnes, Richard Burton and Dante Gabriel Rossetti. It was Whitley Stokes who first recognised the beauty of Edward Fitzgerald's translation of the *Rubáiyát of Omar Khayyám* when he found several copies of the work in a 'bargain box' in 1861, two years after its publication. He sent copies to his friends, including Rossetti, and it soon made its way into the hands of such notable figures as Algernon Swinburne, Robert Browning, Edward Burne-Jones, William Morris and John Ruskin. As a result of Whitley Stokes' espousal of the poem among his pre-Raphaelite friends, the *Rubáiyát* began to attract the attention it deserved. Whitley Stokes studied ancient Celtic manuscripts, and his accurate but beautiful translations helped to reveal genuine Celtic culture to Victorian scholars. There was at the time much interest in Celtic literature and art, an interest that was greatly stimulated in England by Mathew Arnold's influential work *On the Study of Celtic Literature*. This book became one of the canons of the aesthetic movement by contrasting an idealised beauty of Celtic life and art with the utilitarianism of the Victorian period. Oscar Wilde would later speak of the Celtic Revival as possessing the key to a new era of greatness in literature and art:

> And though the mission of the aesthetic movement is to lure people to contemplate, not to lead them to create, yet, as the creative instinct is strong in the Celt, and it is the Celt who leads in art, there is no reason why in future years this strange Renaissance should not become almost as mighty in its way as was that new birth of Art that woke many centuries ago in the cities of Italy.[40]

William Stokes' daughter, Margaret, was an able book illustrator, and it may have been in 5 Merrion Square that Oscar Wilde developed his love of beautifully illustrated books. *The Cromlech on Howth*, Samuel Ferguson's epic work, was the first book that she illustrated. The book was beautifully decorated with illuminated initial letters from the Book of Kells and landscape scenes of Howth, where the Stokes family had a country house named Carrig Breacc.

Acting and writing plays formed an integral part of the social scene in which Oscar Wilde grew up. The manuscript section of the library in Trinity College houses a play entitled *The Sisters-in-Law* by J H

Jellett, a provost of the college and a distinguished scientist. It is a comedy which makes playful fun of the intellectual reputation of the Stokes family. Stokes and many of his colleagues were members of a Shakespearean Society founded by the Reverend Robert Perceval Graves, grandfather of the poet Robert Graves. Meetings were held in the houses of the members and during these sessions excerpts from Shakespeare's plays were performed: 'It was most interesting to note the different way in which these readers . . . interpreted his thoughts and discussed his meanings, while some of the readers, such as Stokes himself, when he took such a part as that of Caliban in the "Tempest" showed no little dramatic power.'[41]

John Pentland Mahaffy, Oscar's tutor and mentor at Trinity College Dublin, was certainly greatly influenced by William Stokes when he was a young student. He was fascinated by Stokes' conversational powers and he used to go on long walks with him near his country home at Howth. Stokes loved to mystify his dinner guests by his use of wit and paradox. Mahaffy went on to become one of the greatest and wittiest conversationalists of the last century, and in 1887 he wrote a book entitled, *The Principles of the Art of Conversation*. Even though it was written years after Mahaffy's youthful conversations with Stokes, one can see the influence of the latter in the following excerpt:

> I have heard a witty talker pronounce it the golden rule of conversation *to know nothing accurately*. Far more important is it, in my mind, to *demand* no accuracy. There is no greater or more common blunder in society than to express disbelief or scepticism in a story told *for the amusement of the company*.[42]

The anonymous witty talker whom Mahaffy quoted was William Stokes. In an obituary sketch of Stokes in *MacMillan's Magazine*, Mahaffy recalled the following incident:

> I remember sitting beside him at dinner, when a scientific man of this kind was boring us with his talk. He turned to me, and said with emphasis: 'There is one golden rule of conversation – *know nothing accurately*.' And this rule he always observed himself except where the interest actually lay in minute and careful

description; then nothing could exceed the life-like picturesque-
ness of his language.[43]

Thus Stokes' sensible warning against pedantry in conversation was
elaborated by Mahaffy in his book. It is fascinating to see how Oscar
Wilde in his essay *The Decay of Lying* developed the theme with even
more enthusiasm:

> Many a young man starts in life with a natural gift for
> exaggeration which, if nurtured in congenial and sympathetic
> surroundings, or by the imitation of the best models, might
> grow into something really great and wonderful. But, as a rule,
> he comes to nothing. He . . . falls into careless habits of
> accuracy, . . . begins to verify all statements made in his
> presence, (and) has no hesitation in contradicting people who
> are much younger than himself.[44]

There can be little doubt that in some measure *The Decay of Lying* was
meant as a parody of Mahaffy's ideas and style, although of course it
also contained Wilde's own thoughts on aestheticism. Wilde chose
the title with tongue in cheek, as Mahaffy had written two essays
entitled *The Decay of Modern Preaching* and *The Decay of Genius*.

According to Wilde in *The Critic As Artist*: 'Conversation should
touch everything, but should concentrate itself on nothing.'[45] He
introduced similar ideas into a number of his works: 'One should
absorb the colour of life,' Lord Henry observed in *Dorian Gray*, 'but
one should never remember its details. Details are always vulgar!'[46] In
the same work Lord Henry remarked: 'as for believing things, I can
believe anything, provided that it is quite incredible.'[47] Oscar's friends
were aware of his own intolerance of people who insisted on a strict
adherence to facts:

> The truth is that there was a certain description of man loathed
> by Wilde. This was the kind of man who insists on precise facts in
> the most casual of talks. Thus, if Wilde, sailing along beautifully,
> should happen to say: 'On the morning of the fifteenth of June,
> Napoleon, seeing that Grouchy did not come up, and that all was
> lost – ', some man might pop his head out and declare in a tone
> which brooked no denial: 'You are wrong, Oscar. It was the

eighteenth of June, and the time was three o'clock in the afternoon.' That kind of thing really had the power of exasperating Wilde beyond endurance.[48]

When he met Sir Arthur Conan Doyle, the creator of Sherlock Holmes, Wilde excused his own disinterest in facts: 'Between me and life there is a mist of words always. I throw probability out of the window for the sake of a phrase and the chance of an epigram makes me desert truth.'[49] Even music could be spoilt by an over emphasis on accuracy! In the opening scene of *The Importance of Being Earnest*, Algernon is playing the piano in his flat in Half Moon Street:

Algernon:	Did you hear what I was playing, Lane?
Lane:	I didn't think it polite to listen, sir.
Algernon:	I'm sorry for that, for your sake. I don't play accurately – anyone can play accurately – but I play with wonderful expression. As far as the piano is concerned, sentiment is my forte. I keep science for Life.[50]

Oscar Wilde condemned the English because they 'are always degrading the truth into facts. When a truth becomes a fact, it loses all its intellectual value'.[51] Likewise he attributed many of the distasteful aspects that he observed in American life to George Washington's passion for the truth:

The crude commercialism of America, its materialising spirit, its indifference to the poetical side of things, and its lack of imagination and of high unattainable ideals, are entirely due to that country having adopted for its national hero a man who, according to his own confession, was incapable of telling a lie.[52]

In Wilde's essay *The Critic As Artist*, Gilbert observes:

To give an accurate description of what has never occurred is not merely the proper occupation of the historian, but the inalienable privilege of any man of parts and culture. Still less do I desire to talk learnedly. Learned conversation is either the affectation of the ignorant or the profession of the mentally unemployed.[53]

While the medical profession tended to dominate Merrion Square during Oscar's childhood, there was always a significant number of influential lawyers living there. One of the most interesting and fascinating residents with a legal training on the square never actually practised law. This was the writer Joseph Sheridan Le Fanu, who established the *Evening Mail* in 1839 and edited it for the next two decades. He also edited the *Dublin University Magazine* between 1869 and 1872. Le Fanu, now remembered as one of the best writers of horror stories, became somewhat of a recluse in his later years. He worked into the early hours of the morning on his stories in his darkened study at 18 (now 70) Merrion Square, sustaining himself with coffee or black tea and working at a desk that had once belonged to his great-uncle, the famous playwright Richard Brinsley Sheridan. *Uncle Silas* and *The House by the Churchyard* are among his best-known stories, and his vampire story *Carmilla* almost certainly inspired Bram Stoker's *Dracula*. Le Fanu had been a close friend of William Wilde's during Oscar's childhood, but in later years as tales began to circulate about the high life and Bohemian soirées at 1 Merrion Square, both men drifted apart. When Oscar was growing up, his parents' home was well known to the citizens of Dublin, and it was pointed out to visitors. Readers of T D Sullivan's *A Guide to Dublin* were informed that 'The corner house, No 1 Merrion Square, north, is the residence of the eminent antiquarian, Sir William Wilde, and his gifted wife, the well known Irish poetess "Speranza" '.[54]

CHAPTER 5

A Dublin salon

The intellect is a delicate-stringed instrument that rusts if not played on, and it is by the collision of mind with mind that we learn our own value, or the need of progress; what we are and what we might be.[1]

Speranza

All women become like their mothers. That is their tragedy. No man does. That's his.[2]

Oscar Wilde

ALTHOUGH NOT THE BIGGEST house in Merrion Square, number 1 was certainly one of the most distinctive, possessing balconies and a sun-room.[3] Anyone waiting outside the house on a Saturday afternoon when the Wildes lived there witnessed a very busy scene, as it was on that afternoon that Speranza held her weekly salon. She established the salon in 1859 when Oscar was five years old. She became a very successful hostess, and often more than a hundred people crowded into her receptions. Visiting celebrities from abroad made their way to the house, and according to one visitor it was 'a rallying place for all who were eminent in science, art, or literature'.[4]

At these receptions Speranza developed her conversational skills, pitting her wits against those of her brilliant guests. 'Never be malicious, it is so vulgar', she once observed, 'epigram is always better than argument in conversation, and paradox is the very essence of social wit and brilliancy; the unexpected, the strange combination of opposites, the daring subversion of some ancient platitude, are all keen social weapons . . . .'[5] They were weapons that her son mastered and used with great skill in conversation and in his plays. In his novel *The Picture of Dorian Gray*, Lord Henry Wotton loved paradox, and as he developed an idea he 'grew wilful; tossed it into the air and transformed it; let it escape and recaptured it; made it iridescent with fancy, and winged it with paradox'.[6] Wilde once wrote to a friend telling him that he loved 'best in the world, Poetry and Paradox dancing together'.[7] He saw life, according to a contemporary, as an aggregation or succession of paradoxes. In the words of Lord Henry Wotton: 'The way of paradoxes is the way of truth. To test Reality we must see it on the tight-rope. When the Verities become acrobats we can judge them.'[6]

Speranza expressed opinions on a wide variety of subjects, including poetry, art and clothes. She argued that dress should have a moral significance, expressing a woman's personality, and that it should not be subject to the 'frivolous mutations of fashions'.[8] A woman's first duty was to discover her own personality and to decide, for example, whether she wished to be 'either a superb Juno, or a seductive Aphrodite, or a Hebe, blooming and coquette, or a Pallas Athene, grand, majestic and awe inspiring'.[8] She had very definite views on the most appropriate dress for women writers:

> The literary dress, should in fact, be free, untrammelled and unswathed. As simple and as easily adjusted as Greek drapery, and fastened only with a girdle or a brooch. No stiff corselet should depress the full impulses of a passionate heart. Grecian women wore a flowing robe without sleeves, girdled at the waist, the hair braided, and sometimes crowned with flowers and sandals on the feet. Art had only to imitate – it could not improve this costume, where grace, beauty and harmony were made visible to the eye.[8]

It is doubtful if Speranza was ever regarded as an authority on fashion and her dress was looked upon as eccentric by most of her contemporaries. When she hosted receptions in 1 Merrion Square, she 'dressed in long, flowing robes of Irish poplin and Limerick lace, and was adorned with gold chains and brooches modelled on the ancient ornaments of Erin's early queens'.[9] Oscar Wilde also considered himself an expert on women's dress and he frequently lectured on the subject.

Speranza was an advocate of women's rights long before it became a common or popular issue. She pointed out that there were two moral codes, one permitting wide latitude for men and the other exacting rigid obedience from women. She campaigned for a better education for women, including the right to study at university. This remained a life-long interest and her signature was the first on a petition, signed by ten thousand women, demanding the admission of women to Trinity College Dublin in 1892.[10] Speranza emphasised the lack of opportunities for women with talent in Victorian society: 'Nothing is done by laws', she argued, 'by government or society towards giving women an honourable status and adequate reward for their gifts and work.'[11] She was optimistic about the future however, and she already noted signs of change, particularly in the literary field: 'Women's intellect, keen, brilliant, and fearless, is rapidly permeating all departments of literature, and making its influence felt upon the mind of the age; an influence which is now mainly exerted in overthrowing old prejudices and conventionalisms, and those venerable social fictions which have long held women in bondage.'[12]

Speranza was encouraged by the views expressed on the subject of women in society at the fifth annual meeting of the National Association for the Promotion of Social Science, which took place in Dublin in August 1861. This organisation, which was founded in 1856 to promote social justice, took a very positive view on the place of women in society, and part of the meeting was given over to discussing the employment of women. The meeting was attended by sixteen hundred delegates from around the world, and was held in The Four Courts. William Wilde and Speranza kept an open house during the meeting, according to their Swedish friend Rosalie Olivecrona: 'During the walk in the morning through the Zoological Garden in the Phoenix Park, which is rather near, I had the opportunity of observing, how our kind friend and his amiable wife, who in her native country is known and valued as a successful authoress, literally went out on the roads and paths encouraging people to come to their table.'[13] The dinner that evening was a lively affair, mixing serious discussion on the day's proceedings with humour, and the Swedish guest was fascinated by the 'quick repartees' that flew across the table.

Speranza, like her illustrious uncle Charles Maturin, usually had the shutters closed and candles lit when she received her guests. The writer Henrietta Corkran who attended Speranza's salon at 1 Merrion Square recalled her hostess's peculiar aversion to daylight: 'She hated what she called "the brutality of strong lights"; the shutters were closed and the lamps had pink shades.'[14] Oscar could also adopt this affectation when he wanted to make an impression. The French writer Jean-Joseph Renaud recalled an occasion when Oscar arrived at a house in Paris. Sitting down with an air of exhaustion, he begged the hostess to close the window shutters and to light candles, as he could not possibly stand the light of day.[15] A young friend who attended some of Oscar's receptions in London noticed that 'the most extraordinary coloured effects of lighting were used to give an aesthetic effect, supposed to have an influence on the thought and conversation of the people present; and, except for the drawback – if so it really were – that one was not always sure who the person one was speaking to was, owing to the dimness, otherwise it must have been very soothing to tired eyes and tired nerves'.[16]

Uncharitable contemporaries assumed that Speranza resorted to the closed shutters and pink shades so that curious guests would not detect any signs of ageing in her face. Mrs Erlynne certainly admitted to adopting this strategy in *Lady Windermere's Fan*:

> Besides, my dear Windermere, how on earth could I pose as a mother with a grown-up daughter? Margaret is twenty-one, and I have never admitted that I am more than twenty-nine, or thirty at the most. Twenty-nine when there are pink shades, thirty when there are not.[17]

Speranza believed that a woman should never be too specific about her age, and this was a belief to which she adhered firmly throughout her life. She adjusted her own date of birth, claiming that she was born in 1826, whereas extant records indicate that she was actually born in 1820 or 1821.[18] Lady Bracknell expressed similar convictions with regard to age in *The Importance of Being Earnest*:

Lady Bracknell (to Cecily):	Come here, sweet child. How old are you, dear?
Cecily:	Well, I am really only eighteen, but I always admit to twenty when I go to evening parties.
Lady Bracknell:	You are perfectly right in making some slight alteration. Indeed, no woman should ever be quite accurate about her age. It looks so calculating . . . . Eighteen, but admitting to twenty at evening parties. Well, it will not be very long before you are of age and free from the restraints of tutelage. So I don't think your guardian's consent is, after all, a matter of any importance.
Jack:	Pray excuse me, Lady Bracknell, for interrupting you again, but it is only fair to tell you that according to the terms of her grandfather's will Miss Cardew does not come legally of age till she is thirty-five.
Lady Bracknell:	That does not seem to me to be a grave objection. Thirty-five is a very attractive age. London society is full of women of the very highest birth who have, of their own free choice, remained thirty-five for years. Lady Dumbleton is an instance in point. To my own knowledge she has been thirty-five ever since she arrived at the age of forty, which was many years ago now.[19]

In *A Woman of No Importance* Lord Illingworth held even more extreme views than Lady Bracknell about women who are truthful about their age:

Mrs Allonby:	He is very nice; very nice indeed. But I can't stand the American young lady.

Lord Illingworth:	Why?
Mrs Allonby:	She told me yesterday, and in quite a loud voice too, that she was only eighteen. It was most annoying.
Lord Illingworth:	One should never trust a woman who tells one her real age. A woman who would tell one that, would tell one anything.[20]

Oscar Wilde inherited his mother's facility to be flexible on the subject of age. She appears to have encouraged this trait in her son, who regularly subtracted two years from his own age. When Oscar won the Newdigate prize at Oxford, his mother wrote that it was a remarkable achievement for a twenty-two-year-old, when she knew that he was nearly twenty-four.

Speranza worked hard to make her salon a success and to make 1 Merrion Square the fulcrum of artistic and literary life in Dublin. Often the rooms became very crowded and it was necessary to leave the coffee and wine on tables in the hall. There was usually a music recital and authors were invited to read from their works. As a hostess Speranza set herself exacting goals:

> The queen regnant of a literary circle must at length become an actress there; she must adapt her manners, her ideas, her conversation, by turns, to those of every individual around her. She must be perpetually demonstrating her own attractions and attainments, or calling forth those of others. She must become a slave to the caprices, envious feelings, contentions, rivalries, selfish aims, ignoble artifices and *exigeants*, pretensions of literati, artistes, and all the notabilities of fashionable circles.[21]

The diaries and memoirs of her contemporaries reveal that she took these self-imposed duties very seriously. She moved constantly among her guests, introducing people and making sure that no one felt left out. She was always generous and lavish in her praise when highlighting the achievements of her guests. The poet Denis Florence McCarthy recorded a visit to 1 Merrion Square with Sir John Gilbert in his diary on 8 May 1878:

> Gilbert and I paid a visit to Lady Wilde at one of her afternoon-

tea receptions. There were several accomplished, learned, and, I have no doubt, beautiful ladies present, but as the room was so dark, I cannot speak with absolute certainty on the last point . . . . Another of Lady Wilde's visitors was the celebrated and many-sided Mr Mahaffy. To this universal genius I was formally introduced, and he to me, by Lady Wilde, she standing between us on the hearthrug, and towering over us in her grand and queenly proportions.[22]

Catherine Jane Hamilton recalled a visit to Speranza's salon in her book *Notable Irishwomen*:

She had *the art de faire un salon*. If anybody was discovered sitting in a corner, Lady Wilde was sure to bring up someone to be introduced, and she never failed to speak a few happy words which made the stranger feel at home. She generally prefaced her introductions with some remarks such as 'Mr A, who has written a delightful poem', or 'Mr B, who is on the staff of the Snapdragon', or 'Miss C, whose new novel everyone is talking about.'[23]

In the original version of *The Picture of Dorian Gray*, which appeared in *Lippincott's Magazine*, the portrayal of Lady Brandon as a hostess corresponds closely to a number of contemporary descriptions of Speranza:

I like to find out people for myself. But poor Lady Brandon treats her guests exactly as an auctioneer treats his goods. She either explains them entirely away, or tells one everything about them except what one wants to know.[24]

Speranza may have expressed her displeasure when she read this, or Oscar may have thought the description was too transparent. In any case, it did not appear in the text when *Dorian* was first published in book form.

Speranza was once asked how she managed to attract so many interesting people to her salon: 'By interesting them', was the reply. 'It's quite simple. All one has to do is to get all sorts of people – but no dull specimens – and take care to mix them. Don't trouble about their morals. It doesn't matter they haven't any.'[25] It was an unusual

contd p71

Speranza in 1848.

William Wilde by Erskine Nicol.
(Courtesy National Gallery of Ireland)

Charles Robert Maturin, the Gothic novelist whose work had a major influence on Oscar Wilde.

21 Westland Row,
Oscar Wilde's birthplace,
by Pat Liddy.
(Courtesy of the artist)

St Mark's Church, Pearse Street, where Oscar Wilde was baptised.

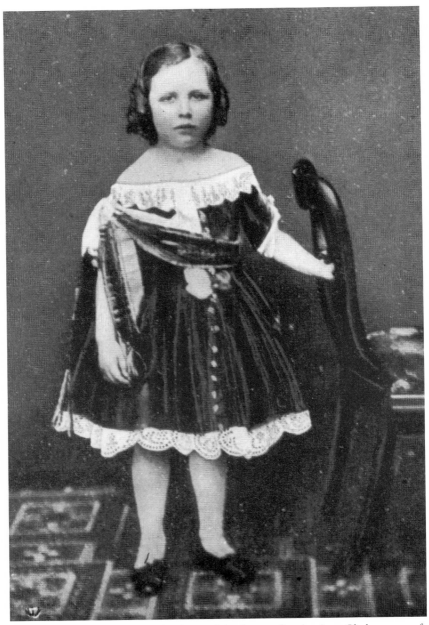

Oscar Wilde as a young child. The photograph has been attributed to Leon Gluckman, one of the first professional photographers in Dublin.

St Mark's Ophthalmic Hospital which was founded by Oscar Wilde's father.
(Drawing by Eamon Sweeney)

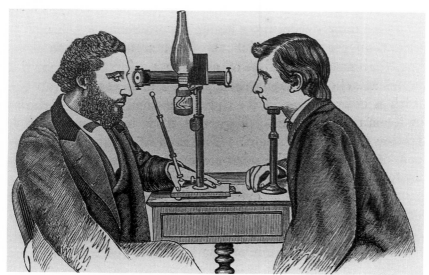

Henry Wilson, Oscar Wilde's natural brother, examining the eye of a young patient.
(Courtesy Royal College of Physicians of Ireland)

59

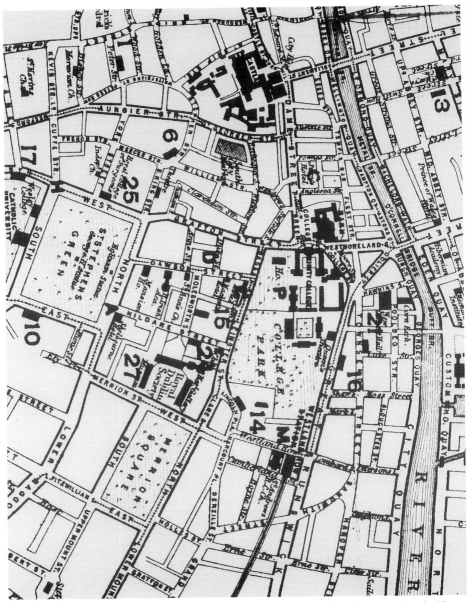

A map of 'medical' Dublin in the nineteenth century. St Mark's Hospital can be seen on Lincoln Place.
(Courtesy Royal College of Physicians of Ireland)

1 Merrion Square at the beginning of the twentieth century.

Night by Thorwaldsen — *a plaque on the wall of 1 Merrion Square. The companion pendant*
Day *by the same sculptor also hangs there. Several castings and reproductions of Thorwaldsen's*
most famous works were made in the last century. There are also copies of the pendants *Night*
and *Day* *in The Wedgewood Room at Dublin Castle.*

'Cupid Received by Anacreon' — one of the overdoor reliefs at 1 Merrion Square.
The original model for this work, executed in Rome in 1823 by Thorwaldsen, is in the Thorwaldsen
Museum in Copenhagen. William Wilde and Speranza visited this museum in 1858.

The physician William Stokes by an unknown artist. Stokes was a close friend and neighbour of William Wilde and he had a major influence on Oscar Wilde's tutor, John Pentland Mahaffy. (Courtesy William Stokes Postgraduate Centre, St James's Hospital, Dublin)

William Wilde (left) and William Stokes (right) share a bottle of beer.
(Courtesy Royal College of Surgeons in Ireland)

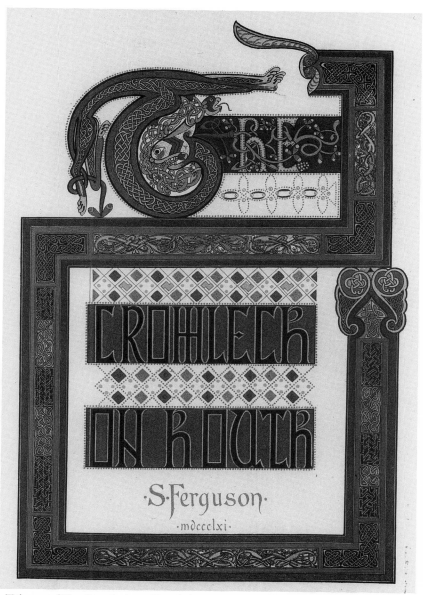

Title page of The Cromlech on Howth *by Samuel Ferguson, illustrated by Margaret Stokes, daughter of William Stokes, with motifs from the Book of Kells. Oscar admired beautifully designed books throughout his life. He was also a great enthusiast of Celtic art. (Courtesy Board of Trinity College Dublin)*

Oscar Wilde as a child. Attributed to the artist Henry O'Neill.

Portora Royal School, Enniskillen, County Fermanagh. The school had a remarkable headmaster when Wilde was a student and it was described as being 'more like a College of a university than a middle-class school'.

Boys parading in the grounds of Glencree Reformatory, County Wicklow, in the nineteenth century. Oscar Wilde was baptised a second time in this reformatory. (Courtesy National Library of Ireland)

TO

MY SONS

WILLIE AND OSCAR WILDE.

"I MADE THEM INDEED,
SPEAK PLAIN THE WORD COUNTRY. I TAUGHT THEM, NO DOUBT,
THAT A COUNTRY'S A THING MEN SHOULD DIE FOR AT NEED!"

Dedication page from Speranza's book of poetry which was published when Oscar Wilde was ten years old.

Illustration of Hag's Castle, Inishmaan, by Oscar's brother Willie Wilde, from his father's book on Lough Corrib and Lough Mask. The figures probably represent Oscar and his father.

Celtic 'sweat house' which was first discovered by William Wilde and his son Oscar when exploring the shores of Inishmaan.

a) *As illustrated in William Wilde's* Lough Corrib and Lough Mask *(1867).*

b) *Photograph of the structure today. (Photograph Mary Coakley)*

The Chapel Royal and the Bermingham Tower, Dublin Castle, by Walter Osborne, from
The Woman's World *which was edited by Oscar Wilde. Dublin Castle was the centre of
English power in Ireland. Speranza attended receptions at the castle and Oscar was taken
to services in the chapel as a child.*

contd from p54

world for children to grow up in, but Oscar appreciated its eccentricity. He once remarked: 'No one can do artistic work when in a thoroughly normal condition.'[26]

One evening a guest mentioned to Speranza that she would like to bring along a friend on the next occasion, explaining that she was 'respectable'. 'You must never employ that description in this house', admonished Speranza, 'only trades people are "respectable".'[27] Lady Bracknell voiced the same sentiments in *The Importance of Being Earnest*:

Lady Bracknell:	Is this Miss Prism a female of repellent aspect, remotely connected with education?
Chausable: (somewhat indignantly)	She is the most cultivated of ladies, and the very picture of respectability.
Lady Bracknell:	It is obviously the same person.[28]

Civilised society, according to Oscar, 'feels instinctively that manners are of more importance than morals, and, in its opinion, the highest respectability is of much less value than the possession of a good *chef*'.[29] In *De Profundis*, Christ condemns the Philistines for 'their dull respectability'![30] Oscar and his friends in London were also careful to distance themselves from the 'middle classes'. Edgar Saltus, who knew Oscar during his 'aesthetic phase' when he dressed in knee-breeches, wore velvet and had long hair, was surprised when he met him later in London: 'He was married, he was a father, and in his house in Tite Street he seemed a bit bourgeois. Of that he may have been conscious. I remember one of his children running and calling at him: "My good papa!" and I remember Wilde patting the boy and saying: "Don't call me that, it sounds so respectable." '[31]

There were physical as well as intellectual similarities between Speranza and Oscar. Leonard Ingleby described Speranza as a very handsome woman: 'The particular feature in her face which commanded instant recognition was the splendour of her dark eyes, full of life, vivacity, and an unquenchable enthusiasm.[32] This description is close to the impression that Oscar made on his Scottish friend, David Hunter Blair: 'I have a vivid recollection of him at our first meeting: the large features lit up by intelligence, sparkling eyes, and broad cheerful smile; altogether an attractive personality, enhanced by his extraordinary conversational abilities.'[33] Oscar was over six feet in height and he was described by a contemporary as 'the tall, beautiful, young Irish giant'.[34] Speranza was also tall, a fact that led George Bernard Shaw to claim that she suffered from gigantism and to ascribe Oscar's homosexuality to the same condition. Gigantism is in fact a very rare condition, caused by overactivity of the pituitary gland. Although repeated in a number of biographies of Wilde, there is absolutely no medical basis for Shaw's diagnosis.

In an article Speranza wrote on 'Genius and Marriage', she concluded that: 'The best chance, perhaps, of domestic felicity is when all the family are Bohemians, and all clever, and all enjoy thoroughly the erratic, impulsive, reckless life of work and glory, indifferent to everything save the intense moments of popular applause.'[35] She then went on to describe an idyllic Bohemian family 'in the art circles of Paris':

> The mother had been a model and a beauty, and still posed as Hebe when she handed a cup of tea to a visitor. The daughters, handsome, brilliant and clever, as the children of artists always are, sing, act, recite, dance, dress better than anyone else. Everything looks picturesque on them . . . . People asked how they managed to pay for everything; but they never paid. That was their magic secret.
>
> Bills, of course, were endless; but when some particularly severe creditor appeared, one of the splendid daughters pleaded with such a bewitching smile that he would 'call next Monday' (it was the family formula), that he retired humbled and abashed from the glorious presence, as if his claim had been an impertinence.[36]

Oscar shared his mother's philosophy and he once observed: 'Where there is no extravagance there is no love, and where there is no love there is no understanding.'[37] Speranza believed that artists should not be bothered by petty financial considerations and she advocated tax exemption for writers and artists:

> The State, surely, ought to consider the importance of preserving genius from low cares; and Parliament might pass a bill to exempt the race of the gifted from taxation. For these brilliant beings are necessary to the world; they supply life, the phosphorus, the divine fire, the grace, beauty, and charm of existence, and the nation in return should relieve them from all the mean burdens or prosaic and parochial claims.[38]

She could empathise with the financial difficulties of writers, as from time to time difficult situations were encountered in Merrion Square when funds ran low. One visitor recalled finding bailiffs in the house:

> There were two strange men sitting in the hall, and I heard from the weeping servant that they were 'men in possession'. I felt so sorry for poor Lady Wilde and hurried upstairs to the drawing-room where I knew I should find her. Speranza was there indeed, but seemed not in the least troubled by the state of affairs in the house. I found her lying on the sofa reading Prometheus Vinctus of Aeschylus, from which she began to declaim passages to me, with exalted enthusiasm. She would not let me slip in a word of condolence, but seemed very anxious that I should share her entire admiration for the beauties of the Greek tragedian which she was reciting.[39]

She never lost her composure in such difficult circumstances. Years later in London, when forced to sell some of her books because of financial problems, she said to the book dealer who called to the house: 'Look round, Mr Spencer, and tell me what you wish to buy.' When he made his choice and inquired the price she answered with dignity: 'Whatever you offer, Mr Spencer.'[40] Oscar inherited his mother's attitude to debtors: 'It is only by not paying one's bills that one can hope to live in the memory of the commercial classes.'[41] He had a similarly cavalier attitude to paying taxes, an attitude illustrated by the following conversation which he had with a taxman:

> 'I want to talk to you about your taxes.'

'What taxes? What makes you think I should pay taxes?'
'Well, sir, you live in this house and sleep here!'
'Ah, yes! But then, you see, I sleep so badly.'[42]

According to the stage directions near the end of Act I of *The Importance of Being Earnest*, Lane, the butler, enters and 'presents several letters on a salver to Algernon. It is to be surmised that they are bills, as Algernon, after looking at the envelopes, tears them up'.[43]

Oscar and his mother both scorned to take an interest in practical matters. A contemporary, Catherine Hamilton, summed up this characteristic of Speranza as follows:

> Trifles everyday trifles, she considered quite beneath her, and yet trifles make up the sum of human life. She had a horror of the 'miasma of the commonplace', her eyes were fixed on ideals, on heroes – ancient and modern – and thus she missed much that was lying near her, 'close about her feet', in her fervent admiration of the dim, the distant and the unapproachable. Her failings were the failings of a noble nature and it is in this light that we must consider her.[44]

One evening when Speranza was entertaining, a visitor asked the time as she wished to catch a train. 'Does anyone here', asked Speranza with a lofty glance around the room, 'know what time it is? We never know in this house about time.'[44] Oscar encapsulated a similar attitude in the phrase 'Punctuality is the thief of time'.[45]

Speranza wrote and spoke primarily for effect; consistency and accuracy were not her strong points. She could write passionately about the rights of women and just as enthusiastically about the duties of the wife of a man of genius. She could praise the revolutionaries of 1848 and she could also praise the non-violent campaigns of Daniel O'Connell who, according to Speranza, knew 'that Irish independence could never be achieved by epileptic fits of mad ferocity'.[46]

A contemporary described Speranza's talent for talk as infectious, and everyone in her presence 'talked their best'.[47] Henrietta Corkran who attended Speranza's salon in Merrion Square recalled that 'her talk was like fireworks – brilliant, whimsical and flashy'.[48] Speranza, like all good talkers, needed an attentive audience: 'I also go now and then to grand gatherings of the Soulless where they polka and eat', she told a friend, 'and I at least talk for it is singular how these dumb souls like to listen.'[49] W B Yeats, who knew Speranza when she was older, was very impressed by her: 'When one listens to her and remembers that Sir William Wilde was in his day a famous raconteur, one finds it in no way wonderful that Oscar Wilde should be the most finished talker of our time.'[50] Oscar's brother Willie was also influenced by his mother's enthusiasm for good conversation. He was described by contemporaries as a delightful talker: 'In his own fashion, his talk was as memorable as his brother's. It did not astonish as much as it charmed.'[51] Speranza and Oscar both liked to astonish. Speranza found her audience at her weekly salon in Merrion Square. Oscar would find a wider audience by creating some of the most brilliant social comedies ever written for the stage.

CHAPTER 6

Portora Royal School

A school should be the most beautiful place in every town and village
— so beautiful that the punishment for undutiful children should be
that they should be debarred from going to school the following day.[1]
Oscar Wilde

OSCAR WILDE WAS SENT TO Portora Royal School at Enniskillen, County Fermanagh, in February 1864 when he was nine years old. His brother Willie was taken out of St Columba's College on the outskirts of Dublin and sent to Portora with Oscar. Enniskillen was a hundred miles north-west of Dublin, but it could be reached by train, as a railway line to the town had been opened in 1859. The school, situated on a height, commanded a view over the town on one side and over a ruined castle on the other. A round tower, which formed part of the monastic ruins on the island of Devenish, could also be seen from the building. The school was well endowed and this ensured the maintenance of an excellent staff of masters. It was one of the four Royal schools of Ireland and enjoyed a good reputation.

Enniskillen was built on an island, in an area rich in military and monastic antiquities. It was a small but thriving market town, which had been the stronghold of the Maguires of Fermanagh from the fourteenth century until the 'plantation of Ulster' in the reign of James I. The Church of Ireland parish church 'nestled in the centre of the town . . . towers above all other buildings of the place, as a hen amongst her chickens . . . . The eastern window presents one of the finest examples of stained glass to be seen in Ireland. The effect of the choir is greatly enriched by the war and time-worn colours of the

Enniskillen regiments, which hang from its sides'.[2] There was a Model School for the local children a little outside the town. Enniskillen also had a courthouse, a barracks, a poorhouse, a convent, a county jail, a county infirmary and a fine Town Hall, which was 'used for balls, public dinners, lectures and other entertainments'.[2] A vegetable and fish market was held daily in the Diamond, the centre of the town, and a fair was held there on the tenth day of each month. There were pleasure gardens situated on Cole's Hill where a military band usually played on Saturdays. There were several hotels and banks, the town boasted three weekly newspapers, and all the Dublin and Belfast daily papers arrived by the one o'clock train. There was also a bookshop in the town.

Most of the students at Portora Royal School were the sons of colonial officials, landed gentry, clergy and professional people. Over the years it educated many students who subsequently gained distinction. Samuel Beckett was a student there in the twentieth century. In Wilde's time, board and education cost sixty guineas a year and there was an extra fee of one guinea a quarter for drawing lessons. On first entering the school, students were instructed to bring with them 'two pairs of sheets, six towels, eight day-shirts, four night-shirts, two hair brushes and combs, one clothes brush, and a small strong dressing box, with lock and key'.[3] The school was divided into Upper and Lower. The Lower School was for boys between the ages of ten and twelve years, and there were three classes. The schoolroom and dormitories of the smaller boys were separate from those of the Upper School, and they also had different hours for work and recreation. There were three classes in the Upper School, each having a separate classroom which was used as a reading room by the boys out of school hours. The curriculum embraced English, classics, mathematics and French. German and Italian were offered as optional subjects . There were two vacations each year, one commencing about 21 June and terminating about 10 August, the other commencing about 21 December and terminating about 28 January.

The school accommodated approximately one hundred boarders and about fifty day pupils. Its grounds of over sixty acres stretched along the banks of Lough Erne, offering the boys excellent facilities for rowing, bathing, fishing and skating. Rowing was by far the most popular sport at the school. Senior boys were allowed to take rowing boats out without supervision, but the smaller boys had to be accompanied by a master. Collecting the eggs of the wild birds that frequented the islands and woods of the region was a favourite pastime, and almost every boy had a collection. The northern end of the lough was only a short distance from the sea so that the islands were visited by large numbers of sea birds.

His contemporaries remembered Oscar Wilde as being boyish in nature. According to one classmate he was 'fairly well liked' rather than popular at the school: 'He was somewhat reserved and distant in his manner, but not at all morose or supercilious. He had rather a quick temper, but it was not very marked.'[4] He was also described as being very active and restless, although he did not take an active part in school games. His interest in sport was confined to occasional rowing on Lough Erne. He was given the nickname 'Grey-crow', which was apparently derived from the name of an island on the lake that was easily reached from the school.[5] The island of Devenish with its ruins was also within easy rowing distance:

> At the extreme end of the grounds of Portora, . . . stands the ruin of an old plantation castle, overlooking the lake. At the foot of this castle was the place of departure for the boats carrying the dead to their last resting-place in the holy island of Devenish, a little lower down in the Lough.
>
> As all were not privileged to accompany the dead on their last voyage, scenes of weeping and wailing were frequently witnessed there, hence the name Portora, 'the Harbour of tears,' or 'Tearful bank,'. . . . At all events, Devenish Island, with its wonderfully preserved Round-tower and all its sacred memories, was a favourite place of resort for the boating excursions of us boys.[6]

The headmaster of the school, Rev William Steele, held the benefice of Devenish, a parish nearby. The Jesuit convert and ascetic John Sullivan, who studied at Portora, described the island of Devenish as 'a remarkable incentive to make us thoughtful in the right direction'.[6]

Religious training was regarded as of supreme importance in Portora. The boarders received regular religious instruction and on Sundays they attended their respective Protestant churches. In a number of biographies of Oscar Wilde, it has been suggested that the ethos at Portora was very illiberal, and it has been condemned for its 'austere Protestantism'.[7] This was not the case, and the headmaster was remarkably liberal for his time. William Steele was born in 1820 and educated at Trinity College Dublin, where he had a very distinguished undergraduate career. He was appointed headmaster of Portora in 1857, a post he held for thirty-four years. It was his ambition to develop a school that would not only be the best in Ireland, but which could compete with the best schools in England. He was a courageous man and he was not afraid to champion the rights of Irish Catholics. Primary education for Catholics in Ireland had improved considerably in the early part of the nineteenth century, but there was still very little provision for second-level education. One of his first acts after his appointment was to open the school to the sons of Catholic parents. Steele had a very tolerant nature and he was most uncomfortable with the bigoted views of many of his contemporaries. At one time he proposed the establishment of two boarding houses in the school grounds, one for Catholic boys and the other for Protestant boys. They would live separately but be taught together. His willingness to remit the fees of children whose parents were encountering financial difficulties was described as 'almost excessive' and it was attributed by one of his former students to 'a magnificent and impulsive generosity and unselfish large-heartedness'.[8]

Steele encouraged his students to be responsible and to behave honourably at all times. Each pupil, depending on age, received from sixpence to two shillings pocket money every week, not an insignificant sum at the time. Steele was popular with the pupils, as one of them, Maurice Dockrell, later recalled: 'His gentlemanly, kindly bearing, his avoidance of all trickery in dealing with us, made him a universal favourite. Surrounding himself also with able lieutenants — men who were not merely scholars but gentlemen — he brought the school to an eminence of which any man might be proud.'[9] He always heralded his approach by shaking a large bunch of keys so that the students would know he was in the vicinity. Another former pupil, Graves Leech, remembered Steele as 'the mirror of a genial, winning courtesy'.[10]

The earliest surviving letter from the pen of Oscar Wilde is one he wrote to his mother from Portora School in September 1868, when he was thirteen years old:

> Darling Mama, The hamper came today, I never got such a jolly surprise, many thanks for it, it was more than kind of you to think of it. Don't please forget to send me the *National Review*. The flannel shirts you sent in the hamper are both Willie's, mine are one quite scarlet and the other lilac but it is too hot to wear them yet. You never told me anything about the publisher in Glasgow, what does he say? And have you written to Aunt Warren on the green note paper?[11]

Aunt Warren was his mother's older sister, who was married to a captain in the British Army and who had no sympathy for Speranza's nationalist or 'green' leanings.

According to one of his classmates, Edward Sullivan, Oscar did not develop any close friendships at Portora: 'He had, I think, no very special chums while at school. I was perhaps as friendly with him all through as anybody, though his junior by a year . . . . Willie Wilde was never very familiar with him, treating him always, in those days, as a younger brother.'[12] At school Oscar was noted for his love of beautiful books and special editions. He liked the novels of Disraeli and he had little good to say about Dickens. He enjoyed reading poetry, but he did not have musical ability. He was regarded as a prodigy by his classmates for his ability to read a book at phenomenal speed and retain the information subsequently. His rapid reading skill and his photographic memory enabled him to accumulate a vast amount of information on a wide range of subjects, which he would later draw on in his writing and conversation. He was noted for his interest in dress, which explains the concern expressed over his scarlet and lilac flannel shirts in his letter to his mother. He was recognised even then as a great talker, with a tendency to exaggerate accounts of everyday events in the school for the amusement of his friends. He regularly held court in the late winter afternoons around a stove that stood in the boy's entrance hall, an area known as the Stone Hall because of the original grey stone flags, and sometimes he enlivened these occasions by mimicking the postures of the figures in the stained-glass windows. During one of these sessions, towards the end of his time in Portora, the group was discussing an ecclesiastical prosecution in the Court of Arches, the court of appeal of the archbishop of Canterbury, when, according to his friend Edward Sullivan, Oscar announced that 'there was nothing he would like better in after life than to be the hew of such a *cause célèbre* and to go down to posterity as the defendant in such a case as "Regina Versus Wilde".'[13] This desire to make a great impression, regardless of personal cost, was a trait which he inherited from his mother. She once remarked: 'I should like to rage through life – this orthodox creeping is too tame for me – ah, this wild rebellious ambitious nature of mine. I wish I could satiate it with Empires, though a St Helena were the end.'[14]

On one occasion Oscar Wilde and Edward Sullivan jousted as knights on the backs of two other boys. Oscar was unhorsed in the tournament and, falling awkwardly, broke his arm. He showed no resentment, however, and both 'knights' remained friends. On another occasion Oscar went into Enniskillen town with three other boys, where they joined an audience listening to an open-air speech. One of the boys manoeuvred his position so that he was able to knock off the orator's hat with a stick, and then all four lads made a dash for it, followed by some furious members of the audience. In his hurry to escape, Oscar accidentally brushed against a disabled bystander, and the unfortunate man lost his balance and fell over. In telling the story later, Oscar recounted how his way had been barred by an angry giant and he described the prodigious feats of valour he had to perform before defeating the monster. Wilde drew on his memory of this event in *The Critic as Artist* when he attributed the invention of social intercourse to the cave man who, although he had not left his cave, was able to convince his listeners that he had slain a mammoth in single combat.

Wilde was not interested in science or mathematics at school and his academic strength lay in languages and the classics. He was particularly interested in the literary aspects of classical studies but he was less enthused by more academic issues such as grammar and textual criticism. He was taught art by William Frederick Wakeman, better known as 'Bully Wakeman', who was a friend of Sir William Wilde and a very able artist. Wakeman had studied under George Petrie, and in 1848 he wrote his *Handbook of Antiquities*. Shortly afterwards he was appointed art master at Portora, where he remained for nineteen years. He wrote and illustrated several books on Irish history and topography and contributed illustrations to William Wilde's books, *The Boyne and the Blackwater, Lough Corrib and Lough Mask* and his *Catalogue of Antiquities in the Royal Irish Academy*. In 1870 Wakeman wrote a book on Lough Erne which he dedicated to Speranza. The Wildes' friendship with Wakeman must have been a significant factor in their decision to send Willie and Oscar to Portora. Oscar profited from Wakeman's teaching and he won a school prize for art. Edward John Hardy was a young teacher at the school during this time. He married a niece of Sir William Wilde and years later Oscar reviewed his book *How to be Happy though Married* for the *Pall Mall Gazette*. Oscar recommended the book as an ideal wedding present, and he concluded the review by describing the author as the 'Murray of matrimony' and the 'Baedeker of bliss'. Another teacher, J F Davies, published an edition of the *Agamemnon* of Aeschylus with a commentary in 1868. This play made a great impression on Wilde; he quoted from it frequently in later years and he wrote a poem entitled 'A Fragment from the Agamemnon of Aeschylus'. Benjamin Purser taught history and geography at Portora, and Wilde was adept at manipulating the lessons with carefully chosen questions so that long periods were spent discussing subjects of particular interest to him. Purser's son, Louis Claude, who was only eighteen days older than Oscar, was at the school at the same time as him. He remarked years later that Wilde had 'a real love for intellectual things, especially if there was a breath of poetry in them, and he often used to inveigle some of the masters (who were, I think, rather highly educated men) into spending the time usually devoted to "hearing us our lessons" in giving a disquisition on some subject he would artfully suggest – for he had engaging manners when he liked – by some apparently innocent question e.g. I remember well: he asked "What was a Realist?" and drew forth a disquisition on Realism and Nominalism and Conceptualism in which we were all asked questions and which proved most illuminating'.[4] Louis Purser was also a brilliant classical scholar and he went to Trinity College with Wilde. Unlike Wilde, however, Purser decided to pursue an academic career. He became professor of Latin at Trinity and his portrait by Leo Whelan now hangs in the provost's office in the university. Purser valued the education he received at Portora and he spoke highly of it in later years:

> Of the very high level of instruction in Classics and Mathematics given at Portora it would be idle to speak: everyone knows of it, but best of all, those who have enjoyed it; and the instruction in English and French . . . in its higher branches were as extensive and complete as that of any school in Ireland. There was, besides, at Portora a far greater width of culture and diffusion of ideas than in any other school with which I have been acquainted; it was in that respect more like a college of a university than a middle-class school.[15]

Portora played a crucial role in Wilde's development and its importance in this respect has been greatly underestimated. It was an ideal environment for a child with an interest in culture, and it complemented the influence of his home.

When Robert Sherard came to Dublin soon after Wilde's death to research a biography, Purser supplied him with his memories of Wilde. He spoke highly of his former classmate and he mentioned how Wilde displayed his mastery of classical Greek during the competition for the school's Gold Medal. 'In the *viva voce* which was on the *Agamemnon* of Aeschylus he simply walked away from us all.'[16]

Wilde's success surprised some of his classmates, as they had not considered him as a serious competitor for academic distinctions.

Later, at both Trinity and Oxford, he would surprise his fellow students in a similar way by the apparent effortlessness of his triumphs. During his years in London and Paris, Wilde never boasted about his academic prowess, and he would get embarrassed if it was drawn to his attention. Vincent O'Sullivan remembers buying some of Wilde's personal effects in Chelsea after the auction of all Wilde's belongings following his arrest in 1895. O'Sullivan later offered the material to Wilde:

> He accepted all except one. It was a history of English literature in two volumes which had been given to him as a prize at his Irish School – the Enniskillen school, as well as I remember – and the arms of the school were stamped in gilt on the cover, and there was a laudatory inscription.
>
> Wilde looked at the volumes with a sort of horror and then began to laugh.
>
> 'However could you imagine! Do take those dreadful things away. Don't keep them yourself. Give them to the cab-driver.'[17]

Wilde wrote in *De Profundis* that among the things he regretted losing most in the auction of the contents of his home in Tite Street was his library 'with its collection of presentation volumes from almost every poet of my time, from Hugo to Whitman, from Swinburne to Mallarmé, from Morris to Verlaine: with its beautifully bound editions of my father's and mother's works, its wonderful array of college and school prizes'.[18]

In later years Oscar Wilde's classmates were proud of his achievements, as can be seen from the following letter written in 1886 by Herbert Beatty, an inspector of national schools:

> Portora has, under Dr Steele, turned out a splendid array of brilliant pupils. To take an example: in my own class were three men who already have come to the front in three different, but all distinguished, walks of life. Mr Louis Purser, FTCD, is not only the most modest but also the most profound scholar in the kingdom. Sir Edward Sullivan, a contemporary of Mr Purser's, is a prominent Dublin politician; and everyone who has laughed

at Mr Oscar Wilde does not know how much he has done, with his Portora training, to popularise classical forms of art.[19]

The classics always fascinated Wilde, and his fluent and beautiful translations in class of the works of Thucydides, Plato and Virgil were remembered afterwards by his school friends. During his penultimate year at the school, he won the Carpenter Greek Testament Prize. The following year both he and Louis Purser were awarded Royal scholarships to Trinity College Dublin. This also gave Wilde the distinction of having his name inscribed in gilt letters on an Honours Board in the school. After his imprisonment in 1895 his name was erased from the board, but it has since been regilded.

CHAPTER 7

Revelations

The Book of Life begins with a man and a woman in a garden. It ends with Revelations.[1]

Oscar Wilde

Children begin by loving their parents; as they grow older they judge them; sometimes they forgive them.[2]

Oscar Wilde

THE WILDE CHILDREN WERE TAKEN out from time to time by a young woman named Mary Travers, who called for them at Merrion Square. She was a friend of their father, but it was a friendship that William Wilde would later wish he had never encouraged. Mary Travers was the daughter of Robert Travers, professor of medical jurisprudence in Trinity College Dublin and acting librarian of Archbishop Marsh's library. Wilde first met her in July 1854 when she was referred to him at 21 Westland Row with an earache by his friend William Stokes. She was a striking nineteen-year-old at the time and she shared a mutual interest in books with the thirty-nine-year-old doctor. William Wilde began to direct her reading and she became a regular caller at his home. It was about this time that Speranza was developing her friendship with William Rowan Hamilton, but whereas one can be fairly confident that this relationship remained on an intellectual plane, one cannot have the same confidence about the relationship between her husband and Mary Travers. Speranza did not appear to be unduly worried and Mary Travers was a welcome visitor at 1 Merrion Square. She also called on Wilde at St Mark's Hospital.

In the early 1860s things began to go wrong. In 1861 Wilde invited Mary to the Queen's University conferring ceremony in St Patrick's Hall in Dublin Castle. The following day, according to Mary Travers, Wilde told her that Speranza had had their carriage followed. The relationship appeared to have cooled for a while, but Mary did spend Christmas Day with the Wilde family at 1 Merrion Square later that year. In February of the following year Speranza took her children to Bray in County Wicklow, where her husband owned a number of houses. While she was away, Wilde sent a note to Mary inviting her to call. According to Mary, when she arrived at Merrion Square Wilde held her tightly in his arms and asked her to address him as William. In March 1862 Oscar, who was then seven, became very ill. During a visit to the house, Mary Travers held Oscar on her lap, and when William Wilde entered the room he told her that her solicitude was making the child better. Soon afterwards he wrote telling her that Oscar had recovered and had benefited greatly from her nursing.

In April 1862 Mary Travers announced her intention to emigrate to Australia. Wilde gave her £40, but she only went as far as Liverpool. He must have been dismayed when she returned as he was now trying, rather ineffectually, to extricate himself from what was becoming a very complex and uncomfortable relationship. She made a second attempt to leave for Australia later in the year, but this proved equally unsuccessful. During this period she was still calling at 1 Merrion Square. On one of these visits Speranza confronted her and asked if she planned to steal her husband, whilst at the same time giving Mary a 'good pinch' in a playful manner. Matters came to a head, however, when Speranza asked Mary to take the three children to a service in the Chapel Royal in Dublin Castle. Mary arrived late on the appointed day and was very annoyed to find that Speranza had already left for Dublin Castle in a carriage with the children and their German governess.

Another episode occurred soon after this which made relations between the two women considerably worse. Mary was in the drawingroom at Merrion Square with a friend of Speranza. The latter was in her bedroom and she sent a maid down to invite her friend to come up to her. Mary also went up to the bedroom, assuming that she too was invited, but Speranza made it very clear that this was not the case. Mary rushed from the house, and as she passed a son of the sculptor John Hogan in the hall, he heard her mutter 'I will pay her off'. Over a period of time her behaviour became more and more bizarre. On one occasion she walked into Wilde's consulting room and drank an overdose of laudanum in his presence. On another visit she placed garlic in the soap trays in the consulting room. She also began to send Speranza letters she had received from Wilde, which Speranza promptly returned. When Speranza refused to see her one afternoon, Mary sat on a marble table in the hall of 1 Merrion Square for two hours; Speranza was trapped upstairs, becoming more furious as time went by, because she had arranged to travel to Bray.

In October 1863 Mary wrote a pamphlet entitled *Florence Boyle Price; or a Warning by Speranza*. The pamphlet told the story of a Dr Quilp who had taken advantage of one of his female patients while she was under the influence of chloroform. A thousand copies were printed and Mary circulated them widely, dropping some into the postbox at 1 Merrion Square. This harassment, although without immediate effect apart from giving rise to some gossip, could not have come at a worse time for William Wilde, who was now approaching the zenith of his career. His work on Celtic antiquities at the Royal Irish Academy was attracting considerable attention, and several distinguished visitors came to see his collection, including the future Edward VII of England, then Prince of Wales. He was also being honoured for his great contributions in many different fields. In 1862 he received the Swedish Order of the North Star, in 1863 he was appointed surgeon oculist to the queen in Ireland, Dublin University awarded him an honorary MD in 1864, and he was knighted in the same year.[3]

Speranza was also riding on the crest of a wave. Her translation of *The First Temptation* by the German author Wilhelmine Canz appeared in 1863. In 1864 a collection of her poems was published under the title *Poems by Speranza*. The work bore the dedication 'To my sons, Willie and Oscar' and underneath were the words:

I made them indeed,
Speak plain the word Country. I taught them, no doubt
That a Country's a thing men should die for at need![4]

William Wilde tried to escape from Mary Travers by going to his country house, Moytura, in the west of Ireland, but he was to have no respite. She sent him a printed announcement of her death and she also sent one to Speranza, with a coffin sketched on it for good measure. Throughout this period she was borrowing and demanding money from Wilde, often in exchange for IOUs. During the subsequent court case Mary referred to 'my IOU', and this was misprinted in *Saunder's News-Letter* as 'my son', an error that has given rise to the mistaken belief that Wilde had a son by Mary Travers – a belief repeated in a number of biographies of the surgeon and of Oscar Wilde.

William Wilde gave an important public lecture entitled 'Ireland, past and present, the land and the people' in Dublin in April 1864. It was an optimistic lecture, in the course of which he voiced his confidence that Ireland would one day have her own parliament, that poverty and crime would decrease, that trade and education would grow and that there would be religious liberty. 'I for one', he declared, 'hold that there is still a good time coming, not for "old" nor "young", but for New Ireland.'[5] However, the outlook for Wilde himself that evening looked anything but good. Mary Travers waited outside the hall while five newspaper boys she had employed distributed her Dr Quilp pamphlets and copies of Wilde's letters to her. One of the boys rang a bell that Mary had borrowed from an auctioneer in Blackrock, lest anyone should fail to notice their presence.

Speranza decided that she would take the children to Bray until the ensuing fuss had subsided, but the newspaper boys were quick on her heels, and the harassment continued. Speranza's patience finally gave when Isola announced that there were boys in the hall selling pamphlets and she wondered how they knew Speranza's name. Afraid to go out with the children any more, she vented her frustration by writing a very unwise letter to Doctor Travers:

Sir: You may not be aware of the disreputable conduct of your daughter at Bray, where she consorts with all the low newspaper boys in the place, employing them to disseminate offensive placards, in which she makes it appear that she has had an intrigue with Sir William Wilde. If she chooses to disgrace herself, that is not my affair; but as her object in insulting me is the hope of extorting money, for which she has several times applied to Sir William Wilde, with threats of more annoyance if not given, I think it right to inform you that no threat or additional insult shall ever extort money for her from our hands. The wages of disgrace she has so basely treated for and demanded shall never be given to her.

Jane F Wilde[6]

Mary found the letter in her father's house and she promptly sued Speranza for libel, demanding a settlement of two thousand pounds. The Wildes refused a settlement and the case opened on 12 December 1864 before Chief Justice Monahan. Isaac Butt and Richard Armstrong led for Mary Travers, and the Wildes were represented by Edward Sullivan and Michael Morris (later Lord Killanin).[7] William Wilde was sued with Speranza, as at the time a husband was considered to be responsible for his wife's civil wrongs. It soon became clear that it was not Speranza but William Wilde who was under attack, as in the opening phases of the trial it was alleged that Wilde had sexually violated Mary Travers in his consulting room in mid October 1862. According to her evidence, he first half-strangled her and then carried out the deed while she was unconscious. Whilst this alleged assault was taking place, there were several patients waiting outside in the hall.

The trial was a *cause célèbre*. According to *The Irish Times*, the police had to take special precautions to prevent overcrowding. Speranza adopted a superior and lofty approach to the proceedings and she occasionally made the courtroom audience laugh when she referred disdainfully to some of Mary Travers' antics. She lost considerable sympathy, however, by her answer to one of Richard Armstrong's key questions:

'When Miss Travers complained to you of your husband's attempt upon her virtue, why did you not answer her letter?

What was your reason?' 'Because I was not interested,' she replied.[8]

This was a major error, and Isaac Butt placed great emphasis on Speranza's apparent indifference when he was summing up for Mary Travers. He also pilloried Sir William Wilde because he did not go into the witness box to defend his honour.

It became apparent during the cross-examination of Mary Travers that she was addicted to laudanum. The judge in his summing-up said that if the alleged assault had been the subject of a criminal charge it would have been thrown out of any court. Yet the jury decided that Speranza's letter was libellous, and Miss Travers was granted damages of a farthing. This was some consolation for the Wildes, but they still had to bear the costs, which came to a sum in excess of the original two thousand pounds sought. Speranza had faced a most unpleasant courtcase with great fortitude. Years later she would expect Oscar to do the same when others, perhaps more prudently, advised him to leave England.

William Wilde's decision not go into the witness box gave rise to considerable speculation at the time. Some assumed that he did not wish to give his own account of what actually happened between himself and Mary Travers, while others felt that he was following the considered legal opinion of his advisers. There was another factor that almost certainly had a major influence on his conduct during the trial. Wilde would not have wished to have the details of his relationships with other women, before his marriage to Speranza, recounted in court. His natural son Henry was twenty-six at this time and was working with him at St Mark's Hospital, and his natural daughters Emily and Mary were sixteen and eighteen years old respectively. Mary Travers knew about his natural children and she used this knowledge on more than one occasion to taunt Wilde. She wrote some appalling doggerel verse which she dropped into the letter box at 1 Merrion Square in an envelope fastened with a pin so that the servants would have access to the contents. The 'poem' began with the lines:

Your progeny is quite a pest,
To those who hate such critters,

> Some sport I'll have or I am blest
> I'll fry the *Wilde breed in the west.*
> Then you can call them *fritters.*[9]

Against this background, Wilde's silence in court is understandable.

Most of his colleagues and the majority of the leading medical journals, including *The Lancet*, rallied to his support. But his public reputation was damaged and it was a very bruising experience for his family. Oscar and Willie and their classmates at Portora would have had access to the newspaper reports of the court action. One of Oscar's friends at the school, Edward Sullivan, was the son of Edward Sullivan who acted as counsel for Speranza. Oscar was ten years old at the time. By coincidence, this was also the age of Oscar's eldest son, Cyril, when he read of Oscar's own disgrace in a Dublin newspaper in 1895.

CHAPTER 8

The west of Ireland

I am sure you would like this wild mountainous country, close to the Atlantic and teeming with sport of all kinds. It is in every way magnificent . . . .[1]

Oscar Wilde

Every Celt has inborn imagination.[2]

Oscar Wilde

WILLIAM WILDE HAD A FISHING lodge on Lough Fee in Connemara on the west coast of Galway. The lake was situated a short distance from the sea and near the Little Killary, a deep inlet flanked by mountains, resembling a Norwegian fiord. The lodge was built on land that jutted into Lough Fee, so that it was virtually surrounded by water. Wilde had acquired the thirteen acres of land on a 150-year lease in 1853, together with three acres of lake. The place was known as Illaunroe, which is Gaelic for 'red island', and it was an ideal location for boating, fishing and swimming. It was this wild, remote and beautiful countryside that Oscar Wilde explored as a child.

Nineteenth-century cities such as Dublin were very unhealthy places for children, and even the children of the affluent were at risk from the many epidemic diseases that were prevalent. The west of Ireland was a much cleaner environment and the Wilde children were taken there for long holidays. 'All my children', wrote Speranza to a friend in 1862, 'have had whooping cough and I have spent a miserable time with them – they are getting better and we are all going off to Connemara for a month.'[3] A few weeks later Oscar

93

became quite ill again and spent five weeks in bed with a fever at 1 Merrion Square.

When Oscar was ten years old his father built a two-storey villa overlooking Lough Corrib in County Mayo. The villa was situated on a 170-acre estate near Cong, which Sir William Wilde had acquired when the property of his mother's family, the Fynnes, was sold. 'Moytura', as Wilde called it, stood at the end of an avenue half a mile long – an important status symbol for an Irish country residence. The house was large enough to accommodate the family and several guests, and it contained fine Italian marble fireplaces. Speranza lent her husband £2500 to help to bring this dream to fruition. In her biography *Crowned Harp*, Nora Robertson, granddaughter of the physician Robert Graves, observed that the hierarchy of Irish social order was not defined in the Victorian period because 'it did not need to be, it was deeply implicit'.[4] Although breeding was essential, it still had to be buttressed by money and property, and it was for this reason that Graves bought a castle in the west of Ireland when he was at the height of his professional career. Wilde emulated his teacher by purchasing the estate near Cong, an action that moved his family from the ranks of the 'loyal professional people' into the ranks of the 'country gentry', with the attendant social advantages. At Moytura, Wilde entertained on a scale that could compete with his dinners in Merrion Square. His knighthood gave his family an even more prestigious place in the social firmament. This family background was an important factor in forming the confident self-perceptions that would later help Oscar to dominate the London social scene. In *De Profundis* he described Lord Alfred Douglas as 'a young man of my own social rank and position'.[5]

Cong was an area rich in archaeological treasures, and William Wilde's medical reputation helped him in acquiring valuable artefacts for the collection of the Royal Irish Academy:

> By the peasantry he was peculiarly loved and trusted, for he had brought back joy and hope to many households. How gratefully they remembered his professional skill, always so generously given; and how, in the remote country districts, he would often cross moor and mountain at the summons of some poor

sufferer, who believed with simple faith that the *Docteur mor* (the great Doctor as they called him) would certainly restore the blessed light of heaven to blind-struck eyes. In return, they were ever glad to aid him in his search for antiquities, and to him came many objects from the peasant class for his inspection and opinion – a fragment of a torque or a circlet; an antique ring or coin – and in this way many valuable relics were saved from loss, and given over to the Academy's Museum.[6]

He was befriended by Lord Ardilaun (Benjamin Guinness) who lived nearby at Ashford Castle and who shared Wilde's enthusiasm for local antiquities. He recorded his researches around Cong in his book *Lough Corrib and Lough Mask* which was published in 1867 and which received considerable public attention. Wilde, both by his writings and personal example, made it fashionable for the affluent to take holidays in the west of Ireland. It would be difficult for a reader to resist his enthusiasm, which is evident from the very first paragraph of his book on the region:

> Westward ho! Let us rise with the sun, and be off to the land of the West – to the lakes and streams – the grassy glens and fern-clad gorges – the bluff hills and rugged mountains – now cloud-capped, then revealed in azure, or bronzed by evening's tints, as the light of the day sinks into the bold swell of the Atlantic . . . But, whether seen in sunshine or in shade-curtained by mist, or with the light of morning playing upon the brown shores and landslips on the mountain side, or when the streamlets form threads of molten silver as they gleam through the purple heather and the yellow-lichened rocks ere they leap into the lake – the land we invite you to is ever beautiful in outline, and graceful in form.[7]

William Wilde set out to write an accurate and informed book that would be a blend of nature, topography, architecture, history, legend and science. He wished to take his readers as 'intelligent tourists' to the west of Ireland, and he made it clear that he had 'no desire to introduce imaginary conversations in broken English, to amuse our Saxon friends'.[7] Because of his great interest in the west of Ireland, his friends sometimes jokingly referred to him as the 'Wilde man of Connemara'.[8]

Wilde had tenants on his land, but the income from rent fell during the period of organised land agitation in the latter part of the nineteenth century. Oscar remembered a story he had heard as a child about an absentee landlord: 'My father used to have a story about an English landlord who wrote from the Carlton to his Irish agent and said "Don't let the tenants imagine that by shooting you they will at all intimidate me".'[9] Oscar would use this story later in his lecture 'Impressions of America', which was first given in London in 1883 following his tour of the United States:

> From Salt Lake City one travels over the great plains of Colorado and up the Rocky Mountains, on the top of which is Leadville, the richest city in the world. It has also got the reputation of being the roughest, and every man carries a revolver. I was told that if I went there they would be sure to shoot me or my travelling manager. I wrote and told them that nothing that they could do to my travelling manager would intimidate me.[10]

From an early age, Oscar and Willie accompanied their father on his archaeological expeditions, and they mixed with the local people. Oscar was to use this experience when he was investigating the possibility of an archaeological studentship at Oxford in 1879. He wrote to one of Mahaffy's friends, A H Sayce, professor of comparative philology at Oxford:

> I think it would suit me very well – as I have done a good deal of travelling already – and from my boyhood have been accustomed, through my Father, to visiting and reporting on ancient sites, taking rubbings and measurements and all the technique of *open air* archaeologica – it is of course a subject of intense interest to me.[11]

In *Lough Corrib and Lough Mask* Wilde described a visit to Inishmaan on Lough Mask with 'his son Oscar' in August 1866, when they discovered a very curious structure among the limestone rocks that sloped towards the lake. It was a square unmortared building, with two crypts on the west face. Wilde described the crypts as 'the most remarkable and unexplicable structures that have yet been discovered in Ireland'.[12] He postulated that it may have been a prison or penitentiary in which some of the refractory brethren of the neighbouring abbey were confined. The building has since been identified as a very good example of a sweat house. Illustrations of the structure were made by Wilde's friend William Wakeman, the art teacher in Portora. Nearby on a small island there was a ruin named Hag's Castle, and the author included an illustration of this from a drawing by his son Willie in which a man with a young boy can be seen in the foreground.

Conor Maguire, the son of the local dispensary doctor at Cong, was a frequent visitor to Moytura, and he often accompanied William Wilde on his expeditions around Connemara. Conor, who was around thirteen or fourteen at the time, remembered Speranza as a very charming lady. He was amused by the shabby old clothes that Sir William wore as he went about the neighbourhood, including 'the funny old caubeen, a soft hat, and a piece of twine round it to keep it on his head'.[13] Of the Wilde brothers, Conor was drawn more to Willie than to Oscar. The former was jolly, sang to his own accompaniment and enjoyed a drink. Oscar, however, stayed more aloof: 'When I met him he always seemed to me very dull company. I suppose he looked on all the people about as a brainless ignorant lot, not worth talking to, whose souls never rose above the weather, the crops, fishing or shooting. Whereas his thoughts were centred on Greek poetry. He had a long solemn face and rarely ever smiled.'[13]

The young Wildes knew the children of many of the leading families in the area, including the Martin family who lived at Ross House near Oughterard, on the opposite side of Lough Corrib. The youngest member of this family, Violet, would write under the pseudonym Martin Ross in a famous partnership with her cousin Edith Somerville. Oscar and his brother occasionally met with the brothers George and Augustus Moore, whose father George Henry Moore was a frequent visitor to Merrion Square and Moytura. The Moores lived on the east side of Lough Carra, in Moore Hall, a large house with a Doric columned portico. George Moore was just two years older than Oscar, but they were never good friends. It has been suggested that this was due to rivalry between Willie and Augustus, both of whom later became journalists in London, but it is very unlikely that this would explain the degree of bitterness that developed between them. On one occasion in later years when Oscar was asked if he knew George Moore, he replied: 'Do I know–him? Indeed, I know him so well that I have not spoken to him for ten years!'[14] The feeling was reciprocated and Moore accused Wilde of literary piracy: '. . . Paraphrasing and inverting the witticisms and epigrams of others.'[14] On hearing that James Joyce had acknowledged his indebtedness to Dujardin several times, Moore observed: 'Such frankness in Irish plagiarists astonishes me. Now, there was Oscar Wilde, another Dublin Jackeen who plagiarised wholesale, without admitting to his thefts.'[15] Ironically, Moore himself was well known to be adept at quoting from the works of others without acknowledgement. Moore's younger brother Augustus admired Oscar, and a sonnet he wrote for him suggests that there may have been an element of infatuation in the relationship. The poem, which bore the title *To Oscar Wilde Author of Ravenna*, was published in *The Irish Monthly* in September 1878. The following are the last six lines:

> I buried Love within the rose I meant
> To deck the fillet of thy Muse's hair;
> I take this wild–flower, grown against her feet,
> And kissing its half-open lips I swear,
> Frail though it be and widowed of its scent,
> I plucked it for your sake and find it sweet.[16]

Augustus or Gus Moore later became a well-known figure in London, and he was a regular patron of the Café Royal. Unlike his brother George, Gus appears to have been a popular character and was remembered as an amusing and clever person who always had a fund of anecdotes to relate about the theatrical world. He was noted for his passion for brightly coloured neckties, and on one occasion when he asked Willie Wilde for his opinion of a very loud tie, Wilde replied: 'Well, my dear Gus, since you ask me, I should have thought that only a deaf man could have worn it with safety.'[17]

At Moytura, Oscar Wilde listened to the stories of Frank Houlihan, a Galway man who worked for his father. Houlihan and others introduced the young Oscar to the oral traditions of Gaelic culture. Later Wilde would delight in telling stories, and many of his prose works such as *The Happy Prince* and his poems in prose were first told to audiences before being committed to paper. *Salomé* was written in this way: 'One day, when he was in Paris, he lunched with some young writers, and he told them his play, inventing and filling in as he talked. This was generally his method. He invented, not in silence, but in talking. Possibly he had inherited the soul of some far away bard who invented his chants as he sang them.'[18] Walter Pater once observed that there was 'always something of an excellent talker about the writing of Mr Oscar Wilde'.[19] Wilde's conversation was admired for its brilliant epigrams and paradoxes, but according to Leonard Ingleby: 'His chief successes were made by the telling of strange and symbolic stories.'[20] Shaw, who did not have the easiest of relationships with Wilde, remembered meeting him by chance when they were both relaxing at Rosherville Gardens: 'Wilde and I got on extraordinarily well on this occasion. I had not to talk myself, but to listen to a man telling me stories better than I could have told them.'[21] According to Henri de Regnier, the French poet and novelist, Oscar was 'an uncomparable teller of tales; he knew thousands of stories which linked themselves one to the other in an endless chain'.[22] Wilde's exposure to Celtic folklore during his early years had a major influence on his work. This influence is particularly apparent in *The Picture of Dorian Gray*, where Celtic symbols are used to invoke a mood of enchantment and there are colourful descriptive passages reminiscent of those used by the bards in ancient mythological tales. Repetition is also used in the manner of oral literature throughout the book. Critics who fail to appreciate this make the common mistake of attributing the vivid passages and use of repetition in *The Picture of Dorian Gray* to an unrestrained style. Folklore and myth form the basis and structure of the novel, setting it apart from other works of the same genre in the English language.[23]

Oscar absorbed much of the folklore of the west of Ireland, and years later he would tell delightful fairy and adventure stories to his children, Cyril and Vyvyan, at bedtime. His son Vyvyan later recalled this period of his childhood:

> He told us about the family house at Moytura, where he was going to take us one day, and of the 'great melancholy carp' in Lough Corrib, that never moved from the bottom of the lough unless he called them with the Irish songs learnt from his father; and he would sing these songs to us. I do not think he sang very well, but to us he had the most beautiful voice in the world; there was one particular song, called 'Athá mé in mu codladh, agus ná dúishe mé', meaning I am asleep, and do not wake me, which I came across again when I was grown up and was trying to learn the Irish language myself. And he invented poems in prose for us which, though we may not always have understood their inner meaning, always held us spellbound.[24]

William Wilde believed that Moytura was situated on the site of the great battle of Magh-Tura. The *Battle of Magh Tura* is considered to be the most important of the early Irish mythological tales. It relates how the gods of the Irish Tuatha Dé Danann fought the demonic horde known as the Fomóirí. Babor of the Evil Eye was slain in single combat during the battle. Babor was reputed to possess magic powers in his evil eye, which could cause havoc among the ranks of an opposing army. The concept of the 'Evil Eye' was familiar in Irish folklore and many believed that great harm could be inflicted by the direct fixed glance of those with this sinister gift or power. Severe punishments were meted out under Brehon Laws to those who used the power of the Evil Eye to harm others. In *Melmoth The Wanderer* Charles Maturin described 'a withered Sybil' who exercised considerable influence over 'the lower orders' by claiming that she had a counter-spell of unfailing efficacy against the Evil Eye. In her book on the ancient legends of Ireland, Speranza wrote that there was nothing more dreaded by the people or considered more deadly in its effects than the Evil Eye, and she went on to try to rationalise the phenomenon:

> The singular malific influence of a glance has been felt by most persons in life; an influence that seems to paralyze intellect and

speech, simply by the mere presence in the room of some one who is mystically antipathetic to our nature. For the soul is like a fine-toned harp that vibrates to the slightest external force or movement, and the presence and glance of some persons can radiate around us a divine joy, while others may kill the soul with a sneer or a frown. We call these subtle influences mysteries, but the early races believed them to be produced by spirits, good or evil, as they acted on the nerves or the intellect.[25]

Oscar Wilde heard many stories when he was young about the dreadful things that happened to innocent victims when they were fixed by the Evil Eye, and these stories made an impact on his sensitive mind. Years later when he was walking through a street in Naples with his friend Vincent O'Sullivan, they saw an old woman approach. 'Unless that old woman asks you for money,' Wilde said, 'do not offer it to her. But if she asks you, be sure not to refuse.'[26] Some days later they were sitting in a restaurant when the old woman came along and, pausing for a while, she stared at them both. Wilde became agitated: 'Did you see that?' he said, 'She has looked in at the window. Some great misfortune is going to happen to us.'[26]

Despite his highly cultured mind, Wilde was very superstitious. 'I love superstitions', he wrote in 1894 when he was at the height of his fame, 'they are the colour element of thought and imagination. They are the opponents of common sense. Common sense is the enemy of romance.'[27] Speranza had translated J W Meinhold's *Sidonia the Sorceress* in 1849, and this book was one of Wilde's favourites as a child. His father collected superstitions in the west of Ireland and he wrote *Irish Popular Superstitions* in 1852 which he dedicated to Speranza. Throughout his life William Wilde never missed an opportunity to collect fairy tales: 'Old men and women, too, when going away cured from his hospital, would ask leave to send eggs or fowl, or some such country gift, and he would bargain for a fairy tale instead.'[28] After her husband's death, Speranza published two further books based largely on material collected by her husband, *Ancient Legends, Mystic Charms, and Superstitions of Ireland* (1888) and *Ancient Cures, Charms and Usages of Ireland* (1890). William Butler Yeats drew

101

on these books when he published his *Fairy and Folk Tales of Ireland* in 1892. In the preface of the work he generously acknowledged his debt:

> But the best book since Croker is Lady Wilde's *Ancient Legends*. The humour has all given way to pathos and tenderness. We have here the innermost heart of the Celt in the moments he has grown to love through years of persecution, when, cushioning himself about with dreams, and hearing fairy-songs in the twilight, he ponders on the soul and on the dead. Here is the Celt, only it is the Celt dreaming.[29]

Oscar's friend Vincent O'Sullivan thought that Wilde may have been influenced during his life by some prediction he had heard during his early years. Certainly his lack of productivity after his release from prison appears to have been influenced by a fortune-teller whom he met three or four years before his downfall: 'I see a very brilliant life for you up to a certain point,' she told him, 'then I see a wall. Beyond the wall I see nothing.'[30] Shortly before the court trials he had consulted another fortune-teller named Mrs Robinson, and unfortunately she prophesised 'complete triumph'. In April 1895 when he was imprisoned in Holloway Gaol he wrote to his friend Ada Leverson: 'With what a crash this fell! Why did the Sibyl say fair things? I thought but to defend him from his father: I thought of nothing else, and now.'[31]

In his short story *Lord Arthur Savile's Crime*, Oscar had shown that an augury can lead to disastrous results if taken too seriously. But in the story, it was Lady Windermere's fortune-teller who ultimately suffered the misfortune:

> Suddenly she looked eagerly round the room, and said, in her clear contralto voice, 'Where is my chiromantist?'
>
> 'Your what, Gladys?' exclaimed the Duchess, giving an involuntary start.
>
> 'My chiromantist, Duchess; I can't live without him at present.'
>
> 'Dear Gladys! you are always so original,' murmured the

Duchess, trying to remember what a chiromantist really was, and hoping it was not the same as a chiropodist.

'He comes to see my hand twice a week regularly,' continued Lady Windermere, 'and is most interesting about it.'

'Good heavens!' said the Duchess to herself, 'he is a sort of chiropodist after all. How very dreadful. I hope he is a foreigner at any rate. It wouldn't be quite so bad then.'

'I must certainly introduce him to you.'

'Introduce him!' cried the Duchess; 'you don't mean to say he is here?' and she began looking about for a small tortoise-shell fan and a very tattered lace shawl, so as to be ready to go at a moment's notice.

'Of course he is here; I would not dream of giving a party without him. He tells me I have a pure psychic hand, and that if my thumb had been the least little bit shorter, I should have been a confirmed pessimist, and gone into a convent.'

'Oh, I see!' said the Duchess, feeling very much relieved; 'he tells fortunes, I suppose?'

'And misfortunes, too,' answered Lady Windermere, 'any amount of them. Next year, for instance, I am in great danger, both by land and sea, so I am going to live in a balloon, and draw up my dinner in a basket every evening. It is all written down on my little finger, or on the palm of my hand, I forget which.'[32]

There was a strong belief in the 'banshee' or 'fairy woman' in the west of Ireland. Her mournful cry, if heard in the middle of the night, betokened certain death to some member of the family. According to Speranza: 'only certain families of historic lineage, or persons gifted with music and song, are attended by this spirit; for music and poetry are fairy gifts, and the possessors of them show kinship to the spirit race — therefore they are watched over by the spirit of life, which is prophecy and inspiration; and by the spirit of doom, which is the revealer of the secrets of death.'[33] Oscar Wilde also believed that the banshee only associated with established families and eschewed the *nouveau riche*. He told Vincent O'Sullivan that he had heard the banshee in 1 Merrion Square when he was a child. He woke up crying: 'Why are they beating that dog? Tell them to stop beating the dog',[34] and the next day a member of the family died. When a warder stepped on a spider as it crossed the floor of his cell in Reading Gaol, Wilde was horrified. He told the warder that killing a spider brought very bad luck. He also told O'Sullivan that his mother appeared to him in his prison cell on the night of her death: 'She was dressed for out-of-doors, and he asked her to take off her hat and cloak and sit down. But she shook her head sadly and vanished. When they came to tell him of her death he said quietly: "I knew it already".'[34]

After the Travers' law suit, William Wilde spent an increasing amount of time in the west of Ireland, and his natural son, Henry Wilson, began to take on much of his clinical practice in the hospital. In February 1867 the Wilde family suffered a major blow when Isola died of fever at the young age of nine years. She had been staying at The Glebe, Edgeworthstown, County Longford, with her aunt Emily, who was married to the rector, the Reverend William Noble. Oscar was grief-stricken by the death of his sister, whom he described as 'a golden ray of sunshine dancing about our home'.[35] He made frequent and long visits to her grave in the village cemetery, and some time later he wrote a poem to her memory, called 'Requiescat', which began with the lines:

> Tread lightly, she is near
> Under the snow;
> Speak lightly, she can hear
> The daisies grow . . . .[36]

Years later, when Oscar died in Paris, an envelope was found in his possession containing a lock of his sister's hair.

Speranza was devastated by the death of her only daughter, and two years after the loss she wrote to a friend on paper edged with black: 'My two sons were home for the vacation – fine clever fellows – the eldest quite grown-up looking – I thank God for these blessings. Still, a sadness is on me for life – a bitter sorrow that never can be healed.'[37]

Just four years after Isola's death, tragedy struck again when

William Wilde's natural daughters Emily and Mary lost their lives. The girls were attending a ball at Dromaconner House on the road between Smithboro and Monaghan when the muslin crinoline worn by one of the sisters caught fire. The other sister rushed to help and both were engulfed in flames. The girls were taken outside and rolled in the snow, but despite these efforts they were too badly burnt to survive. According to an account of the event written years later by the painter John Butler Yeats, the girls' mother, whom he said had a small black-oak shop in Dublin, came down to be with them before they died. He also said that William Wilde's groans could be heard by local people outside the house: 'There is a tragedy, all the more intense, because it had to be buried in silence. It is not allowed to give sorrow words.'[38] Emily was twenty-four years old and Mary was twenty-two. Both girls were buried in Drumsnatt churchyard under a headstone that bore an inscription from the Book of Samuel: 'They were lovely and pleasant in their lives and in their death they were not divided.'

CHAPTER 9

Victorian Dublin

The birds sat on the trees and sang so sweetly that the children used to stop their games in order to listen to them. 'How happy we are here!' they cried to each other.[1]

Oscar Wilde

DURING OSCAR'S CHILDHOOD, Dublin was the second largest city in Great Britain and Ireland, with a population of around 258,000. Despite the loss of its parliament earlier in the century, it still had many of the advantages of a capital city – advantages that would not have been found in provincial English cities such as Birmingham and Manchester. Social and intellectual life was stimulated by the range of classes, attitudes, professional occupations and literary and artistic activity in the city. The lord lieutenant, representing the monarchy, presided over the viceregal court in Dublin Castle. Although depleted in numbers, there was still a significant number of titled aristocrats living in the city. There were eight military barracks in Dublin and the officers were popular figures on social occasions. Of the professional classes, law, medicine and the Church were the most influential. Dubliners grudgingly conceded that London was bigger, but that was all: 'They confidently asserted that social life in Dublin was equal, and in some respects superior to London.'[2]

Dublin possessed a bustling port, a busy stock exchange, and it was a terminus for a rapidly expanding railway network. Brewing was a very important industry, and Guinness's brewery was the largest in the country. But the biggest employer in Dublin at that time was the printing industry. Transport around the city was still dependent on the horse, and every substantial Georgian mansion had three or four horses in its stables. Horse-drawn hackney transport was a major part of everyday life. There was a constant movement of carriages around Merrion Square, and rows of cabs waited outside the houses. One of the jarvey men from the cab rank across the street from the Wildes' home recalled that when Oscar was older he would not drive in a cab drawn by a white horse as he thought it would bring bad luck. Ireland's first railway was opened in 1834 and it connected Westland Row with Kingstown (Dún Laoghaire). Within thirty years, all the main railway lines had been laid, making it easy for parents like the Wildes to bring their children with them on holidays to the west of Ireland.

One of the significant achievements of the early Victorian period was the invention of the first practical photographic process, known as the daguerreotype, by Louis Daguerre of Paris. Around the same time an Englishman named Henry Fox Talbot patented another photographic technique using paper negatives, which became known as a calotype. 'Professor' Leon Gluckman, who was probably from Hungary or Germany, was the most outstanding of the early daguerreotypists in Dublin. He practised as a professional photographer and he had rooms in Sackville Street. He charged twelve shillings and sixpence for a portrait. Portrait likenesses done by this technique were once-off, unique, positive images on thin sheets of silver-plated copper. The daguerreotypes of Speranza and of Oscar Wilde as a child have both been attributed to Gluckman. Oscar's first portrait shows the wonder of a very young child caught up for an instant in the mid-nineteenth-century technological revolution, of which photography was but one more facet. Oscar is wearing a dress in the photograph, as it was common practice at the time to dress boys in this way. Boys wore a miniature version of adult female dress, and in the Victorian era this was often very elaborate. In some parts of Ireland the custom was associated with stories of fairy changelings and it was believed that if boys were dressed like girls, the fairies would not steal them.[3]

The novelist Maria Edgeworth has left us an impression of the 'wonderful mysterious operation' of being daguerreotyped: 'You are taken from one room into another upstairs and down and you see various people whispering and hear them in neighbouring passages and rooms unseen and the whole apparatus and stool on a high platform under a glass dome casting a snapdragon blue light making all look spectres . . . .[4] As might be expected, William Wilde and his neighbours in Merrion Square were fascinated by the new process. One of the earliest surviving Irish calotypes is a photograph taken around 1846 of William Wilde and William Stokes enjoying a drink of beer. The Earl of Dunraven took a camera on expeditions with Wilde and Stokes to explore Irish sites of archaeological and historical interest around Ireland, and his very fine photographs were subsequently published in a book that was edited by Margaret Stokes.

The takeover of Merrion Square by the intellectual elite of the city was confirmed fifteen years after the Union when the Duke of Leinster sold Leinster House to the Dublin [later Royal Dublin] Society and a large lecture theatre was built on the south side of the house. During the second half of the last century, Leinster House became the cultural nucleus of the city. This development took place within a short distance of the Wildes' home. The National Gallery of Ireland was formally opened in the grounds of Leinster House by the lord lieutenant, the Earl of Carlisle, on 30 January 1864, when Oscar was nine years old. The new gallery excited considerable public interest and in the first year it was visited by nearly 170,000 people.

A visit to the sculpture and picture galleries must have been an adventure for the young Oscar Wilde. The sculpture gallery was situated in the main hall on the ground floor, where casts of Greek and Roman originals were arranged between the Corinthian columns. The walls and ceiling of the picture gallery overhead were painted maroon, in imitation of the Grand Gallery in the Louvre. This gallery, known as 'The Queen's Gallery', housed the main collection and, although small at the beginning, it included several works by some of the great European masters, including Boulogne the Elder, Pietro della Vecchia and Padovanino. Many of the themes were biblical, and it is noteworthy in view of Oscar's later interest in Salomé and St John the Baptist that the collection boasted no fewer than four paintings of the saint. *St John in the Wilderness*, which was acquired in 1863, was attributed originally to Titian, but subsequently was identified as an important copy after Titian by Gian Antonio Guardi. The second, *St John in the Wilderness*, bought the following year, was painted by Simone Cantarini (1612-48) of the Bolognese School, and *A Landscape with the Baptism in the Jordan* by Salvator Rosa was acquired in 1856. *The Beheading of John the Baptist* was acquired in 1864 and catalogued as a Caravaggio. In 1971, however, it was identified as the work of the seventeenth-century artist Mattia Preti. This painting was included in a collection of some of the gallery's 'most precious masterpieces' which toured the USA in 1992, and it has been praised for its clarity and dignity.[5]

One of the original paintings acquired by the gallery, *St Sebastian*, depicts the young saint in his last agony, his body pierced by arrows. It has been attributed to a follower of Ribera.[6] Another painting of St Sebastian, by Luca Giordano, was presented to the gallery in 1868 by the third Duke of Leinster when Oscar Wilde was fourteen years old. Wilde had a life-long fascination with the story of the martyred saint. When he visited Italy in 1877 he sought out the Pallazo Rosso in Genoa so that he could see Guido Reni's *San Sebastian,* and in one of his early poems he described Keats as a young martyr: 'Fair as Sebastian, and as early slain.' Years later, Wilde took Sebastian as his Christian name when he adopted an alias after his release from Reading Gaol. *The Beheading of John the Baptist* by Preti and *St Sebastian* after Ribera are still two of the most visually arresting paintings in the National Gallery's collection of old masters.

One of the advantages of living in Merrion Square was that residents had a key to the private gardens that formed the centre of the square. Writing about the park in 1859, just five years after Oscar's birth, William Pryce Maunsell remarked: 'A few ladies take within its railings their solitary constitutional walk; an occasional gentleman is seen crossing it, producing his key at the gate and locking it after him as he would a wine cellar.'[7] This was a fine park where the young Wildes, Willie, Oscar and Isola, could run and explore without encountering children from the lower classes, and where the adults could walk without being annoyed by the paupers and beggars who thronged the streets of the city in the years following the Famine.

It was a very rarefied environment, and yet not far from this magnificent square were some of the poorest slums in Europe. A writer reporting on the conditions of the poor in 1845 observed: 'Nothing marks their poverty more than when congregating round their public fountains, struggling to have their supply. There are many lanes and courts in which a tumbler of water could not be had for drinking.'[8] Misery was widespread in the overcrowded tenements, and there was a marked difference between their poverty and the elegance of the great squares. 'The inhabitants of Merrion Square', observed a physician, 'may be surprised to hear that in the angle between Mount Street and Holles Street there is now a family of ten in a very small room of whom eight have had fever in the last month.'[9]

Oscar grew up surrounded by this poverty, but he was protected from its harsh realities as he played in the garden of Merrion Square. He could empathise with the thoughts of the prince in his most famous story for children, *The Happy Prince*:

> In the day time I played with my companions in the garden, and in the evening I led the dance in the Great Hall. Round the garden ran a very lofty wall, but I never cared to ask what lay beyond it, everything about me was so beautiful. My courtiers called me the Happy Prince, and happy indeed I was, if pleasure be happiness. So I lived, and so I died. And now that I am dead they have set me up here so high that I can see all the ugliness and all the misery of my city, and though my heart is made of lead yet I cannot choose but weep.[10]

The theme of one of Oscar's other very fine children's stories *The Selfish Giant* also centres around a beautiful garden, from which the village children are excluded:

> 'My own garden is my own garden,' said the Giant; 'any one can understand that, and I will allow nobody to play in it but myself.' So he built a high wall all round it, and put up a notice-board.

TRESPASSERS
WILL BE
PROSECUTED

He was a very selfish Giant.

The poor children had now nowhere to play. They tried to play
on the road, but the road was very dusty and full of hard stones,
and they did not like it. They used to wander round the high
walls when their lessons were over, and talk about the beautiful
garden inside. 'How happy we were there!' they said to each
other.[11]

In *De Profundis* he returned to the theme of the garden when
examining his own life. He remembered a conversation with fellow
students in Oxford, during which he recalled himself saying:

I wanted to eat of the fruit of all the trees in the garden of the
world, and that I was going out into the world with that passion
in my soul. And so, indeed, I went out, and so I lived. My only
mistake was that I confined myself so exclusively to the trees of
what seemed to me the sun-lit side of the garden, and shunned
the other side for its shadow and its gloom . . . . There was no
pleasure I did not experience. I threw the pearl of my soul into
a cup of wine. I went down the primrose path to the sound of
flutes. I lived on honeycomb. But to have continued the same
life would have been wrong because it would have been
limiting. I had to pass on. The other half of the garden had its
secrets for me also. Of course all this is foreshadowed and
prefigured in my books. Some of it is in *The Happy Prince*, some
of it in *The Young King*.[12]

Another writer, the novelist Elizabeth Bowen, who lived in Georgian
Dublin during her early childhood, has left us a detailed description
of the effect that the environment had on her:

The perspectives of this quarter of Dublin are to any eye, at any
time, very long. In those first winters they were endless to me.
The tense distances that one only slowly demolished gave a
feeling of undertaking to any walk. Everything in this quarter

seemed outsize. The width of the streets, the stretch of the squares, the unbroken cliff-like height of the houses made the human idea look to me superhuman. And there was something abstract about this idea, with its built-up planes of shadow and light.

At the same time, the complexion of these façades humanly altered from day to day. The neighbourhood seemed infused with a temper or temperament of its own, ... Some days, a pinkish sun-charged gauze hung even over the houses that were in shadow; sunlight marked with its blades the intersections of streets and dissolved over the mews that I saw through archways. On such days, Dublin appeared to seal up sunshine as an unopened orange seals up juice. The most implacable buildings were lanced with light; the glass half-moons over the darkest front doors glowed with sun that, let in by a staircase window, fell like a cascade down flights of stairs.[13]

The Wilde children were often taken by their mother to swim at nearby Sandymount, or at Bray, which was further south along the coast. They spent a number of summers at Glencree in the Wicklow mountains, just south of Dublin, in a farmhouse near the newly opened Glencree reformatory for Catholic boys. The reformatory was originally one of a series of barracks built to guard the military road which was constructed immediately after the 1798 rebellion. It ceased to be used as a barracks in 1825, and in 1859, the year of the Wildes' first visit, it became a reformatory for Catholic boys. A priest at the institute, the Reverend Father Prideaux Fox, formed a friendship with Speranza, and she began to attend Mass at the reformatory with her children. Speranza admired the Catholic Church, which in the post-Emancipation years became a major patron of the arts in Ireland. 'Indeed', wrote Speranza in the *Dublin University Magazine*, 'the sole patron of the Arts is the Catholic Church and considering the scant and insufficient means supplied by the faithful and impoverished people, it is marvellous to what an amount we are indebted to it for all that is best in architectural, pictorial or sculptured art throughout the country. Catholicism alone has comprehended the truth that Art is one of the noblest languages of religion.'[14]

Fox was a man of considerable intellectual ability. He was born in 1820 into an influential Quaker family in Devon. Charles Dickens was a boyhood friend, and this friendship continued when Fox went to London to study dentistry. At twenty-three, Fox shocked both his family and friends when he decided to join the Catholic Church. He studied for the priesthood, and in 1853 he was ordained a priest in the Oblate Order. He became a founder member of the Order's house in Inchicore, Dublin, and he won acclaim as a preacher in Ireland. Later in his life he counted John Henry Newman, Henry Manning and Frederick Faber among his friends. Between 1866 and 1872 he was superior of the reformatory at Glencree. Before this he had been at the centre of a public outcry which had reached the House of Commons at Westminster. Fox had been dismissed from his post as chaplain to the South Dublin Union when he had publicly championed the cause of some young female inmates who had been subjected to obscene treatment by the male attendants of the workhouse. Speranza would have admired his courageous stand on behalf of these despised and vulnerable women. When an old man, Father Fox recalled his friendship with Speranza and its consequences:

> When stationed at the reformatory I sometimes called on Sir William Wilde, who was reputed to be one of the cleverest oculists of his time. He was bitterly opposed to reformatories, and made no secret of his animosity; not so, however, his talented and patriotic wife, Lady Wilde, who was better known by her nom de plume, Speranza. She used to take lodgings every summer for herself and her children at a farm house, at the foot of the vale of Glencree, belonging to a worthy family of the name of Evans, intimate friends of mine. On my calling there one day she asked my permission to bring her children to our chapel to assist at Mass on Sundays. As we had a tribune in the chapel from which the boys and the altar could be seen without actual communication I readily acceded to her request, and after Mass was over, I enjoyed many a pleasant hour with this

excellent lady. I am not sure whether she ever became a Catholic herself, but it was not long before she asked me to instruct two of her children, one of them being that future erratic genius, Oscar Wilde. After a few weeks I baptized these two children, Lady Wilde herself being present on the occasion. At her request I called on their father and told him what I had done, his sole remark being that he did not care what they were so long as they became as good as their mother.[15]

The baptisms did not change the children's religious practice, and the family continued to attend Church of Ireland services, usually at St Stephen's Church in Upper Mount Street. Years later, Oscar would remark to friends that he had a recollection of having been baptised a Catholic as a child. He would also use the theme of a second baptism to great effect when writing *The Importance of Being Earnest*:

Jack:	Ah! that reminds me, you mentioned christenings, I think, Dr Chausable? I suppose you know how to christen all right? (Dr Chausable looks astounded). I mean, of course, you are continually christening, aren't you?
Miss Prism:	It is, I regret to say, one of the Rector's most constant duties in this parish. I have often spoken to the poorer classes on the subject. But they don't seem to know what thrift is.
Chausable:	But is there any particular infant in whom you are interested, Mr Worthing? Your brother was, I believe, unmarried, was he not?
Jack:	Oh yes.
Miss Prism: (bitterly)	People who live entirely for pleasure usually are.
Jack:	But it is not for any child, dear Doctor. I am very fond of children. No! the fact is, I would like to be christened myself, this afternoon, if you have nothing better to do.

114

Chausable:	But surely, Mr Worthing, you have been christened already?
Jack:	I don't remember anything about it.[16]

The Wildes were regular theatre-goers and Speranza once admitting that she had a 'passion for acting'.[17] Dublin's leading theatre during Oscar Wilde's childhood was the Theatre Royal in Hawkin's Street, which was built in 1820 to replace the old Theatre Royal in Crow Street. It was a large theatre, capable of seating some two thousand people, the acoustics were excellent, and it was said to have had 'a particularly fine stage'.[18] The Queen's Theatre in Brunswick Street, a close rival, was built a few years later, and several other theatres soon followed. Among these were the Tivoli, La Scala (later known as the Capitol), the Gaiety and the Palace (now the Olympia) – only the latter two still survive as theatres today. Many of these venues were used for performances other than drama, such as music-hall variety and operettas. There was no strong native drama company comparable to the highly regarded Smock Alley of the previous century, although the early Victorian period produced some Irish playwrights and actors, such as James Sheridan Knowles and Tyrone Power, who established reputations outside the country.

Barry Sullivan was one of the best-known Irish actors of the mid nineteenth century. He was an actor of the old school who delivered his lines with flamboyant movements. In the early 1870s, while Oscar was at Trinity College, Sullivan returned to Dublin for a very successful three-week engagement. Crowds flocked to see him play Sir Giles Overreach in *A New Way to Pay Old Debts*. Trinity students were enthusiastic supporters of the theatre. In 1874, when Barry Sullivan had another very successful run, he was 'chaired' back to his hotel on the last night by the students in a torch-light procession. Two years later the actor Henry Irving was given a similar reception: there was a special 'university night' when the students decided to show their admiration for Irving by booking all the seats at the Theatre Royal. After the play they took the horses from the actor's carriage and pulled it through the streets to his hotel. Oscar had left

Dublin for Oxford at this stage, but the event demonstrates the interest displayed in the theatre by the Trinity students of the period.

The works of Shakespeare were the most frequently performed plays, but the theatres also relied heavily on the dramas written by the great Irish playwrights of the eighteenth century, such as Sheridan, Congreve and Farquhar. Irish theatre received a considerable boost in the mid nineteenth century when the plays of the prolific Dion Boucicault began to appear on stage. The Boucicault family were of Huguenot origin and Dion Boucicault was born in Dublin in 1820. He decided to pursue a career in the theatre as an actor and playwright. His early works attracted considerable attention on both sides of the Atlantic, and Queen Victoria became a great admirer, going five times to see one of his plays, *The Corsican Brothers*.

Boucicault embarked on a most successful American tour in 1853 and spent seven years travelling with his company between the major cities, but it was *The Colleen Bawn*, which he wrote in 1860 as an adaption of Gerald Griffin's novel *The Collegians*, that brought Boucicault to the pinnacle of success. When the play opened in New York, Boucicault acted the part of the comic rogue Myles na Coppaleen, and audiences were enthralled by the brisk and witty dialogue. The play was such a success that it was decided to stage it in London in September 1860, where it achieved a record run. He then brought the play to Dublin where it opened at the Theatre Royal, Hawkin's Street, on Easter Monday, 1 April 1861, and played to full houses for twenty-four nights. Boucicault was treated like a national hero and every time he left his hotel large numbers of admirers followed him through the streets. He was entertained by the Wildes at 1 Merrion Square. Oscar was six at the time and old enough to be caught up in the general excitement associated with having such a famous playwright and actor in the house.

In 1872 Boucicault returned to Dublin to perform a season of his Irish plays in the Gaiety. His plays were reviewed favourably in the *Dublin Mail* by a young reviewer named Bram Stoker, who was later to achieve fame himself as the author of *Dracula*. Boucicault followed the success of the *Colleen Bawn* with two other plays in an Irish trilogy, *Arrah-na-Pogue* in 1865 and *The Shaughran* in 1874. According to his biographer Richard Fawkes, Boucicault's conversational skills were greatly admired, and the cleverest lines in his plays were those he used himself in conversation. Some of his plays, such as *Forbidden Fruit*, were precursors of the dialogue comedies of Oscar Wilde. Wilde's dialogue, however, was superior to Boucicault's, and it was generally acknowledged by his contemporaries that Wilde's skill at comic dialogue had been unmatched since Congreve. Wilde, unlike Boucicault, had no interest in using the 'stage Irishman' in order to amuse his audiences. 'The Celtic element in literature is extremely valuable', he once wrote, 'but there is absolutely no excuse for shrieking "Shillelagh" and "O-Garrah!"' [19]

The Beheading of John the Baptist *by Mattia Preti, one of the paintings that the young Oscar Wilde would have seen in the National Gallery of Ireland. The story of the beheading of John the Baptist forms the theme of Wilde's play* Salomé.
(Courtesy National Gallery of Ireland)

St Sebastian, *after Ribera. Another dramatic painting that Wilde would have seen in the National Gallery of Ireland, which was situated a short distance from his home on Merrion Square. Wilde was fascinated by the story of St Sebastian's martyrdom and he took the name Sebastian as an alias when he was released from Reading Gaol.*
(Courtesy National Gallery of Ireland)

Moytura House on the shores of Lough Corrib which was built by William Wilde and where Oscar spent several holidays during his childhood and teenage years.

Oscar Wilde, from a drawing by George Francis Miles.

121

The entrance of Trinity College Dublin in 1892.

Trinity College janitors in their full regalia photographed in 1892.
(Courtesy Board of Trinity College Dublin)

Student room in Trinity College Dublin in the nineteenth century.
(Courtesy Board of Trinity College Dublin)

Botany Bay, Trinity College, where Oscar Wilde had rooms.
(Courtesy Board of Trinity College Dublin)

The Examination Hall, Trinity College Dublin, in the last century.
Oscar Wilde sat his examinations in this hall. (Courtesy Board of Trinity College Dublin)

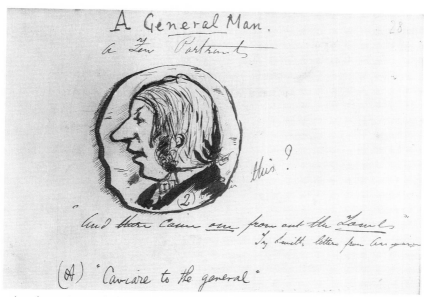

A student caricature of John Pentland Mahaffy, from The Suggestion Book of the Philosophical Society. *(Courtesy Board of Trinity College Dublin)*

Student caricature of Thomas Kingsmill Abbot, from The Suggestion Book of the Philosophical Society. *Abbot, who had a European reputation for scholarship, was one of Wilde's teachers at Trinity College. (Courtesy Trinity College Dublin)*

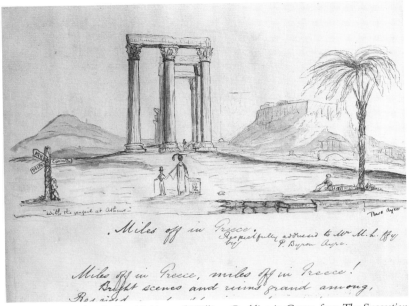

Student cartoon of Mahaffy with his pupil William Goulding in Greece, from The Suggestion Book of the Philosophical Society. (Courtesy Board of Trinity College Dublin).

The museum building, Trinity College Dublin. This building was inspired by the writings of John Ruskin and was finished in 1854, the year of Oscar Wilde's birth. Ruskin described the building as 'the noblest thing' ever done from his teaching.

126

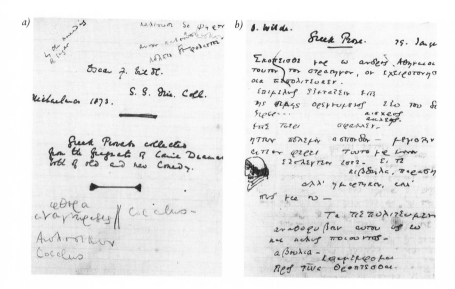

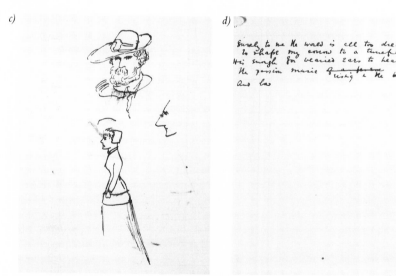

A selection of pages from Oscar Wilde's Trinity College notebooks. (Courtesy William Andrews Clark Library)

a) Notes on Greek proverbs, Michaelmas term 1873.
b) Notes on Greek prose.
c) Figure sketches.
d) Draft of the first lines of Wilde's poem 'Heart's Yearnings'.

Pencil on paper sketch of Oscar Wilde by Alexander Stuart Boyd, drawn in 1883.
(Courtesy National Gallery of Ireland)

Florence Balcombe, from a drawing by Oscar Wilde. Florence was Oscar Wilde's first love.

Bram Stoker, author of Dracula, *was a regular visitor to 1 Merrion Square.*
A graduate of Trinity College Dublin, he married Florence Balcombe on 4 December 1878.

Illaunroe, the Wildes' cottage on Lough Fee in the west of Ireland.
Oscar Wilde spent several holidays there, including one with his friend the artist
George Francis Miles.

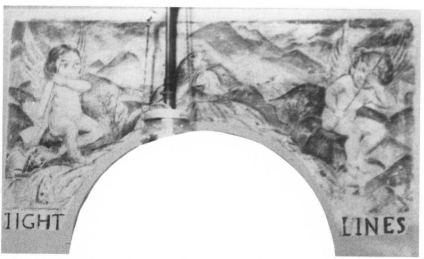

Mural by George Francis Miles painted in the hall at Illaunroe when he was on holiday there
with Wilde.

Edward Carson. A fellow student with Oscar Wilde at Trinity College, he became a very successful barrister and was merciless in his cross-examination of Wilde at the Old Bailey.

Oscar Wilde at the Parnell Commission, from a drawing by S P Hall. Wilde had great admiration for the Irish politician Charles Stewart Parnell and he supported his Home Rule policies. (Courtesy National Portrait Gallery, London)

Denis Florence McCarthy, one of the poets of 1848 and a friend of Speranza. His poem 'A New Year's Song' had a significant influence on Wilde when he was writing 'The Ballad of Reading Gaol'.

Trinity College Dublin

It has frequently been said that Ruskin moulded my father's character at Oxford, but it would be more accurate to say that Ruskin watered the seeds that had been sown by Mahaffy.[1]

Vyvyan Holland

In examinations the foolish ask questions that the wise cannot answer.[2]

Oscar Wilde

OSCAR WILDE MATRICULATED AT Trinity College Dublin on 10 October 1871, just six days before his seventeenth birthday. The university, situated in the centre of the city, was founded in 1592 by Queen Elizabeth I, and its campus occupies almost forty acres. In its constitution and academic life it resembles Oxford and Cambridge. From its foundation it was linked with the Anglo-Irish ascendancy, and many of its graduates held powerful positions in the country. However, this loyal university also educated some of the country's leading patriots, such as Henry Grattan, Robert Emmet and Thomas Davis. Among the busts ranged along its famous library is one of Theobald Wolfe Tone, leader of the Society of the United Irishmen. It is a university which takes pride in a long list of distinguished alumni. Several of its former students, among them Jonathan Swift, William Congreve, Oliver Goldsmith and George Farquhar, went on to become leading literary figures.

Wilde entered the university when it was undergoing some profound changes. These changes sought to bring it abreast of modern intellectual developments, but at the same time protect much of the old collegiate life and traditions. The resulting tensions produced vigorous debate. Students were encouraged to express their views on many subjects, and great stress was placed on fluency of expression in the oral examinations. John Pentland Mahaffy has left us an interesting pen-picture of the college life of students and fellows at the time:

> As Irishmen they are fluent talkers, and as Trinity College men they are independent talkers, free to utter their opinions, not guided by precedent, differing readily, even from their teachers . . . . A man is judged by his conversation, by his ability to take in new ideas . . . . So it is of course among the fellows. They criticise one another openly and readily, but always with perfect honesty . . . . But the stranger who dines at the fellows' table, and enters the common room, is, I believe, pleased by the vigour and liveliness of the conversation . . . an assembly of young Irishmen will have their jokes about everything, and no one escapes.[3]

There were about eleven hundred students on the register when Wilde entered Trinity, and although courses were open to students of all religions, approximately 90 per cent of them were Protestant. Some two hundred of the students lived within the walls of the college, another four hundred lived in Dublin, and the remaining five hundred lived some distance from the city and came to Dublin periodically to sit their examinations. The accommodation in college was much sought after and many students, Oscar Wilde among them, spent part of their undergraduate career living on the campus.

In the entrance examination, Wilde excelled in Greek, Latin and history, but did not do as well in mathematics. He was beaten for first place by his classmate from Portora, Louis Claude Purser. By a strange irony of fate Edward Carson, who would later play a key role in Wilde's first trial at the Old Bailey, entered Trinity in the same year. Many years earlier, when the Wilde and Carson families were on holiday in Dungarvan, County Waterford, Oscar had shared a nanny with Edward Carson and had played with him on the beach. In November 1871 Wilde, along with six others, was elected a

'Queen's Scholar', and during his first term he won a composition prize worth £2 for Greek verse and he was also awarded a premium for composition at the end of term examination.[4] During this first term he was a reasonably conscientious attender at lectures; he attended twenty-one of twenty-eight lectures given by Thomas Kingsmill Abbot, professor of moral philosophy, who was described by Mahaffy as 'the most learned man in Europe', and thirty of thirty-four lectures in classics given by John Pentland Mahaffy. Abbot translated several works of Immanuel Kant, including the *Theory of Ethics*, which contained a memoir of the philosopher, and he criticised George Berkeley's theory of vision in a book entitled *Sight and Touch*.

During the second term, Hilary term 1872, Wilde became more casual about his attendance at lectures. He attended only five of thirty-nine lectures in classics given by Arthur Palmer and two of seventeen lectures in English literature given by Edward Dowden. Dowden was the first professor of English literature in Trinity and he took up the post in 1867 at the age of twenty-four. He may have resented Wilde's lack of interest in his lectures, as he had a considerable reputation as a lecturer. However, Dowden stressed the moral and psychological aspects of literary criticism and he had little interest in the aesthetic and sensuous aspects of poetry. During Wilde's time in Trinity, Dowden was working on his first major contribution to literary criticism. This was published in 1875 under the title *Shakespeare, His Mind and Art*. When W B Yeats was collecting letters of support for Wilde after the latter's arrest in 1895, Dowden was one of the few people who refused to write one. Wilde's attitude to lectures may have been influenced by the philosophy of education expounded by his tutor John Pentland Mahaffy. Many years ahead of his time, Mahaffy questioned the value of formal lectures as a method of teaching:

> The actual teaching of science and of languages might possibly be obtained from books or private tutors, but the moral atmosphere in which a man lives and talks and idles – this it is which moulds his character more than any books, and this it is too which the reader cannot easily gather from calendars or

> examination papers . . . . Above all, we still hold fast to our old
> plan of giving considerable weight to oral examination, and still
> value elegant and fluent viva voce translations. Despite of the
> disfavour with which this sort of examining is regarded in
> English Universities, we are still convinced that it is perhaps the
> best test of intelligence, and a very good test of scholarship.[3]

Despite his cavalier approach to lectures, Wilde did very well at his
examinations. On 29 April 1872 he was first of nine students in the
first rank for classics. He was awarded a diploma on vellum by the
university in 1872 (this was auctioned at Sotheby's in 1911). Wilde
was elected to a Foundation Scholarship on 9 June 1873 which gave
him an annual sum of £20 payable quarterly, together with several
privileges. There were fifty candidates when Wilde sat the
examination for this coveted distinction. Trinity College was
founded as a corporation consisting of the provost, the fellows and
the scholars. The scholars, who are members of the corporation, are
called *foundation scholars*, or scholars of the house, to distinguish them
from students holding other scholarships. In the examination for
prizes in 1873, Wilde's name was again in the first rank. Wilde's
academic performance, twice achieving 'first of the firsts', was
particularly notable, as there were several very gifted students in his
class, including Louis Claude Purser, a future professor of Latin in
Trinity College Dublin, and William Ridgeway, a future professor of
archaeology in Cambridge. If Wilde had decided to stay in Trinity he
would almost certainly have been elected to a fellowship. The late W
B Stanford, a leading classical scholar and pro-chancellor of Trinity
College, concluded that Wilde was 'the best educated in classics of all
the major figures in the Anglo-Irish literary tradition'.[5]

Some of Wilde's Trinity notebooks have survived and are now in
the William Andrews Clark Memorial Library in Los Angeles. They
include notes on Greek, Latin, mathematics and logic. The figure
drawings and other sketches scattered throughout the pages reveal
that, as with other students, Wilde's attention wandered during his
lectures! In a notebook dated Michaelmas 1873 there is a draft of the
first four lines of a poem which he later entitled 'Heart's Yearnings':

> Surely to me the world is all too drear,
> To shape my sorrow to a tuneful strain,
> It is enough for wearied ears to hear
> The passion music rising in the brain.[6]

The poem contained forty lines when it was finished, but it was not published during Wilde's lifetime (see Appendix). It was thought that the poem was written in Oxford in 1876, but his notebook proves that he began the work while he was still a student at Trinity. Indeed the surviving fragment in his college notebook is one of the earliest extant examples of a poem by Wilde.

During his first year at the university, Wilde lived at home in Merrion Square with his parents. On occasion he invited fellow students to his mother's receptions, where they would meet many of the most talked about people in Irish art and literature. Oscar said to one fellow student: 'Come home with me, I want to introduce you to my mother. We have founded a society for the suppression of virtue.'[7] This statement has often been quoted to imply that Wilde was brought up in an amoral atmosphere. This was not the case however, and although Speranza liked to shock her listeners, there is no evidence to suggest that there was anything amoral about her conversation or behaviour. After the first year, Oscar occupied rooms in the college, which he shared with his brother Willie. The rooms were situated in the quadrangle known as 'Botany Bay', and are believed to have been on the first floor of number 18. They consisted of two bedrooms, a sittingroom and a pantry. Sir Edward Sullivan, a contemporary of Oscar Wilde's at Trinity, and before that at Portora, has left us the following description of Oscar's room:

> He had rooms in the College at the north side of one of the older squares, known as Botany Bay. These rooms were exceedingly grimy and ill-kept. He never entertained there. On the rare occasions when visitors were admitted, an unfinished landscape in oils was always on the easel, in a prominent place in his sitting room. He would invariably refer to it, telling one in his humorously unconvincing way that 'he had just put in the butterfly'.[8]

His remark about the butterfly was an allusion to Whistler's distinctive way of signing his paintings. Wilde would later use the same easel to produce a similar effect in his rooms at Oxford.

The furniture in the rooms at Trinity varied depending on the taste and means of the occupant. Every room had its own tobacco-jar and pipe-rack, as most students smoked. The students had male servants or 'skips' to perform the more menial day-to-day tasks – the 'skips' were usually army pensioners and they were not noted for their efficiency. Their name was said to be derived from the verb to 'skip' because their advanced age made such an activity most improbable. It is more likely however, that 'skip' was derived from a combination of the words 'scout' (a college servant in Oxford) and 'gyp' (a college servant in Cambridge). They were inferior in social rank to the college janitors, who wore velvet hunting caps and liveries of dark blue, with brass buttons bearing the college arms.

Students looked upon the property of those sharing the same house as common, and it was generally regarded as a significant breach of etiquette to restore borrowed items of food, 'the characters of lender and borrower being so easily interchanged'.[9] The students dined on Commons in the college hall at 6pm in winter and 6.30pm in summer. Before dinner, a scholar ascended a pulpit at the right-hand side of the fellows' table to say Grace in Latin. Parties, or 'sprees' as they were called, were organised regularly in the rooms to celebrate various events, real or imagined, and as one can gather from the following 'invitation' printed in the college magazine, alcohol was not banned on these occasions.

43, Trinity College

Dear Sir,

A movement having been inaugurated for the purpose of putting down drink, a meeting of its supporters will be held on Saturday next in the above rooms at nine o'clock pm. You are requested by attendance to show your interest in this absorbing question, and we hope at the close of the meeting to be in a position to exhibit some examples of the baneful effects of intemperance.

Yours truly,

Josiah Snooks[10]

Such sprees usually went on all night.

As well as studying for his classical examinations, Wilde 'devoured with voracity all the best English writers'. He was particularly enthused by Swinburne's poetry, and a poem he wrote about this time, entitled 'Ye Shall Be Gods', was modelled on Swinburne's lyric 'Before the Beginning of Years' from *Atlanta in Calydon*.[11] Wilde was often seen brandishing a copy of John Addington Symond's works on the Greek authors. He also read William Morris and the early verse of Dante Gabriel Rossetti. As a consequence, he became very familiar with the aesthetic outlook of the pre-Raphaelites. His enthusiasm for these writers and painters was shared by several other Trinity students at the time. Wilde had a phenomenal memory and a remarkable ability to absorb a wide range of diverse reading material with considerable rapidity. Yet no one could accuse him of being a bookworm as 'He mixed freely at the same time in Dublin society functions of all kinds, and was always a very vivacious guest at any house he cared to visit'.[8] A story, passed down in the family of Daniel O'Connell, suggests that Wilde possessed a certain social arrogance even at this stage. The incident occurred during a ball in a Georgian house on Hardwicke Crescent. Wilde was dancing a minuet with a granddaughter of Daniel O'Connell, and when the music stopped he bowed to his partner with one hand in his pocket. She stood still while all the other couples sat down, so that Wilde had to take his hand out of his pocket and bow again. He was later heard to describe her as 'A dreadful woman'![12]

Although Wilde became a member of the Philosophical Society, he did not take a very active part in its proceedings, and he was not known to take an interest in any of the social, religious or political issues that preoccupied many of the other students at the time. A fellow student, Horace Wilkins, remembered him as being rather awkward and ungainly, but very good humoured and generous.

Wilkins also remembered an occasion when Wilde showed that he could account for himself quite capably in a fight:

> He wrote a poem which he read at one of the class symposiums. It struck me as a beautiful thing but when he had finished reading, the bully of the class laughed sneeringly. I never saw a man's face light up with such savagery of hate as Wilde's. He strode across the room and, standing in front of the man, asked him by what right he sneered at his poetry. The man laughed again, and Wilde slapped him across the face. The class interfered, but inside of an hour the crowd was out behind the college, arranging for a fight. Wilde, in a towering rage, was ready to fight with howitzers if necessary, but the bully wanted to fight with nature's weapons. No one supposed that Wilde had a ghost of a show, but when he led out with his right, it was like a pile-driver. He followed the surprised bully up with half a dozen crushers, and that ended it. Talk about that man being 'a pallid young man'! When I see these allusions in the newspapers, I always think of his fighting qualities. I think he would make an ox shake his head and blink.[13]

His classmates were surprised by Wilde's physical prowess because he did not take part in any sporting activities in the college. An army officer who had been at Trinity with Wilde remembered him in a less belligerent mood:

> One night we heard a frightful row in his room. Myself and another man rushed to his door. He was half undressed and jumping about the floor. 'What on earth is the matter?' we asked. 'There's a huge fly in my room', replied Oscar, 'a great buzzing fly. I can't sleep till I drive it out.'[14]

Charles Eason, who was awarded a scholarship in the same year as Wilde, recalled him as 'a very good natured man, and most extraordinarily amusing. Everybody liked him'.[14] Wilde received special instruction from a classical scholar named John Townsend Mills, who had fallen on hard times. On one occasion when Wilde saw his tutor wearing a tall hat that was completely covered in black crêpe, he expressed his sympathy. Mills explained that no one had died, but that he was using the crêpe purely to keep his battered hat intact. Sir Edward Sullivan thought that this incident was in Oscar Wilde's mind when he had John Worthing wear crêpe around his hat in mourning for his fictitious brother in Act II of *The Importance of Being Earnest*.

Wilde was elected a member of the College Historical Society on 19 November 1873. This society, known as the 'Hist', was founded by Edmund Burke in the eighteenth century and it is the oldest university debating society in Ireland and Great Britain. Its membership included such illustrious names as Henry Grattan, Wolfe Tone, Robert Emmet and Isaac Butt. Bram Stoker was the auditor of the society when Oscar Wilde became a member. Stoker was a frequent visitor to 1 Merrion Square, where he created a very favourable impression on Speranza. He was intrigued by William Wilde's descriptions of his early travels and explorations in Egypt. The surgeon delighted in recounting his exploits and the subject became a regular topic during Stoker's visits. More than thirty years later, Stoker would use the Egyptian information gleaned at Wilde's dinner table when, following the success of *Dracula*, he wrote his second book on a weird and supernatural theme. The book was entitled *The Jewel of Seven Stars* and the plot was set among the tombs of Egypt, tombs that William Wilde had explored at first hand.

Edward Carson joined the 'Hist' in the same year as Oscar Wilde. There is no evidence to suggest that Wilde took an active part in debates, but Carson became a very enthusiastic contributor. The minute books show that the young Carson had radical ideas: he spoke against capital punishment, he condemned Cromwell, he believed in equal rights for women, and was in favour of the disestablishment of the Church of Ireland. Oscar later claimed that he and Carson were very good friends at Trinity and that they walked about the campus arm in arm. Carson denied such a close friendship and said that he disapproved of Wilde's flippant attitudes. This was also Mahaffy's memory of the relationship between the two men: 'There was no comraderie between them. They were utterly different types. Carson was a plodding quiet student whose intellect blossomed later on in life, whereas Wilde was all verve and *joie de vivre*. I heard that Carson once took part in a rag and that he occasionally played a game of draughts, but I found it hard to believe that he had enough animal spirits for either pastime.'[15]

Wilde arrived at Trinity at a time when a remarkable group was emerging in the classical school of the college. The pioneering members of this group were John Pentland Mahaffy, Arthur Palmer and Robert Yelverton Tyrrell. Mahaffy and Tyrrell had a major influence on Wilde's development, as he later acknowledged:

> I got my love of the Greek ideal and my intimate knowledge of the language at Trinity from Mahaffy and Tyrrell; they were Trinity to me; Mahaffy was especially valuable to me at that time. Though not so good a scholar as Tyrrell, he had been in Greece, had lived there and saturated himself with Greek thought and Greek feeling. Besides he took deliberately the artistic standpoint towards everything, which was coming more and more to be my standpoint. He was a delightful talker, too, a really great talker in a certain way – an artist in vivid words and eloquent pauses.[16]

The classical school at Trinity was developed from an ambitious base, which set out to embrace the critical traditions of Cambridge, the philosophical scholarship of Oxford and the comparative philosophy of the Germans. The first publication to herald this new era of classical learning was Mahaffy's *Twelve Lectures on Primitive Civilisations*, which was published in 1868, just three years before Wilde entered the university. Mahaffy followed this achievement with another eighteen brilliant and provocative books on Roman and more especially Greek history within seventeen years. Wilde's notebooks reveal that he studied in depth many of the ideas treated in Mahaffy's books during his years at Trinity and later at Oxford. His published essays however reveal that he did not always come to the same conclusions as his Trinity tutor. Mahaffy was thirty-two when he became Wilde's tutor in 1871. At the time he was junior dean, one of the university's preachers for the year, and an examiner in classics. The main duty of a tutor in Trinity is to counsel and advise students about the intricacies of university life and to act as an advocate for them if necessary.

Many of the students entering the university at that time came from privileged backgrounds and Mahaffy believed that they should use the opportunities presented to them to cultivate their minds in the broadest sense, as he himself had tried to do. He was born in Vevay, Switzerland, in 1839, and spent his early years at a number of locations on the Continent, where his father was chaplain to various English-speaking communities. His family lived for a time at the German spa town of Bad Kissingen, where the young Mahaffy met some very fascinating visitors from all over Europe, including the future Tsar Alexander II and Ludwig, King of Bavaria. These early contacts with some of the leading dignatories of Europe gave him a confidence that he never lost. The family returned to Ireland in 1848 when revolution was sweeping over central Europe. Mahaffy was educated at home before he entered Trinity College at the age of sixteen in 1855. In an address delivered before the undergraduate Philosophical Society of which he was president in 1858, Mahaffy encouraged his listeners to read widely so that they would be more likely to develop reflective and original traits. He reminded them that the college course did not give one an education, it only provided the material or basis for the process: 'The age is an age of progress, an age of change. The lower classes are rising rapidly on all sides, by the cultivation of their intellects. We have been placed above them in birth and station; let us endeavour to excel them as much in mind as in circumstances.'[17]

Mahaffy became a junior fellow in 1864 at the early age of twenty-five, and five years later he was appointed to the Chair of Ancient History. The core of the academic staff of the university was formed by the thirty-five junior and senior fellows. The fellows did most of the teaching in the BA course, and the seven senior fellows with the provost formed the board or governing body of the college. At that time it was required that fellows would take holy orders, so Mahaffy was ordained a clergyman in the Church of Ireland. He had an ambivalent attitude towards orthodox religion and he used to say that he was not a clergyman 'in any offensive sense of the word'.[18] An evangelical Protestant once asked him if he was 'saved'. 'Yes', answered Mahaffy, who spoke with a lisp, 'but it was such a vewwy nawwow squeak that I never boast about it.'[19]

Mahaffy was a young man in a hurry. He resented the number of old professors holding lucrative senior fellowships in Trinity who, by virtue of their long lives, blocked his own chances of promotion. As an undergraduate in 1858 he tabulated the ages of the provost and fellows, and using two sets of actuarial tables he worked out the chances of places becoming available over the following years to five decimal places. Unfortunately for Mahaffy, the senior fellows were very long lived and he had to keep updating the figures in his notebook over the following forty years. He vented his frustrations in his book *Social Life in Greece*, which was published in 1874. Describing how the old people in some parts of Greece took hemlock when they felt themselves becoming useless, he added pointedly: 'How desirable would such a practice appear in some of our public services and institutions.' Forty years later, in 1914, Mahaffy did not allow this philosophy to prevent him from becoming provost at the age of seventy-five!

In 1865 Mahaffy married the daughter of a wealthy Dublin solicitor. Surprisingly Mrs Mahaffy did not relish the social intercourse of Dublin society. She did not like dining out and rarely accepted invitations to other people's houses. Contrary to Victorian conventions, however, she did not allow her lack of interest to inhibit the activities of her husband, who has been aptly described as 'one of nature's guests'.[20] As a result, he managed to combine the social advantages of a bachelor's freedom with the security of a loving wife and family. This was a model which his protégé Wilde would also find attractive.

Mahaffy was renowned for his snobbery, and his conversational skills made him a welcome guest at the tables of the aristocracy. On one occasion he wrote a letter to a friend which began: 'I am down here on a spree shooting with the de Vescis nothing but Lords in the house except myself, Drogheda, Ormonde, Kingston, Castletown, . . . and their wives. So I am really in a snob's paradise, if that were my object.'[21] According to Mahaffy's friend, the Oxford scholar A H

Sayce: 'no one enjoyed more than he did visiting the country houses of Great Britain, where he found ancient traditions, good manners, interesting personages, excellent cuisine and, not unfrequently, splendid libraries.'[22]

He became so famous as a conversationalist that he was in demand in royal circles:

> Until you heard Mahaffy talk, you hadn't realized how language could be used to charm and hypnotize. With this gift, there were no doors which could not be opened, no Society which was proof against its astonishing effect. Kings and Queens, famous men and beautiful women, all must come under its powerful and compelling spell.[23]

He was a friend of the King of Greece and he was invited to Sandringham and Windsor by King Edward VII who appreciated his memories of Germany and Greece in the period of Prince Edward of Saxe Weimar. After visits such as these, he entertained his colleagues with anecdotes in the university's Common Room. One of his stories related to a visit to Windsor at the time of the coronation:

> I was in the drawing-room with seven kings and seven queens. I was talking to Her Majesty the Queen of Spain and I was paying her a pretty compliment. 'Madam', I said, 'Spanish is the language of Kings; French is the language of diplomacy; Italian is the language of love; German I speak to my horse.' As ill luck would have it, the Kaiser was standing nearby and he turned to me saying: 'What's that you say'. I was taken aback for a second but I quickly recovered and replied: 'Her Majesty and I are already on terms of intimacy: we have a secret.'[24]

Cecily voiced similar views on German as a language in the opening lines of Act II of *The Importance of Being Earnest*:

Miss Prism [calling]:	Cecily, Cecily! Surely such a utilitarian occupation as the watering of flowers is rather Moulton's duty than yours? Especially at a moment when intellectual pleasures await you. Your German

	grammar is on the table. Pray open it at page fifteen. We will repeat yesterday's lesson . . . .
Cecily [coming over very slowly]:	But I don't like German. It isn't at all a becoming language. I know perfectly well that I look quite plain after my German lesson.[25]

There can be little doubt that Mahaffy embellished many of his stories for the entertainment of his colleagues in the Common Room. He confessed that he had been whipped only once as a child 'and that was for telling the truth'. 'It cured you, Mahaffy', was the quick response of one of the senior fellows.[26]

Mahaffy was an imposing figure of about six feet three inches in height. In Wilde's time he was known as 'The General' because of his many accomplishments, both intellectual and sporting. He was very interested in music, he spoke French and German fluently, he was a connoisseur of wine and an acknowledged authority on old silver and antique furniture. He was a great enthusiast of eighteenth-century Dublin architecture and was a founder of the Irish Georgian Society. He had captained the Trinity cricket eleven and as a marksman he was selected to shoot with the Irish team at an international competition in Wimbledon. He was also a very skilful angler. He was not, however, unaware of his talents, and he once remarked, 'Take me all round. I am the best man in Trinity College.'[27]

Although Mahaffy was a very able scholar and the author of several books, he placed success in society above academic achievement: 'There can be no doubt', he wrote, 'that of all the accomplishments prized in modern society that of being agreeable in conversation is the very first.'[28] Wilde was certainly impressed by Mahaffy's wit and conversational abilities and to a certain extent he modelled himself on his tutor. Surviving records of Mahaffy's conversation, however, reveal sentences that are more like aphorisms, and they do not possess the sparkle of Wilde's polished epigrams. 'In Ireland the inevitable never happens and the unexpected constantly occurs' was one of

Mahaffy's better-known paradoxes.[29] Wilde's wit was never calculated to offend whereas Mahaffy could be very wounding. On one occasion a guest at a function exclaimed on being introduced to Mahaffy:

> 'Oh, Dr Mahaffy. I hear you are *so* amusing. Do say something funny to me.'
> 'Well', came the retort, 'I am delighted to have you beside me. Is that funny enough?'[15]

Contemporaries such as Robert Tyrrell believed that Wilde had been greatly influenced by Mahaffy. Speranza also shared this view, and according to her it was Mahaffy who gave the first 'noble impulse' to Oscar's intellect and who inspired him to aim for the higher things of life rather than follow the pursuits of lesser mortals. Mahaffy recognised Wilde's brilliance at classical studies. He told Gerald Griffin that Wilde's 'aptitude for, and keen delight in, Hellenic studies attracted me towards him. He was one of the few students I knew who could write a really good Greek composition . . . . In Greek you have to diagnose the substance that underlies the form of the English you are transposing. And again, Wilde was one of the very few students who could grasp the nuances of the various phases of the Greek Middle Voice and of the vagaries of Greek conditional clauses.'[30]

Robert Yelverton Tyrrell won a scholarship to Trinity, where he had an outstanding undergraduate career. The son of a clergyman from County Tipperary, he was a few years younger than Mahaffy and he had just been appointed to the Chair of Latin at the early age of twenty-five when Oscar entered the university. Apart from his interest in Latin, he was also a brilliant Greek scholar and he was appointed regius professor of Greek in 1880. His great work *The Correspondence of Cicero* was said to have brought fame to his college and brought many a student to the verge of despair.[31] The Greek scholar, the late W B Stanford, described Tyrrell's academic record in Trinity as 'the finest career in classical literature that the College has known'.[32] Tyrrell was also admired for his wit. After reading Browning's translation of the *Agamemnon* of Aeschylus, he is said to have remarked that 'he found the Greek most helpful in explaining its obscurities'.[33] On another occasion when he was asked: 'Is it true, as the Archbishop says, that you got drunk at his dinner table?', he replied, 'Oh, no, I took the obvious precaution of coming drunk.'[33] The surgeon and writer Oliver St John Gogarty, who knew both Mahaffy and Tyrrell, acknowledged the former as one of the greatest intellects of his time, but described Tyrrell as 'the wittiest man of his day'.[34] The writer Stephen Gwynn has encapsulated the difference in scholarly emphasis between Wilde's two most influential teachers at Trinity:

> Greek and Latin, which to Tyrrell were exquisite examples of linguistic form, embodied in the strict bounds of two great literary periods, were to Mahaffy the keys to the history of two great world-civilisations which intertwined through many centuries and ramified out in a hundred directions. Tyrrell's interest was in Latin and Greek; Mahaffy's in the Greeks and Romans.[35]

When Oscar Wilde was in Reading Gaol, Tyrrell signed a petition on his behalf, which many others including Mahaffy refused to sign. After signing, he said to Frank Harris, who had organised the petition: 'When you next see Oscar, please tell him that my wife and I asked after him. We both hold him in grateful memory as a most brilliant talker and writer, and a charming fellow to boot. Confusion take all their English Puritanism.'[36] His response contrasts with that of Mahaffy who, when asked about his former friend and pupil, replied: 'We no longer speak of Mr Oscar Wilde.'[37] In old age, Mahaffy's attitude mellowed and he admitted that 'despite his extravagant garb and his effeminate way, . . . I rather liked Wilde'.[38] On another occasion he told Louis Claude Purser that Wilde 'was a delightful man to talk to on matters of scholarship, his views were always so fresh and unconventional'.[39]

Tyrrell founded a college magazine named *Kottabos*, a name taken from a Greek after-dinner wine-game. The magazine published lyrics, verse, translations and parodies. Wilde contributed six poems to the magazine between 1876 and 1879, including the sonnet

'Wasted Days'. His older brother Willie also sent poetry to *Kottabos*, and one of his poems was entitled 'Salomé' – a theme that would later provide the inspiration for one of Oscar's plays. The following are the opening lines of Willie's sonnet

> The sight of me was as devouring flame
> Burning their hearts with fire, so wantonly
> That night I danced for all his men to see!
> Fearless and reckless; for all maiden shame
> Strange passion-poisons throbbing overcame
> As every eye was rivetted on me,
> And every soul was mine, mine utterly –
> And thrice each throat cried out aloud my name![40]

Oscar was not very complimentary about his brother's poetic efforts: 'Your sonnets follow all the accepted rules', was his verdict. 'Anyway, they each have fourteen lines, with two rhymes in the octave and two in the sextet. All the same, Willie, you had better stick to prose.'[41] Willie Wilde won a number of prizes at Trinity, including a gold medal for ethics, before leaving to study law at the Middle Temple in London in 1872.

Samuel Haughton was a Trinity fellow who would have been well known to Oscar Wilde. He was registrar of the medical school and he had a particular interest in using mathematics to solve biological problems. He was a friend of William Wilde and both men shared many interests. On one occasion they were travelling together by train to a meeting in London and they wished to relax in comfort. Haughton informed the guard that he was accompanying 'a lunatic' to London who could prove dangerous if provoked. A separate compartment was organised for the two men immediately! Haughton was very humane and he was horrified by the way in which condemned men were executed, as many of those hanged at the time died by slow strangulation. He argued that a longer drop would result in instant death, and he used his mathematical and anatomical skills to devise a formula for a 'long drop', which was subsequently widely used by executioners. His book *Principles of Animal Mechanics*, published in 1873, described in detail the horrors of hanging. Mahaffy borrowed from this book to describe the agonies of a condemned man in his own work, *Social Life in Greece*, the proofs of which were corrected by Oscar in 1874. Mahaffy's vivid description could be read as a fitting introduction to 'The Ballad of Reading Gaol'.[42]

Oscar Wilde began to develop his interest in aesthetics or the philosophical study of beauty during his undergraduate years at Trinity. Aesthetics is a subject upon which philosophers have written since the time of Plato and Aristotle. Modern aesthetic thought developed under the influence of thinkers such as the Earl of Shaftesbury, Alexander Baumgarten, Immanuel Kant and Georg Wilhelm Friedrich Hegel. Two of the most influential early books on aesthetics were written in Dublin: Francis Hutcheson's *An Inquiry into the Original of Our Ideas of Beauty and Virtue*, published in 1725, and Edmund Burke's *A Philosophical Inquiry into the Origin of Our Ideas on the Sublime and Beautiful*, published in 1757. Burke's treatise is thought to have been written while he was still at Trinity College. When Wilde entered Trinity, the university had a course on aesthetics and during his second year there John Pentland Mahaffy published the first volume of his commentary on Kant's philosophy, under the title *The Aesthetic and Analytic*. The aesthetic movement developed in the nineteenth century as a reaction to the materialism of the industrial age. Its roots were set in aesthetic philosophy, and members of the movement sought to promote beauty in life and art. In England, aestheticism was championed in the works of artists and writers such as Dante Gabriel Rossetti, Edward Burne-Jones, Algernon Charles Swinburne and Walter Pater.

The architecture of one of the buildings at Trinity was inspired by John Ruskin, who was Slade professor of fine arts at Oxford and one of the champions of beauty and art in England. Ruskin had a number of Irish connections, one of the most remarkable being his love for the young Rose La Touche of Harristown, County Kildare. He was well informed about Ireland through his life-long friend Henry Acland, regius professor of medicine at Oxford. Acland was a very cultured man and a friend of both William Wilde and William Stokes. He wrote a biography of Stokes and he was also involved in facilitating Oscar Wilde's eventual move from Trinity to Oxford. Ruskin and Acland were close friends of the Irish architect Benjamin Woodward. The beautiful museum buildings designed by Woodward at Trinity and at Oxford were the direct result of the friendship between these men. The Museum Building in Trinity is Venetian in character, as Woodward was strongly influenced by Ruskin's books *Stones of Venice* and *Examples of the Architecture of Venice*, both of which were published in 1851. Both Ruskin and Acland were very impressed by Woodward's ability and they invited him to design the Museum Building at Oxford.

The building at Trinity is decorated externally with some very fine carved stone, the beauty of which vindicated Ruskin's emphasis on the importance of using direct observation of nature to inspire the chisel of the craftworker. There is also some very fine stone work inside the building, where the architecture is distinctly Moorish in design. It is one of the loveliest buildings in Trinity College: 'Architecturally as well as sculpturally it is beautifully detailed: pilaster lies against pilaster, and capital against capital so that the respective profiles converse, while leaves and flowers and animals curl and dart along the mouldings, pausing, at least once, to retell an Aesop fable.'[43] Ruskin visited the college to see the building in 1861, and he described it as 'quite the noblest thing ever done from my teaching'.[44] When he returned to Dublin in 1867 to lecture on 'The Mystery of Life and Its Arts' he told his audience:

> Among several personal reasons which caused me to desire that I might give this, my closing lecture on the subject of art here, in Ireland, one of the chief was, that in reading it, I should stand near the beautiful building, – the engineers' school of your college, – which was the first realization I had the joy to see, of the principles I had, until then, been endeavouring to teach . . . .[45]

Records of debates of the Philosophical Society at the time show that the students had a keen interest in aesthetics. Among the papers read to the society was one by Willie Wilde on 'Aesthetic morality'. Willie was not the first member of the Wilde family to take an interest in aesthetics, as his mother had translated the German novel

The First Temptation in 1863. This book described the life of a young man who made himself an apostle of the aesthetic movement with tragic consequences. The Suggestion Book of the Philosophical Society during Oscar's time in Trinity has been preserved in the college. Members of the society could jot down observations and comments about other members in this book. Wilde is lampooned for winning the Berkeley Gold Medal, which is described as The Aesthetic Medal. Remarks about Ruskin's 'Queen of the 'air' and Spenser's 'Fair-'airy Queen' suggest that Wilde was already adopting an aesthetic pose while at Trinity. There is a thinly veiled reference to lilies and to the hair-styles of 'certain fair individuals'.[46] The Suggestion Book also contains a caricature of Wilde. Richard Ellmann pointed out in his biography of Wilde that all this evidence leads to the conclusion that 'six months before he went up to Oxford, Wilde was an exponent of aestheticism, and flaunted his doctrine with a certain style which needed mockery'.[47]

Wilde crowned his academic career at Trinity by winning the blue ribbon of classical scholarship, the Berkeley Gold Medal. William Wilde was delighted with his son's success and he organised a party to celebrate it. He sent an invitation to their old family friend, Sir John T Gilbert: 'We are asking a few old friends upon Moytura cheer (poteen) on Thursday, and also to cheer dear old Oscar on having obtained the Berkeley gold medal last week with great honour. You were always a favourite of his, and he hopes you will come.'[48] In later years the Berkeley medal would see Wilde out of many a tight corner, as it was pawned by him in times of acute financial difficulties.[49]

CHAPTER 11

Expanding horizons

Go to Oxford, my dear Oscar: we are all much too clever for you over here.[1]

John Pentland Mahaffy

WILLIAM WILDE PROBABLY LOOKED benignly on his son's enthusiasm for the aesthetic movement, but he was becoming very worried about Oscar's growing interest in the Catholic Church. Catholicism was in favour with intellectuals of the period, largely due to the influence of John Henry Newman, whom Oscar admired. William Wilde was uneasy about his son's friendship with members of the Jesuit order in Dublin, particularly as Oscar had begun to attend Mass. By sending his son to Oxford, William Wilde hoped that matters other than Catholicism would attract his attention.[2] Oscar won a classical demyship or scholarship to Magdalen College, Oxford, in June 1874. The scholarship was worth ninety-five pounds per annum and it was tenable for five years. As a consequence, Oscar left Trinity after three years without taking a degree.

After the Oxford scholarship examination, Wilde relaxed on a holiday with his mother and brother in London, during which they visited a number of literary figures, including Thomas Carlyle. They then crossed to the Continent and spent some time in Geneva and Paris. Flushed with success and confidence, Wilde began work on his poem 'The Sphinx' while staying at the Hotel Voltaire in Paris. When they returned to Dublin their high spirits were dampened by the realisation that William Wilde was far from well; he felt weak and languid and he rarely ventured outside the house.

Oscar spent the remainder of the summer of 1874, while waiting to begin his studies at Oxford, correcting the proofs of Mahaffy's book *Social Life in Greece* at the latter's retreat in Howth. In the preface to the first edition, dated 4 November 1874, the author thanked Wilde for having 'made improvements and corrections all through the book'.[3] There is a passage in the work that comes very close to Wilde's philosophy of art for art's sake, an approach to morality that Mahaffy later rejected. In this passage the author described the 'degradation' of Homer into a moral teacher when critics read theories of life and duty into his work, and he claimed that it would be just as great a blunder 'to dilate on the moral purposes of Shelley and Keats'.[4]

The first edition contained a passage on homosexuality, which was described as: 'that strange and to us revolting perversion, which reached its climax in later times, and actually centred upon beautiful boys all the romantic affections which we naturally feel between opposite sexes, and opposite sexes alone.'[5] Mahaffy went on to argue that the phenomenon occurred because in early Greek society men were much more cultured than women, and as a consequence men could not find intellectual fulfilment in relationships with unsophisticated women:

> We have as yet no Asphasia to advocate the higher education of women. We have in many cities a tendency to seclude women, and prevent them from being companions to their lovers. Thus their natural place was invaded by those fair and stately youths, with their virgin looks, and maiden modesty, who fired Solon and Theognis, and Socrates and Epaminondas – in fact, almost every great Greek in their greatest days.[6]

Dorian Gray used similar imagery when describing the love he bore for Lord Henry Wotton, a love that 'had nothing in it that was not noble and intellectual'.[7] Oscar himself used the same reasoning in his famous reply to the prosecuting counsel when asked during his trial 'What is the "Love that dare not speak its name"?':

> 'The Love that dare not speak its name' in this century is such a great affection of an elder for a younger man as there was between David and Jonathan, such as Plato made the very basis

of his philosophy . . . . It is beautiful, it is fine, it is the noblest form of affection. There is nothing unnatural about it. It is intellectual, and it repeatedly exists between an elder and younger man, where the elder has intellect and the younger man has all the joy, hope, and glamour of life before him. That it should be so, the world does not understand. The world mocks at it and sometimes puts one in the pillory for it.[8]

Mahaffy was aware that he was breaking new ground when discussing homosexuality, and he pointed out that it was one of the leading features of Greek life that was usually omitted by historians. He seemed determined to make up for this neglect, because he returned to the subject a second time in the book and devoted twelve pages to it. He acknowledged that modern society was shocked by 'the peculiar delight and excitement felt by the Greeks in the society of handsome youths', but added that the Greeks would be equally shocked by the behaviour of men and women in Victorian ballrooms.[9] 'As to the epithet *unnatural*,' he wrote, 'the Greeks would answer probably, that all civilisation was unnatural, that its very existence pre-supposed the creation of new instincts, the suppression of old, and that many of the best features in all gentle life were best because they were unnatural.'[10] He praised wealthy Greek parents for the interest they took in the education of their sons, as they did not, like affluent contemporary parents, cast their sons 'into public schools with the full knowledge that they will there lose all their simplicity and innocence'.[11] His remarks on homosexuality were taken out of the next edition because of adverse comments and because Mahaffy was anxious to ensure that the book was 'suited to all classes of readers'.[12] In the final paragraph of the book, Mahaffy declared his intention of writing a volume on Greek art and its relationship to the everyday life of the average Greek. He felt that practical lessons could be learned from this exercise which would be: 'of the greatest importance in our modern life. The aesthetical education of our lower classes cannot be reformed without a thorough psychological study of the genesis of national taste, and for this the principal materials must be found among the Greeks.'[13] When Wilde wrote *The Picture of Dorian Gray* in 1890, with its aesthetic themes and homosexual undertones, he took the name of his hero from one of the main ethnic groups of the ancient Greeks, the Dorians.[14]

During his first term at Oxford, Wilde attended the lectures of John Ruskin on the 'Aesthetic and mathematic schools of art in Florence'. The lectures were held in the University Museum, which was designed by Benjamin Woodward. In common with many other students, Wilde was very impressed by Ruskin, and he must have been disappointed when Ruskin left for Venice at the end of his first term at the university and remained away for the following year. Under the influence of Ruskin's artistic tastes, Wilde decorated his rooms, which had a lovely view over the river Cherwell, with *objets d'art* that he had acquired at home and abroad. Here he started social evenings, which were modelled on those he had known at Merrion Square and which were attended by fellow students who were interested in art, music and poetry. Wilde continued his classical and philosophical education at Oxford, where he came under the influence of scholars such as Max Muller, Walter Pater, William Wallace and Benjamin Jowett. His Oxford notebooks highlight both the range and depth of his knowledge. They reveal that his aestheticism was not just derived from Walter Pater and John Ruskin, as has often been suggested, but was based 'on a carefully reasoned philosophical and political stance'.[15]

Contrary to expectations, Wilde's interest in Catholicism grew rather than diminished during his early years in Oxford. He was fascinated, like his mother, by the ritual and pageantry of the Catholic Church. In *De Profundis* he wrote:

> When one contemplates all this from the point of view of art alone one cannot but be grateful that the supreme office of the Church should be the playing of the tragedy without the shedding of blood, the mystical presentation by means of dialogue and costume and gesture even, of the Passion of Our Lord, and it is always a source of pleasure and awe to me to remember that the ultimate survival of the Greek chorus, lost elsewhere to art, is to be found in the servitor answering the priest at Mass.[16]

His friend David Hunter Blair was received into the Catholic Church during Wilde's second term as a freshman at Oxford. Blair, heir to a baronetcy in Scotland, later renounced his wealth and eventually became the abbot of a Benedictine monastery. Wilde was fascinated by Blair's decision to become a Catholic. Blair, in turn, was fascinated by Wilde's conversational abilities and attractive personality, which he thought were inherited from his remarkable parents. Blair met Wilde's parents and his brother Willie at Magdalen when they came on a visit to Oxford. He remembered them as 'an interesting and delightful family circle'.[17] In February 1875 Wilde became a member of the Apollo Lodge, the Freemason's Lodge of Oxford University. William Wilde was a leading mason and he must have been reassured and pleased when his son was raised to the second degree on 24 April, and to the third, that of Master Mason, on 25 May. It was an unusual lodge, very high church, with old French Jacobite connections and with a great emphasis on ritual.[18]

In June 1875 Oscar went to Italy, where he was joined by Mahaffy. Mahaffy was taking a Cambridge undergraduate named William Goulding on a grand tour of the classical world at the request of his father, a wealthy Irish businessman. They explored the north of Italy together, staying in Florence, Venice, Padua, Verona and Milan. From Florence, Wilde wrote to his father, giving him detailed information on antiquarian topics such as sarcophagi, illuminated manuscripts, old coins, swords and goblets. He was inspired to write a poem after a visit to the beautiful Franciscan monastery of San Miniato in Florence, which was published later by the *Dublin University Magazine*. In Venice he had breakfast on board the P & O steamer *Baroda* on the invitation of the ship's doctor, a young Irishman named Fraser. Wilde sent long and perceptive descriptions of his experiences to his mother. He went to see the Ambrosian Library in Milan where he looked at some old manuscripts, including a very early Irish work which had been collated by the Celtic scholar Whitley Stokes. Wilde developed acute financial problems at Milan, so he could not join Mahaffy and Goulding on their journey to Greece. He had to undertake an eighteen-hour journey by stage-coach over the

Simplon Pass and into Lausanne. He wrote in some desperation to his mother:

> Will be in Paris Monday. Have now £2 to bring me, after paying 38 francs for the *diligence* just this moment. I have only had *one* letter from you since I left, and one from Sir William. I suppose there are some at Florence since I left. If there is no money at Paris for me I will not know what to do, but I feel sure there will be the genial £5.[19]

Despite his financial worries, Wilde was able to compose a poem, 'Rome Unvisited', at Arona on Lake Maggiore, in which he expressed his disappointment at not being able to see Rome. The last verse contained a pious hope:

> O joy to see before I die
> The only God-anointed King,
> And hear the silver trumpets ring
> A triumph as He passeth by.[20]

On his return to England, Wilde recounted his Italian experiences to Hunter Blair. He went with him to hear Cardinal Henry Manning preach, and he also discussed his thoughts about conversion with some priests, but he hesitated to take the final steps to conversion. Photographs of the Pope and Cardinal Manning were given a conspicuous place in his room. Dorian Gray, like his creator Oscar Wilde, was fascinated by the ritual of Catholicism:

> It was rumoured of him once that he was about to join the Roman Catholic communion; and certainly the Roman ritual had always a great attraction for him.
> But he never fell into the error of arresting his intellectual development by any formal acceptance of creed or system, or of mistaking, for a house in which to live, an inn that is but suitable for the sojourn of a night, or for a few hours of a night in which there are no stars and the moon is in travail.[21]

During Oscar's second year at Oxford, his father's health deteriorated. William Wilde struggled to continue with his work, but this became increasingly difficult. He finally succumbed on 19 April 1876. Speranza described his last weeks in a letter to a friend:

> Then he became weaker, and for the last six weeks never left his bed. He himself still hoping and planning as usual for his loved Moytura, but still he grew weaker day by day, no pain, thank God, no suffering – the last few days he was almost unconscious, quiet and still and at last passed away like one sleeping – gently and softly – no struggle – with his hand in mine and his two sons beside him.[22]

There was one other person in the sickroom whom Speranza does not mention, but whose presence she tolerated during her husband's last illness. Dying, like living, at 1 Merrion Square was out of the ordinary. Oscar told his first biographer Robert Sherard:

> Before my father died, in 1876, he lay ill in bed for many days. And every morning a woman dressed in black and closely veiled used to come to our house in Merrion Square, and unhindered by my mother, or any one else, used to walk straight upstairs to Sir William's bedroom and sit down at the head of his bed and so sit there all day, without ever speaking a word or once raising her veil. She took no notice of anybody in the room, and nobody paid any attention to her. Not one woman in a thousand would have tolerated her presence, but my mother allowed it, because she knew that my father loved the woman and felt that it must be a joy and comfort to have her there by his dying bed. And I am sure that she did right not to grudge that last happiness to a man who was about to die, and I am sure that my father understood her indifference, understood that it was not because she did not love him that she permitted her rival's presence, but because she loved him very much, and died with his heart full of gratitude and affection for her.[23]

Was this veiled woman in black the mother of his two daughters who had died in the tragic accident five years earlier? Every year for over twenty years, a woman dressed in black travelled from Dublin to Monaghan to visit the grave of the two sisters. She never said who she was, but once she told the sexton 'they were very dear to me'.[24]

The mysterious woman was not mentioned in Wilde's will, but when his accounts were examined after his death it was noted that he had borrowed one thousand pounds in 1874, and no one could trace this money subsequently. It is possible that the money was for this veiled woman, whom he could hardly acknowledge openly in his will without embarrassing Speranza.

William Wilde's funeral took place on Saturday, 22 April 1876, to the family vault at Mount Jerome cemetery. His sons Willie and Oscar and his brother-in-law, the Reverend William Noble, were at the graveside. Henry Wilson stood discreetly among the others at the funeral. Oscar must have felt proud of his father when he saw the number of Church and civic dignitaries who attended or were represented. These included the lord mayor, the lord chancellor, the lord chief justice, the president of the Royal Irish Academy, members of parliament, fellows of Trinity, and Sir Arthur Guinness. William Stokes was there, as was John Pentland Mahaffy and Dr Henry Gogarty, father of the writer Oliver St John Gogarty. Isaac Butt was present with his son. Sir Samuel Ferguson wrote a long elegy when he heard of his friend's death.[25]

Speranza was exhausted and very low after her husband's death. She knew that things would never be the same for the family:

> For us the loss is one that plunges our life into darkness. I feel like one shipwrecked. A wife feels the position more fatally than all others – a broken desolate life, a changed fortune, and in the midst of grief the necessity coming for all the exertion that legal affairs demand. It is a sad sorrow to me to leave this house – yet – it must be done. A married man lives on day by day and cannot think of the morrow. Probably at least £3,000 a year goes down in to the grave with him. This forces a sad change in a family. Happily my sons are of age. They will be self-supporting soon, I trust – but while my eyes are blinded with tears, my brain, alas, is filled with many sad bewildering cares and anxieties for the future.[22]

William Wilde's will brought some unpleasant surprises. Number 1 Merrion Square was heavily mortgaged and Speranza found herself in a difficult financial situation. Wilde's total assets, including the properties at Merrion Square, Moytura, and Illaunroe, amounted to less than seven thousand pounds, and he left substantial debts running into thousands of pounds. Owing to some confusion over a deed, his widow was left in a very difficult position. Life had not been easy for her with the loss of her daughter and the stress of the Travers' case. Now she found herself facing old age with very inadequate financial resources. 'My mother', Oscar wrote, 'who knew life as a whole, used often to quote to me Goethe's lines – written by Carlyle in a book he had given her years ago, and translated by him, I fancy, also:

Who never ate his bread in sorrow,
Who never spent the midnight hours
Weeping and waiting for the morrow, –
He knows you not, ye heavenly powers.'[26]

Her friends immediately set about getting a pension for her from the Civil List. She did not rank highly on the government's priorities however, and she had to wait fourteen years before being granted an annuity of seventy pounds. Willie inherited the house on Merrion Square and Oscar was left four houses, numbers 1 to 4 Esplanade Terrace, Bray, which had been built by his father in 1861. Willie also inherited Moytura, which was charged with an annuity of two hundred pounds a year for Speranza, but because of the political agitation over absentee landlords and the ownership of land, it was very difficult to get rents from the fourteen tenants. Lady Bracknell in *The Importance of Being Earnest* expressed sentiments with which Speranza would have empathised:

What between the duties expected of one during one's lifetime, and the duties exacted from one after one's death, land has ceased to be either a profit or a pleasure. It gives one position, and prevents one from keeping it up. That's all that can be said about land.[27]

The properties at Moytura and Bray were also mortgaged. Oscar was to share the fishing lodge at Illaunroe with his half-brother Henry Wilson. It appeared that William Wilde had been living off his capital for some years before his death. Speranza wrote to Oscar: '. . . now we must face the inevitable. We could not keep up this house and the female servants, fires, gas, rent – there is a mortgage – under £500 a year. Nothing is to be had out of wretched Moytura. I am in a very distracted state of mind. What is to be done?'[28] Financial worries, which Speranza always abhorred, now seemed to press on her from all directions.

In July 1876 there was some good news when Oscar was awarded a first in classical moderations at the end of his second academic year:

> My poor mother is in great delight and I was overwhelmed with telegrams on Thursday from everyone I know. My father would have been so pleased about it. I think God has dealt very hardly with us. It has robbed me of any real pleasure in my First, and I have not sufficient faith in Providence to believe it is all for the best – I know it is not. I feel an awful dread of going home to our old house, with everything filled with memories.[29]

Later in the month he returned to Dublin, and after a brief stay at Merrion Square he set out on a fishing holiday in the west of Ireland, planning to stay at Illaunroe. He intended to edit an unfinished work of his father's, *The Life of Gabriel Beranger*, before the following Christmas. 'Luckily', he wrote, 'the life of Beranger is three-quarters finished; so I will not have much trouble. Still it is a great responsibility; I will not be idle about it.'[30] Despite his good intentions, he did not complete the work, and it was his mother who eventually accomplished the task. Beranger was an artist of Franco-Dutch parentage who painted landscapes and archaeological subjects in the second half of the eighteenth century.[31] Speranza showed her loyalty to Sir William Wilde by the praise she lavished on him in the introduction to the completed biography:

> Sir William Wilde was no visionary theorist – nor mere compiler from the labours of other men. His singularly penetrating intellect tested scrupulously everything that came before him, yet with such clear and rapid insight that nothing seemed laborious to his active and vivid intellect. His

convictions were the product of calm rational investigation, and facts, not theories, always formed the basis of his teaching.[32]

Oscar Wilde's letters at this period reveal that he spent much of his time discussing religion with his mother and his friends. His mother thought dogma was not necessary except for 'the people' and she rejected the concept of a priest and sacrament standing between her and God. In a letter from Merrion Square to one of his Oxford friends, Oscar discussed the Holy Ghost, the Incarnation, St Augustine and John Henry Newman, and he concluded with: 'I am now off to bed after reading a chapter of S. Thomas à Kempis. I think half-an-hour's warping of the inner man daily is greatly conducive to holiness.'[33] At this stage of his life he balanced his intellectual interests with some sporting pursuits such as lawn tennis, at which he considered himself 'awfully good'. When he was staying at 1 Merrion Square, he rode most evenings to the beach at Sandymount, where he enjoyed a swim in the sea. He told a friend that although he always considered himself immortal in the sea, he felt slightly heretical when he saw all the Roman Catholic boys swimming around him wearing St Christopher medals as protection from drowning.

Whenever Wilde was in Dublin he availed of the opportunity to call on his old school friend Edward Sullivan at his rooms in Trinity. On these occasions Wilde talked enthusiastically about his visits to London, and particularly about the theatrical performances he had seen. 'I remember him telling me', Sullivan wrote, 'about Irving's *Macbeth*, which made a great impression on him; he was fascinated by it. He feared, however, that the public might be similarly affected – a thing which, he declared, would destroy his enjoyment of an extraordinary performance.'[34]

During August 1876 Wilde was busy correcting the proofs of Mahaffy's book *Rambles and Studies in Greece* at the professor's home, Earlscliff, in Howth:

> I am with that dear Mahaffy every day. He has a charming house by the sea here, on a place called the Hill of Howth (one of the crescent horns that shuts in the Bay of Dublin), the only place

near town with fields of yellow gorse, and stretches of wild myrtle, red heather and ferns . . . . Mahaffy's book, of Travels in Greece will soon be out. I have been correcting his proofs and like it immensely.[35]

Wilde began to tire of all the lawn tennis, swimming and riding, and he longed to go to the west. He waited for his brother Willie, who was now a barrister and on the circuit, and he was also expecting an Oxford friend, the painter Frank Miles. It was agreed that all three would then set out together for Galway. In the meantime, Wilde met a young woman named Florence Balcombe at her home at 1 Marino Crescent, Clontarf, and he was immediately attracted to her. We learn from a letter he wrote to his Oxford friend Reginald Harding that he accompanied her to a service at St Patrick's Cathedral on 16 August:

> I am just going out to bring an *exquisitely pretty girl* to afternoon service in the Cathedral. She is just seventeen with the *most perfectly beautiful face I ever saw and not a sixpence of money.* I will show you her photograph when I see you next.[36]

Her father, a retired lieutenant-colonel, had fought in the Crimea, and it is more than likely that she was named after Florence Nightingale. Florence Balcombe was considered one of the three most beautiful women of the age by the British artist and novelist George du Maurier. Later in the month of August Wilde went to Moytura:

> Frank Miles and I came down here last week, and have had a very royal time of it sailing. We are at the top of Lough Corrib, which if you refer to your geography you will find to be a lake thirty miles long, ten broad and situated in the most romantic scenery in Ireland.
>
> Frank has never fired off a gun in his life (and says he doesn't want to) but as our proper sporting season here does not begin till September I have not taught him anything. But on Friday we go into Connemara to a charming little fishing lodge we have in the mountains where I hope to make him land a salmon

and kill a brace of grouse. I expect to have very good sport indeed this season.[37]

Wilde described the scenery between Moytura and Illaunroe as the most romantic in Ireland. Miles was delighted with Illaunroe. He painted some sunsets and he also painted a frescoe on the wall of the fishing lodge, showing two naked cherubs angling, one on each side of an entrance archway facing the front door. Underneath is the inscription 'Tight Lines'. No doubt inspired by Miles, Wilde himself did some painting during the holiday, working patiently on a watercolour of the view from Moytura House for Florence Balcombe. He also worked on a book review which Mahaffy had promised to read before it was sent to the publisher. However, Wilde found himself 'too much occupied with rod and gun for the handling of the quill . . . . I have only got one salmon as yet but have had heaps of sea-trout which give great play. I have not had a blank day yet. Grouse are few but I have got a lot of hares so have had a capital time of it.'[38]

When Wilde returned to Merrion Square he was delighted to read a very friendly and encouraging letter from his mother's friend, the poet Aubrey de Vere. Apart from praising Wilde's early poems, de Vere offered to use his influence to have one of Oscar's Italian poems, 'Rome Unvisited', published in *The Month*. When the poem was published in September 1876, it was praised by John Henry Newman.[39] The Fenian John Boyle O'Reilly, another friend of Speranza, had the same poem published in an American magazine of which he was editor, entitled *The Boston Pilot*. It was the first work of Wilde's to be published in America. Wilde's star was beginning to rise, and when he returned to Dublin for the Christmas vacation in 1876 he noticed that many people in the city thought he was a fellow of Magdalen. He was quick to take advantage of this new situation. He suddenly 'tired' of going to private evening parties and began to dine out instead. He found this much more satisfactory, as he observed that everyone listened to all he had to say with great attention.

CHAPTER 12

Turbulent years

This is an era in my life, a crisis. I wish I could look into the seeds of time and see what is coming.[1]

Oscar Wilde

THROUGHOUT HIS YEARS AT OXFORD, Catholicism continued to interest Wilde. In March 1877 he planned to visit Rome, and he saw this visit as a time for decisions. Mahaffy, along with his friends William Goulding and George Macmillan, a member of the English publishing firm, were travelling to Greece, and it was arranged that Wilde should accompany them as far as Genoa. During the journey George Macmillan wrote to his father telling him of Oscar's leanings towards Catholicism and his plan to visit Rome to see the 'glories of the religion':

> Mahaffy is quite determined to prevent this if possible, and is using every argument he can to check him. At first he tried hard to persuade him to come to Greece with us, pointing out to him by the way all the worst faults of Popery. Finding this not altogether effective, though it had some weight, he changed his tack, and when Wilde began to say that perhaps he would come, Mahaffy said 'I won't take you. I wouldn't have such a fellow with me,' which of course, as Wilde is somewhat of a wilful disposition, has raised in him a firm determination to come, and I quite expect he will, and hope so.[2]

Wilde did change his mind as Macmillan predicted, but before leaving Italy they visited Genoa and Ravenna. On 2 April 1877,

168

Mahaffy wrote a letter to his wife telling her how he had managed to change Wilde's plans:

> We have taken Oscar Wilde with us, who has of course come round under the influence of the moment from Popery to Paganism, but what his Jesuit friends will say, who supplied the money to land him at Rome, it is not hard to guess. I think it is a fair case of cheating the Devil.
>
> He has a lot of swagger about him which William Goulding vows he will knock out of him as soon as he gets him on horseback in Arcadia. We call him Snooks on account of this – to his much disgust.[3]

Wilde could now appreciate the beauty of that ancient world about which he had heard so much since early childhood. They visited Olympia and they crossed the Peloponnese on horseback, a journey that took them a week. They then visited Argos and Nauplia before sailing to Aegina and Athens. The travellers also visited Mycenae before leaving Greece. Wilde was enthralled by the whole experience and he listened with great interest as Mahaffy enthused over the beauty of Olympia and the wonder of the Acropolis. He could hardly have had a better or more informed guide than his former tutor, who was finishing an educational process that he had begun in Trinity. Wilde visited Rome on his return journey, where he was met by his friends William Ward and David Hunter Blair. He was introduced to the grandeurs of Rome by the enthusiastic Blair who also secured a private audience for them with Pope Pius IX. The pontiff blessed Wilde and expressed the hope that he would follow his friend into the City of God. Wilde was deeply moved and immediately after the audience he locked himself in his room and wrote a sonnet. Even at the height of this religious ecstasy, he continued to keep his options open. Later that evening he insisted on alighting from the carriage at the Protestant cemetery where he prostrated himself on the turf to venerate the grave of John Keats. This experience also inspired a sonnet. Although Wilde was impressed by his visit to Rome, it was Mahaffy's rather than Hunter Blair's strategy that prevailed. Later, when Wilde and Blair met in Oxford, the latter was disappointed:

> I realized that he was changed. He had become Hellenized,
> somewhat Paganized, perhaps, by the appeal of Greece to his
> sensitive nature; and Rome had retired into the background.[4]

Wilde returned to Oxford a month after the beginning of term. As a
consequence, he was fined forty-seven pounds by the dons of
Magdalen and he was rusticated or sent down for the rest of the term.
The money was returned to him the following year when he took
First Class in the 'Honours Finals'. When Mahaffy returned to
Dublin he also ran into trouble. During a discourse in the college
chapel Mahaffy described St Paul as an 'impudent little Hebrew' and
he added that he could not forgive him for not having attended the
excellent university at Antioch.[5] The authorities suspended Mahaffy
from preaching, much to the annoyance of Tyrrell, who complained
'Ever since his sermons were discontinued, I suffer from insomnia in
church'.[5]

Oscar viewed the decision of the authorities in Oxford to rusticate
him as an illustration of their boorishness, and he described Bramley,
the dean, as an old woman in petticoats. He had failed to convince
the dean that being in Mahaffy's company on a tour of Greece was
just as good as going to lectures in Oxford. He returned home to
Dublin, where he found some rather sceptical friends:

> My mother was of course awfully astonished to hear my news
> and very much disgusted with the wretched stupidity of our
> college dons, while Mahaffy is *raging*! I never saw him so
> indignantly angry; he looks on it almost as an insult to himself.
>
> The weather is charming, Florrie more lovely than ever, and
> I am going to give two lectures on Greece to the Alexandra
> College girls here . . . . As I expected, all my friends here refuse
> to believe my story, and my brother who is down at Moytura at
> present writes me a letter marked '*Private*' to ask 'what it *really* is
> all about and *why* I have been rusticated' treating my
> explanations as mere child's play . . . . I am going down I hope
> for my May fishing soon, but I am overwhelmed with business
> of all kinds.[6]

Part of his business was to get some of his poetry accepted by a reputable London magazine. With this aim in view, he sent a poem 'On the recent massacres of the Christians in Bulgaria' accompanied by a very flattering letter to the English politician William Ewart Gladstone. Wilde, who was twenty-two at the time, deliberately underestimated his age in the letter:

> I am little more than a boy, and have no literary interest in London, but perhaps if *you* saw any good stuff in the lines I send you, some editor (of the *Nineteenth Century* perhaps or the *Spectator*) might publish them: and I feel sure that you can appreciate the very great longing that one has when young to have words of one's own published for men to read.[7]

Around the same time as Gladstone received the letter from his admirer who was 'little more than a boy', Keningale Cook, the editor of the *Dublin University Magazine*, received a rather arrogant letter from 'an Oxford man'. Wilde was returning the proofs of his description of the first exhibition at the Grosvenor Gallery in London which opened on 1 May 1877:

> Naturally, one of the great sorrows of youthful artists is that they always 'expurgate' bits of their articles, the very bits that they think best. However, I am glad to get the article published in your July number before the Gallery closes. Please have all my corrections attended to. Some of them are merely 'style' corrections, which, for an Oxford man, must be always attended to . . . .
>
> I hope we come to terms about this article – and others. Believe me I am most anxious to continue my father's connection with the *D.U.M.* which, I am sure, under your brilliant guidance will regain its lost laurels.[8]

After the publication of his article on the Grosvenor Gallery, Wilde suggested that he would write a similar article on the National Gallery of Ireland, which was just a short distance from his home on Merrion Square, but the offer was rejected on the grounds that the *Dublin University Magazine* 'had a greater circulation outside Ireland than in'.

Wilde was also correcting the proofs of his poem 'Heu Miserande

Puer' which was inspired by his visit to the grave of Keats in Rome. The poem was published in *The Irish Monthly* in July 1877.[9] He was very encouraged by the praise he received from several Catholic priests who had read his religious poetry, and he was particularly pleased when he learned that one of his sonnets had been recited nine times at the Glencree Reformatory in the Wicklow mountains on the day it first arrived there. It was this reformatory that he had often visited as a child with his mother.

Wilde sold his property in Bray in 1877 for around three thousand pounds. The sale was not without its complications because he had involved too many agents and a conflict of contracts resulted. Speranza struggled on, hoping that Oscar's brother Willie would settle down and start providing a steady income. Things were not going smoothly, however, and Speranza wrote to Oscar telling him: 'We have done with Dublin. This is what is now in my head. What profit or respect has a man here?'[10]

On Saturday 9 June 1877 Wilde attended a dinner given by Henry Wilson at his home. Henry had succeeded William Wilde as senior surgeon at St Mark's Hospital and he was working on a projected second edition of his father's book on ear surgery. He was concerned about Oscar's religious leanings and at some stage the brothers may have discussed the fact that Oscar, to quote himself, was 'on the brink' of joining the Catholic Church. Henry probably felt that he owed it to his father to stop this happening at all costs. He himself was well known for his hospitality and the dinner was attended by many of his friends. He had spent the afternoon riding and he appeared to be in excellent health. However, later in the evening he began to feel unwell, and by Sunday morning he was struggling for his life. Despite the efforts of six of his colleagues who stayed with him constantly, he died on the evening of Wednesday 13 June.

One of his last acts was to finish the annual report for St Mark's Hospital. Many of the eminent citizens of Dublin followed the funeral cortège, including the lord mayor in his state coach. Oscar and his brother Willie were the chief mourners, as Henry was not married. After the funeral Oscar wrote to a friend telling him that he was very much down in spirits and depressed. He went on:

My brother and I were always supposed to be his heirs but his will was an unpleasant surprise, like most wills. He leaves my father's hospital about £8,000, my brother £2,000 and me £100, on condition of my being a Protestant!

He was, poor fellow, bigotedly intolerant of the Catholics and seeing me 'on the brink' struck me out of his will. It is a terrible disappointment to me; you see I suffer a good deal from my Romish leanings, in pocket and mind.

My father had given him a share in my fishing lodge in Connemara, which of course ought to have reverted to me on his death; well, even this I lose 'if I become a Roman-Catholic for five years' which is very infamous. Fancy a man going before 'God and the Eternal Silences' with his wretched Protestant prejudices and bigotry clinging still to him.[11]

The board of governors of St Mark's Hospital convened a special meeting after Wilson's death to record the 'expression of their deep regret, and of their sense of the very great loss which the hospital and the public have sustained in his premature death'.[12] According to an obituary notice in the *British Medical Journal*, Wilson bequeathed seven thousand pounds to St Mark's subject to a life interest to two female relatives. It is possible that one of these relatives was his mother.

The following month Wilde was cheered by a letter he received from Walter Pater praising his article on the Grosvenor Gallery and expressing a desire to make his acquaintance on Wilde's return to Oxford. Wilde was also planning to get away from Dublin in July to do some fishing in the west of Ireland and he invited his friend William Ward to join him so that they could study together. He told Ward that he would have to rough it at Illaunroe, but that he would have all the basic necessities. He also guaranteed him magnificent scenery and sunsets, plenty of fishing and bathing and a diet of whiskey and salmon.

Ward resisted the temptations and did not travel to Ireland. Some weeks later Wilde wrote to him from Illaunroe Lodge:

I need not say how disappointed I was that you could not come and see this part of the world. I have two fellows staying with me, Dick Trench and Jack Barrow, who took a lodge near here for July and came to stay with me about three weeks ago. They are both capital fellows, indeed Dick Trench is I think my oldest friend, but I don't do any reading someway and pass my evenings in 'Pool, Ecarté and Potheen Punch'. I wish you had come; one requires sympathy to read . . . .

The weather is fair but not good for fishing. I have only got one salmon but our 'bag' yesterday of 'twelve white trout and twenty brown' was not bad. I have also had capital hare-shooting, but mountain-climbing is not my forte.[13]

He also wrote a letter to his friend Reginald Harding in which he announced that he had become an 'awful misanthrope', and which ended cheerfully:

One week more of this delightful, heathery, mountainous, lake-filled region! Teeming with hares and trout! Then to Longford for the partridge, then home . . . . Write to me at the Square.[14]

This enthusiasm for fishing and shooting contrasts with a reply he made years later when asked if he ever took part in outdoor sport: 'I am afraid I play no outdoor games at all, except dominoes . . . . I have sometimes played dominoes outside French cafés.'[15]

Wilde was in Dublin for the Christmas vacation in 1877. He joined forces with one of his father's associates, John T Gilbert, in trying to get financial support for the ageing and poverty-stricken artist Henry O'Neill. Wilde wrote an article on the artist in *Saunder's News-Letter* praising both his art and his book *The Sculptured Crosses of Ancient Ireland*. The article was unsigned and it appeared in *Saunder's* on 29 December. Wilde praised *The Sculptured Crosses of Ancient Ireland* as one of the very finest productions of modern Irish art. 'And of the delicacy and carefulness of Mr O'Neill's pencil', he wrote, 'we can give no better proof, to those who have not seen his books, than the fact that Mr Ruskin, whose flawless and exquisite taste is so well known, paid as much as fifty guineas some years ago, for a small collection of his drawings.'[16] Wilde went on to praise the influence that O'Neill's work had had on 'funereal art', as Irish crosses could be seen in cemeteries all over the country replacing the urns and sarcophagi that were formerly so common. He appealed for support for the artist:

> Ill-health, however, the fatal apathy of the public in appreciating genius, and the narrow jealousy of an antiquarian clique, have brought Mr. O'Neill in his old age to his present penury and distress. It remains for the Irish public to make reparation for past injustice. Ireland is under a debt to Henry O'Neill. He has benefited his country, in rescuing her from the imputations of barbarism in early ages, and he has a right to ask for assistance.[16]

Although the appeal brought in some money, it was not enough, and Wilde had his article republished in *The Nation* on 12 January 1879.

In March 1878 Wilde was in Dublin again, but he found it hard to concentrate on work. He returned to Oxford where he spent most of the Easter vacation studying at Magdalen. His concentration did not improve and he felt ill and wretched. He went to stay at the Royal Hotel in Bournemouth and he gradually began to feel better, as is apparent from this letter which he sent to Florence Balcombe in April 1878:

> I send you a line to wish you a pleasant Easter. A year ago I was in Athens and you sent me I remember a little Easter card – over so many miles of land and sea – to show me you had not forgotten me.
>
> I have been greatly disappointed in not being able to come over, but I could only spare four days and as I was not feeling well came down here to try and get some ozone. The weather is delightful and if I had not a good memory of the past I would be very happy.[17]

On 10 June it was announced that Wilde had won the Newdigate Prize, one of the most coveted undergraduate awards at Oxford, for his poem 'Ravenna'. He immediately sent his mother a telegram informing her of his success. She responded with characteristic enthusiasm:

> Oh Gloria, Gloria! Thank you a million times for the telegram. It is the first pleasant throb of joy I have had this year. How I

long to read the poem. Well, after all, we have *Genius* – that is something attorneys can't take away . . . I am proud of you.[18]

Wilde recited sections of the poem before the vice-chancellor in the Sheldonian Theatre on 26 June. It was a very special occasion for him, and his brother Willie and Mahaffy were both in the audience. *The Oxford and Cambridge Undergraduate Journal* reported the following day that the audience was very appreciative, listening to Wilde with rapt attention and applauding frequently. His Irish friends were very proud of his accomplishment and it was reported in *The Irish Monthly* under the heading 'An Irish winner of the Newdigate':

> This announcement had some interest for such Irish readers as recognised in this latest winner of the undergraduate Blue Ribbon of Literature a youthful countryman of their own, the youngest son of Sir William Wilde and 'Speranza', himself a faithful but too infrequent contributor to this Magazine.[19]

It was a very busy time for Wilde, but the euphoria associated with the achievement was soon banished by a court case over the sale of his property in Bray. The case was heard on the eighth, the eleventh and the twelfth of July and Wilde appeared to have little confidence in the outcome. He wrote to William Ward from the St Stephen's Club in Westminster: 'As for me I am ruined. The law suit is going against me and I am afraid I will have to pay costs which means leaving Oxford and doing some horrid work to earn bread. The world is too much for me.'[20]

Within a matter of days Wilde's fortunes had improved considerably. On 17 July, judgement in the lawsuit was given in his favour. Two days later, on 19 July, he learned to his great delight that he had achieved the coveted First in Greats. It was a brilliant end to his academic career in Oxford and he characteristically described it as a display of fireworks. In the autumn, Wilde travelled to the west of Ireland. He wrote to the Reverend Matthew Russell, editor of *The Irish Monthly*, from Illaunroe Lodge: 'I am resting here in the mountains – great peace and quiet everywhere – and hope to send you a sonnet as a result.'[21]

Later that year there were further tribulations in store when Wilde learned that Florence Balcombe planned to marry Bram Stoker. Florence and Bram lived just a short distance from each other on Marino Crescent in Clontarf. Wilde wrote to her from his home in Merrion Square:

Dear Florrie,

As I shall be going back to England, probably for good, in a few days, I should like to bring with me the little gold cross I gave you one Christmas morning long ago.

I need hardly say that I would not ask it from you if it was anything you valued, but worthless though the trinket be, to me it serves as a memory of two sweet years – the sweetest of all the years of my youth – and I should like to have it always with me. If you would care to give it to me yourself I could meet you any time on Wednesday, or you might hand it to Phil, whom I am going to meet that afternoon.

Though you have not thought it worth while to let me know of your marriage, still I cannot leave Ireland without sending you my wishes that you may be happy; whatever happens I at least cannot be indifferent to your welfare: the currents of our lives flowed too long beside one another for that.

We stand apart now, but the little cross will serve to remind me of the bygone days, and though we shall never meet again, after I leave Ireland, still I shall always remember you at prayer. Adieu and God bless you.[22]

Florence agreed to meet him, but she asked him to come to a house in Harcourt Street that was owned by Bram's brother Thornley. The latter was a surgeon in the city, and he was rapidly establishing a considerable reputation for his skill. The proposed venue did not suit Wilde, and he wrote again offering to meet her instead at her own home on the Crescent. He enclosed a letter he had received from her eighteen months previously, which he had always carried with him. He told her that the sentiments expressed in the letter seemed strange and out of tune with events, and that he would send back all her letters on his return to Oxford.

Florence was unhappy with the venue proposed by Oscar and she implied in her response that he was seeking a clandestine meeting with her. Oscar was aggrieved:

Dear Florence,

As you expressed a wish to see me I thought that *your mother's house* would be the only suitable place, and that we should part where we first met. As for my calling at Harcourt Street, you know, my dear Florence, that such a thing is quite out of the question; it would have been unfair to you, and me, and to the man you are going to marry, had we met anywhere else but under your mother's roof, and with your mother's sanction. I am sure that you will see this yourself on reflection; as a man of honour I could not have met you except with the full sanction of your parents and in their house.

As regards the cross, there is nothing 'exceptional' in the trinket except the fact of my name being on it, which of course would have prevented you from wearing it ever, and I am not foolish enough to imagine that you care now for any memento of me. It would have been impossible for you to keep it.[23]

Florence Balcombe married Bram Stoker on 4 December 1878 at St Anne's Church in Dublin. Wilde claimed that the rejection hurt him deeply. This may have been true, but it is possible that he also relished the drama of the situation. He once told a young friend who came to him for advice about an *affaire*: 'It is much better to have loved and lost than to have loved and won.'[24] He further dampened the ardour of his confidante by observing: 'There is one thing infinitely more pathetic than to have lost the woman one is in love with, and that is to have won her and found out how shallow she is.'[24] Two years later, when Florence was making her first stage appearance in London, Oscar asked the actress Ellen Terry to arrange for Florence to wear some flowers from him during the performance without letting her know who sent them:

I should like to think that she was wearing something of mine the first night she comes on the stage, that anything of mine should touch her. Of course if you think – but you won't think she will suspect? How could she? She thinks I never loved her, thinks I forget. My God how could I![25]

In June 1888 he sent Florence an inscribed copy of *The Happy Prince and Other Tales*, which had just been published. Some years later he also sent her an inscribed copy of his play *Salomé*.

As Oscar had indicated in his letter to Florence, the Wildes were now preparing to leave Dublin. Speranza was determined that the city that had witnessed her greatness would not see her decline. Number 1 Merrion Square was sold early in 1879, and Speranza wrote to her friend Rosalie Olivecrona in April informing her of the imminent move: 'We have arranged to leave Ireland and this is my last note from the old family mansion in Merrion Square – Both of my sons prefer residing in London, the focus of light, progress and intellect.'[26] Speranza left Ireland in May, and henceforth the family base was in London. She never returned to Ireland and Wilde visited only on two occasions. Dublin held too many memories, whereas London was a city of exciting opportunities. Oscar Wilde was already making an impression there.

CHAPTER 13

'A most recalcitrant patriot'

I live in London for its artistic life and opportunities. There is no lack of culture in Ireland, but it is nearly all absorbed in politics. Had I remained there my career would have been a political one.[1]

> Oscar Wilde

No artist desires to prove anything. Even things that are true can be proved.[2]

> Oscar Wilde

LONDON OFFERED WILDE A MUCH bigger stage for his self-ordained role as an apostle of the aesthetic movement. He began to mix in fashionable society and he associated with some of the most beautiful women of the period, such as Lillie Langtry, Ellen Terry and Sarah Bernhardt. He soon attracted attention. He was caricatured by George du Maurier in *Punch*, and when Gilbert and Sullivan wrote the opera *Patience*, which satirised the aesthetes, it was generally assumed that the character Bunthorne was modelled on Wilde. He became an advocate of the concept that art existed for its beauty alone, thus rejecting John Ruskin's view that art should be informed by a moral purpose.

In *The Decay of Lying*, Wilde elaborated on the doctrines of his new aesthetics. 'Art never expresses anything but itself' and 'Life imitates art far more than art imitates life' were basic tenets. He attacked realism in art, pointing out that objective truths were not a concern of the true artist, who worked from the imagination. He held that art always lies, as it does not present an exact description of the real world outside the imagination of the artist. In art, lies are superior to truth, and masks more revealing than faces. Mahaffy had justified lying in conversation on the grounds 'that recreation, not instruction, is the aim of conversation'.[3] 'Never tell a story because it is true', he once remarked, 'tell it because it is a good story.'[4] Wilde, his protégé, went further, and came to the conclusion 'that Lying, the telling of beautiful untrue things, is the proper aim of Art'.[5]

Wilde decided to live his life according to aesthetic principles and to follow Walter Pater's advice by burning with the intensity of a 'gem–like flame'. This philosophy ultimately had disastrous consequences for him. Gilbert informs Ernest in his essay *The Critic As Artist* that:

> To be good, according to the vulgar standard of goodness, is obviously quite easy. It merely requires a certain amount of sordid terror, a certain lack of imaginative thought, and a certain low passion for middle–class respectability. Aesthetics are higher than ethics. They belong to a more spiritual sphere. To discern the beauty of a thing is the finest point to which we can arrive.[6]

Speranza established a salon in London which, although on a much more modest scale than her gatherings in Merrion Square, attracted a steady flow of visitors. It became particularly popular with Irish artists and writers, whether living in London or just passing through. Others came hoping to meet Wilde as his fame grew. London offered Wilde an exciting challenge and new fields to conquer, but Speranza knew that she would never regain the position she had held in Merrion Square. She wrote mournfully: 'Alas now I only feel the agony and loss of all that made life endurable, and my singing robes are trailed in London clay.'[7] Wilde was so absorbed in his new world, however, that he took no interest in Irish affairs. As a student at Oxford he had begun to disregard the distinction between England and Ireland. He annoyed the Reverend Mathew Russell SJ, editor of *The Irish Monthly*, by referring to 'our English land' in his poem on Keats:

> I am sorry you object to the words 'our English land'. It is a noble privilege to count oneself of the same race as Keats or Shakespeare. However I have changed it. I would not shock the feelings of your readers for anything.[8]

Oscar wrote his first play in 1880 and he gave it the title *Vera*, after the play's heroine. Although the play was set in late-eighteenth-century Moscow, many of Vera's lines bore the hallmarks of Speranza's revolutionary rhetoric. The drama of the play arises from the tension between the plot of a revolutionary group planning to assassinate the czar and his son the czarevich and Vera's love for the latter. Vera is torn between her loyalty to the revolution and her loyalty to the czarevich, who promises reform by constitutional methods. Like Speranza, Vera was equally at home at the palace and at the secret meetings of the revolutionaries. Vera arrived at one meeting wearing a cloak over her ball gown. During his childhood, Wilde must have often puzzled over the enigma of the crowds cheering his mother for her nationalist sympathies as she travelled to viceregal functions at Dublin Castle. Speranza was also very much aware of her unusual double role. 'I went to the last Drawingroom at the Castle', she told a friend, 'and Lord Aberdeen smiled very archly as he bent to kiss my cheek, which is the ceremony of presentation. I smiled too and thought of Alea Jacta Est.'[9] Vera is described as 'the priestess of liberty' in the play, and in Act III she proclaims: 'Here on thy altar, O Liberty, do I dedicate myself to thy service; do with me as thou wilt.'[10] Wilde took this directly from one of his mother's letters to him, in which she declared that she 'had stood a priestess at the altar of freedom'.[11] Many years previously she had used similar rhetoric at the end of her revolutionary article, 'Jacta Alea Est', in which she called for armed rebellion:

> We must crush all vices – annihilate all evil passions – trample on them, as a triumphant CHRIST with his foot upon the serpent, and then the proud hallelujah of Freedom will rise to heaven from the lips of a pure, a virtuous, a regenerated, a God-blessed people; and this fair land of ours, which now affrights the world with its misery, will be one grand temple, in which we shall all kneel as brothers – one holy, peaceful, loving fraternity – sons of one common country – children of one God – heirs together of those blessings purchased by our blood – a heritage of freedom, justice, independence, prosperity and glory.[12]

Vera resolves her difficult dilemma when she decides to save the life of the czarevich by sacrificing her own life in a rather melodramatic scene at the end of the play. The London opening of the play, planned for early 1882 under the direction of Dion Boucicault, was cancelled because of political sensitivities. This was the first of Wilde's plays to fall foul of political censorship, albeit unofficial in this instance. Wilde was planning an American lecture tour and he hoped that he might be able to arrange to have the play performed in the United States. He had Dion Boucicault's encouragement in this venture, but when the play was eventually performed in America in 1883, it was not a theatrical success.

It was his lecture tour in North America in 1882 that brought Wilde face to face with his Irishness. He landed in New York on 2 January and spent twelve months travelling around the continent lecturing to different groups. He was castigated by the *Irish Nation* in New York at the beginning of his tour for lecturing on what he referred to as the 'English' Renaissance, at a time when 'hideous tyranny overshadows his native land'.[13] It was the considered opinion of the *Irish Nation* that Speranza's son had sadly misapplied his talent. Wilde soon took stock of the situation and realised that many Americans would be interested in him not for his advocacy of the beautiful but because of his links with Ireland. He rose to the occasion and he was soon enjoying the adulation he received as 'Speranza's son'.

The Irish Americans had decided to support the Land League movement, whose aim was to win land ownership for the Irish tenant farmers. Stories of evictions fuelled anti-British feeling in America and large sums of money crossed the Atlantic to support the tenants in their conflict. The League's leader in Ireland, Charles Stewart Parnell, and many of his colleagues, had been arrested in October 1881, and they were still in Kilmainham Gaol in Dublin when Wilde began his American tour. Wilde realised, as did his mother, that the Irish Americans were becoming a new and significant force in the age-old dispute between England and Ireland. Under these circumstances he was only too happy to dilate on 'Anglo-Saxon stupidity' in his lectures and to give nationalist answers

183

to the many reporters who interviewed him about relations between England and Ireland. He complained to a reporter in New York that the English took his epigrams as earnest and his paradox as prose. Observations such as this won him many Irish-American friends, but they did not endear him to the readers of the English papers that reported on his American tour. Naturally Speranza was delighted with her son's high profile, but Mahaffy disapproved and he wrote to Speranza saying that Wilde should have sought his advice before embarking on the tour.

At different cities Wilde was met by reception parties composed of the leading Irish citizens and several Irish Americans hosted dinner parties for him. At Saint John in Canada, Wilde was reminded of a painful episode in his own family history when Dr Boyle Travers, brother of Mary Travers, was a guest at a dinner given in Wilde's honour. The fact that Wilde's uncle was a Confederate probably explains in part Wilde's own sympathy for the southern side in the American Civil War. He told a reporter during his lecture tour: 'We in Ireland are fighting for the principle of autonomy against empire, for independence against centralization, for the principles for which the South fought . . . . The principles for which Mr Davis and the South went to war cannot suffer defeat.'[14] In Boston Wilde met the Irish poet John Boyle O'Reilly and he explored with him the possibility of getting Speranza's collection of poetry published in America. A former Fenian, O'Reilly was an influential figure and editor of the *Boston Pilot*. 'I think my mother's work should make a great success here', Wilde wrote, 'it is so unlike the work of her degenerate artist son. I know you think I am thrilled by nothing but a dado. You are quite wrong but I shan't argue.'[15]

Oscar also met Dion Boucicault in Boston and the latter offered sufficient financial support to free Wilde from his commitments to D'Oyly Carte who had sponsored his American lecture tour. Boucicault described the meeting to a friend:

> Oscar is helpless, because he is not a practical man of business, so when I advised him to throw over Carte, and offered to see him through financially if he did so, he felt afraid. I offered him a thousand pounds or two if he required it, but he says he will

play out his contract to April . . . . I do wish I could make him less Sybarite – less Epicurean. He said this morning 'Let me gather the golden fruits of America that I may spend a winter in Italy and a summer in Greece amidst beautiful things.' Oh dear – if he would only spend the money and the time amongst six-per-cent bonds! I think I told him so but he thinks I take 'a painful view of life'.[16]

Boucicault felt protective towards Wilde, as he pointed out that he had known him since he was a child at his knee in Dublin. He recognised Wilde's potential but he felt that Wilde lacked proper management to exploit it. He also sent Wilde a 'candid' critique of *Vera*, advising him that he had not shaped his subject well enough before beginning the play and that there was too much discussion rather than action. It is uncertain whether Boucicault's advice had any influence on Wilde when writing his subsequent plays, but it has been suggested that Wilde was indebted to him in another context. The writer and theatre-director Christopher Fitz-Simon has drawn attention to the similarities between the structure of *The Importance of Being Earnest* and a farce by Boucicault entitled *A Lover by Proxy*, which was written in 1842:

A Lover by Proxy concerns two effervescent young men, Lawless and Blushington, who live in town; and two delightful young ladies, Harriet and Kate, who live in the country at Richmond: substitute Algernon and Jack (and Algernon's flat in Half Moon Street), and Cecily and Gwendolen (at the Manor House, Woolton), and the parallel is complete – except that Wilde made Gwendolen despise the country. An aunt of forbidding demeanour, Miss Penelope Prude, clearly gave Wilde the idea for *two* formidable females, Lady Bracknell and Miss Prism. Where Boucicault's play strives after obvious effects, Wilde's has the appearance of achieving them with a graceful ease; where the dialogue of one is quite flavourless, the other recalls 'a delicate exotic fruit'; where Boucicault's characters could be entertaining only if played by actors of poise and charm, Wilde's are implicitly amusing, vital, and brimming with the energy of the naturally articulate.[17]

Wilde, like many other writers including Shakespeare, borrowed from different historical and literary sources, and the borrowed material was usually absorbed into a work of far greater brilliance. Of Shakespeare's borrowings, Wilde observed:

> Shakespeare had chronicles and plays and novels from which to work, but they were merely his rough material. He took them, and shaped them into song. They become his, because he made them lovely.[18]

Robert Ross remembered that Wilde openly acknowledged his own borrowing:

> Wilde complained to me one day that someone, in a well-known novel, had stolen an idea of his. I pleaded in defence of the culprit that Wilde himself was a fearless literary thief. 'My dear fellow,' he said, with his usual drawling emphasis, 'when I see a monstrous tulip with four wonderful petals in someone else's garden, I am impelled to grow a monstrous tulip with five wonderful petals; but that is no reason why someone should grow a tulip with only three petals.'[19]

When a novelist spoke of adapting Bunyan, Wilde gave him the following advice:

> Never say you have 'adapted' anything from anyone. Appropriate what is already yours – for to publish anything is to make it public property – but never adapt, or, if you do, suppress the fact. It is hardly fair to Bunyan, if you improve on him, to point out, some hundreds of years after, how much cleverer you are than he; and it is even more unfair, if you spoil what he has said, and then hold him accountable.[20]

In *The Critic As Artist* Gilbert pointed out that even in ancient Greece people without true artistic ability interfered in matters of literature and art: 'for the accusations of plagiarism were endless, and such accusations proceed either from the thin colourless lips of impotence, or from the grotesque mouths of those who, possessing nothing of their own, fancy that they can gain a reputation for wealth by crying out that they have been robbed.'[18] Recent analysis of

Wilde's society comedies has shown that the playwright 'borrowed' more extensively from his own work than from the work of any other author.[21]

On Wednesday, 21 November 1883, Wilde returned to Dublin to give two lectures at the Gaiety Theatre. He stayed at the Shelbourne Hotel and gave the first lecture on 'The house beautiful' on the day after his arrival. The eighteen-year-old W B Yeats was in the audience, but more importantly for Oscar, a pretty young woman named Constance Lloyd was also there to listen to him. Constance was a niece of Charles Hare, first Baron Hemphill, who had lived near the Wildes on Merrion Square. A distinguished classical scholar, he was called to the bar in 1860 and he crowned a brilliant career by becoming solicitor-general for Ireland. Oscar had been seeing Constance in London, and she was now, by coincidence, on holiday in Dublin with her grandmother Mary Atkinson, at 1 Ely Place. On the evening of his first lecture, Oscar returned to his old university and dined on Commons at the top table with the fellows of Trinity College.

Constance also attended his lecture on 'Impressions of America', which was held on Friday afternoon. One newspaper critic commented on his 'strongly-marked English accent' and on the fact that he spoke with considerable rapidity. According to another reporter: 'Oscar spoke in a quiet conversational tone, but yet so distinctly and in such a key that it reached the limits of the theatre.'[22] Most of the press coverage of the lectures was very favourable, and no doubt Wilde was pleased to be a celebrity in his native city. On Sunday, 25 November, he walked the short distance from the Shelbourne Hotel to see Constance at 1 Ely Place. Later, when he walked back to the hotel, he was engaged to be married.

Speranza was delighted when she heard of the engagement. 'I would like you to have a small house in London', she told Oscar, 'and live the literary life and teach Constance to correct proofs, and eventually go into Parliament.'[23] The marriage took place on 29 May 1884 at St James's Church, Paddington. Oscar and Constance had two children, Cyril who was born in July 1885 and Vyvyan who was born in November of the following year.

In January 1883 a group of enthusiasts led by Francis A Fahy established the Southwark Irish Literary Club in London with the intention of cultivating Irish history, art and literature. The club organised a series of lectures, which were given by experts in the field of Irish literature. One of the more memorable lectures took place in September 1887 when Justin McCarthy MP read a paper on 'The literature of '48'. The occasion was a special one because Charles Gavan Duffy, who had returned from exile in Australia, was in the chair. Oscar Wilde was among the group who greeted Duffy on his arrival. Some members of the club saw irony in this, as they viewed Wilde as 'the representative of a movement with which Young Ireland could have had no sympathy; – the very head centre of aestheticism himself – more curious still, that this same representative should be the son of "Speranza" '.[24]

The Southwark club formed the nucleus of the Irish Literary Society, which was established in the early 1890s. This society played an important role in the Celtic Revival and it attracted some very gifted writers, such as W B Yeats, Stopford Brooke, T W Rolleston, Dr John Todhunter, Lionel Johnson and Alfred Perceval Graves. W P Ryan, who wrote the first detailed account of the society in 1894, recalled:

> When it was suggested that Oscar Wilde should be invited to join the Society, one who knew him said that he would certainly put off the matter with a quip or a paradox, which, however, would be a good one, and worthy of being entered in the minute-book. This friend was a false prophet, for Oscar Fingal O'Flaherty Wills Wilde was soon an honoured name on our register.[25]

Willie Wilde also joined the society and Speranza was elected as the first honorary member. Several members of the society were members of the famous 'Rhymers' Club', and Oscar Wilde occasionally took part in the activities of this club, which had a definite Celtic bias. Wilde, like Yeats, was a firm believer in the hereditary genius of the Celtic race. If some of his contemporaries saw an incongruity between Wilde's enthusiasm for the Celtic

Revival and his advocacy of aestheticism, Wilde saw the two interests as complimentary. He idealised Celtic life, writing that 'in the whole of Celtic myth and legend . . . the loveliness of the world is shown through a mist of tears, and the life of a man is no more than the life of a flower'.[26] In an early biographical sketch published in *The Biograph* in 1880, Wilde is described as:

> a believer in the religion of beauty, a marked figure among the newest group of aesthetics, a dweller in the high places of feeling. To take this position he is specially fitted by reason of a singularly enthusiastic temperament and an exceptional education. He is the offspring of a fervid and emotional race, and the child of two persons of unusual character. In him the strong emotional tendency of the Irish nature which with most of the race feeds personal feeling alone becomes, through intellectual development, an ardour for art and its glories.[27]

Wilde certainly saw himself as a leader of a new Celtic school of literature. In May 1893 he wrote to George Bernard Shaw thanking him for a copy of his play *Widowers' Houses*:

> I must thank you very sincerely for Op. 2 of the great Celtic School. I have read it twice with the keenest interest. I like your superb confidence in the dramatic value of the mere facts of life. I admire the horrible flesh and blood of your creatures, and your preface is a masterpiece − a real masterpiece of trenchant writing and caustic wit and dramatic instinct. I look forward to your Op. 4. As for Op. 5, I am lazy, but am rather itching to be at it.[28]

Wilde's biographer Heskett Pearson identified *Lady Windermere's Fan* as Op. 1, *Widowers' Houses* by Shaw as Op. 2, *A Woman of No Importance* as Op. 3, *The Philanderer* by Shaw as Op. 4, and Op. 5 as *An Ideal Husband*. Wilde sent Shaw a copy of *Lady Windermere's Fan* with the inscription: 'Op. 1 of the Hibernian School London '93.'

Wilde's enthusiasm for Celtic art and design was genuine and lasting. At a dinner in the House of Commons in 1891 he told some Scottish and Welsh members 'that as to break bread and drink wine together is, as Christ saw, the simplest and most natural symbol of comradeship, *all* of us who are Celts, Welsh, Scotch, and Irish, should inaugurate a Celtic dinner, and assert ourselves, and show these tedious Angles or Teutons what a race we are, and how proud we are to belong to that race'.[29] When an Englishman remarked in Wilde's hearing that in the nineteenth century the Macs had done everything and the Os nothing, Wilde replied: 'You forget. There are O'Connell and O Wilde.'[30]

Wilde's influence on the writers of the Celtic Revival is often underestimated. For instance, Yeats' aesthetic theory and his obsession with the importance of the mask or anti-self for the artist were derived almost wholly from Wilde. Yeats was invited by Wilde to join his family for dinner on Christmas Day 1888. After the dinner, Wilde read from the proofs of his essay *The Decay of Lying*, which was being prepared for publication at the time. Yeats was captivated as he listened to Wilde, and the experience had a major influence on the poet's subsequent artistic development. John Millington Synge's great work of the Celtic revival, *The Playboy of the Western World*, the plot of which revolves around 'the power of a lie', was also influenced by Wilde's ideas in *The Decay of Lying*.[31]

Wilde returned to Dublin for the last time to give a number of lectures in January 1885. Before travelling, he received an invitation from Florence Balcombe's sister, Phillipa Knott, to spend some time with them in Dublin. He accepted the invitation, saying that he looked forward to meeting Florrie and all at the Crescent again. Wilde's first lecture at the Gaiety, on the subject of 'Beauty, taste and ugliness in dress' was attended by about five hundred people. During the lecture Wilde praised the traditional Irish hooded cloak, describing it as a very admirable garment and declaring that 'it was decidedly Irish in very remote times, as their sculptures in Kilconnell Abbey proved'.[32] Wilde included more references of Irish interest in his second lecture, 'Art in modern life'. He praised the Celtic and Islamic contributions to non-representational art and, according to the following report of the lecture, he received applause from his audience when he praised Irish art over English art.

> It was always possible for a nation by artistic power to give to the commonest material vastly increased value. There was no reason

why we in Ireland should not do this. There was in all the Celtic races this power of decoration. Whether they viewed the remains of ancient art in the Royal Irish Academy or in the museums of Northern Europe, they would be struck by the far greater sense of beauty evinced in the early Celtic work than in the old English art, which was deficient in delicacy and sense of proportion. [Applause.] And there was no reason why they should not show that those perceptions of the beautiful, and capacities of delicate handling as to hue and colour, were not dead.[33]

A report on the lectures in the *Freeman's Journal* declared that the audience was very appreciative, and the critic went on to observe 'Evidently people have ceased to regard Mr Wilde as the eccentric apostle of a momentarily fashionable craze, to be seen, heard, and laughed at. They have, apparently, come to discover that underneath the extravagances credited to the aesthetic cult there lie principles of truth and beauty applicable to the pursuits and incidents of everyday life.'[34] Wilde's lectures at the Gaeity also received notice in the first issue of *The Dublin University Review*. The writer confessed that he was surprised that the lectures did not attract bigger audiences as he thought their quality was very good. He went on to speculate on the reasons for the apparent lack of interest, and he warned Wilde about the consequences of being earnest! 'In the first place the British public, though fond of a joke, has little respect for the joker; and when, as is the present case, the latter turns out to be in earnest, it is very apt to regard him as a fool.'[35] The same reviewer observed that it was widely believed that aestheticism was proving 'a good thing' for its chief apostle, and that a true prophet was not usually financially successful. 'However a few more lectures as unfortunate, from a commercial point of view, as those recently delivered in this city, will materially remedy this defect, and will help to restore Mr. Wilde to public favour. Meantime he will not regard the decrease in his receipts, for, as he stated in the second lecture, "True art is economical".'[35]

Although to the outsider the marriage of Oscar and Constance appeared to be a success, things soon began to go wrong. Oscar grew tired of Constance and eventually she was replaced in his affection first by Robert Ross and later by Lord Alfred Douglas, known to his friends as Bosie. Difficulties also developed between Oscar and his brother Willie. Willie had been called to the bar in Dublin, but he gave up legal practice for a career as a journalist. He lived with Speranza in London until he married. During their early years in England, Willie used every opportunity to promote his gifted younger brother. With the passage of time their relationship deteriorated. Oscar thought that Willie took advantage of Speranza by constantly borrowing from her. Then he heard that Willie had been making fun of him in New York. This led to a major rift which upset Speranza greatly, and she appealed to her sons to forget their enmity.

Between 1887 and 1889 Oscar, like his brother, seemed to be concentrating on a career in journalism. He became editor of *The Woman's World* and he pledged to deal 'not merely with what women wear, but with what they think, and what they feel'.[36] The new editor made sure that there was a place in the magazine for Irish women. He published work by his mother and by some of her friends, such as an article on Alexandra College by Lady Samuel Ferguson. He also published essays on places of Irish interest, such as Dublin Castle, with illustrations by Walter Osborne, and on the sea-side town of Youghal, County Cork. He supported Irish industry by including detailed accounts of traditional Irish crafts, under titles such as 'Irish modern art', 'The poplin-weavers of Dublin', 'The knitters of the Rosses', 'Lace-making in Ireland' and 'A few hints on Mountmellick embroidery'. In the second volume he included a collection of fairy stories written by his mother under the title *Irish Peasant Tales.*

During this period Wilde did a considerable amount of book reviewing. Some of his criticisms could be very incisive, but he claimed that he always wished to be fair, adding on one occasion the proviso 'as fair as an Irishman with a temperament ever wants to be'.[37] He could also be very generous and he was particularly generous to the young W B Yeats. He reviewed Yeats' *Irish Fairy and Folk Tales* in *The Woman's World* in February 1889, and he praised the work highly: 'It is delightful', he wrote, 'to come across a collection of purely imaginative work, and Mr Yeats has a very quick instinct in finding out the best and the most beautiful things in Irish folklore.'[38] In the following month he reviewed *The Wanderings of Oisín and Other Poems* in both *The Woman's World* and the *Pall Mall Gazette*. Again Wilde was fulsome in his praise: 'He is essentially Celtic, and his verse, at its best, is Celtic also . . . . It is impossible to doubt, after reading his present volume, that he will some day give us work of high import.'[39]

In 1887 Wilde wrote devastating reviews of two books by John Pentland Mahaffy: *Principles of the Art of Conversation* and *Greek Life and Thought*. He dismissed *The Art of Conversation* as a clever little book: 'It fascinates in spite of its form and pleases in spite of its pedantry, and is the nearest approach, that we know of, in modern literature to meeting Aristotle at an afternoon tea.'[40] He claimed that the book on Greece was inaccurate and provincial, and he went on to say that Mahaffy 'is clever, and, at times, even brilliant, but he lacks reasonableness, moderation, style and charm'.[41] This attack is difficult to understand, as Wilde had written to Mahaffy the previous year asking his former tutor to recommend him as a suitable person to be an inspector of schools. Wilde did not get the job and he may have thought that Mahaffy had not used his influence on his behalf. On the other hand, the motivation for the review may have been a desire to show his independence of his old tutor. There were some fundamental differences between the two men, particularly on Irish politics and culture. Mahaffy strenuously opposed Home Rule for Ireland and he had no appreciation of the richness of Gaelic culture. At the time, it appeared that Home Rule might become a reality because of Gladstone's support. In reaction, Mahaffy had become an enthusiastic Tory, and his book on Greece bristled with extreme unionist prejudice. 'There is always something peculiarly impotent about the violence of a literary man', Wilde observed in his review.[41] Shortly afterwards Wilde reviewed a book by another old family friend in the same magazine. This was *Early Christian Art In Ireland* by Margaret Stokes. It is curious that there are similarities in the approach of both reviews. According to Wilde, Margaret Stokes' handbook would fill a useful niche on Irish art, 'the works of Sir William Wilde, Petrie and others being somewhat elaborate for the ordinary student.'[41] He enthused about the beauty of Celtic art and design, but he pointed out that: 'There is, of course, nothing particularly original in Miss Stokes's book, nor can she be said to be a very attractive or pleasing writer, but it is unfair to look for originality in primers, and the charm of the illustrations fully atones for the somewhat heavy and pedantic character of the style.'[42] It is possible that these two reviews were an expression of Wilde's rejection of the cultural philosophy of the Dublin of his youth. The appreciation of art for its own sake found little support in this philosophy. In a milieu where serious-minded individuals brought Irish medicine and science to an international level of excellence, art also should have its purpose. 'In the pursuit of art', wrote the physician William Stokes, 'we would avoid getting into that condition which has been suitably termed "mental luxury"; one which generates selfishness, on the one hand, and indolence on the other – a condition in which we become recipients, but not artificers, and in the dreamy, idle contemplation of the beautiful become the slaves of a refined sensualism . . . . We are not to worship art, but to use it as a means to some great end.'[43]

Whatever Mahaffy felt about the reviews at the time, it did not end his friendship with Wilde, as some years later he went to the opening night of one of Wilde's plays at the Haymarket Theatre in London, and he subsequently wrote a complimentary note to the playwright. Wilde responded with generosity:

> My dear Mahaffy, I am pleased you like the play, and thank you for your charming letter, all the more flattering to me as it comes not merely from a man of high and distinguished culture, but from one to whom I owe so much personally, from my first and my best teacher, from the scholar who showed me how to love Greek things.
>
> Let me sign myself, in affection and admiration, your old pupil and your old friend, Oscar Wilde.[44]

Although not given to over-exertion, Wilde's brother Willie also made an impact in the world of journalism. He became a leader-writer on the *Daily Telegraph* and he wrote for *The World* and *Vanity Fair*. His greatest journalistic achievement was his reporting of the Parnell Commission in 1889. *The Times* had accused Parnell of being associated with a terrorist conspiracy in Ireland, and they supported their allegations with a number of letters. These charges were investigated by the Parnell Commission. Oscar Wilde was sufficiently interested in Parnell to attend some of the sessions, and he was sketched by S P Hall as one of the celebrities at the inquiry. Speranza saw Parnell as a man of destiny, and Oscar also supported the Home Rule movement, although he never took an active role in politics. Thirteen volumes of the Parnell Commission were among the books found in Wilde's library when many of his possessions were auctioned in April 1895. Parnell was cleared of any complicity in terrorist activity by the Commission, but shortly afterwards Captain O'Shea named him as co-respondent when he instituted his suit for divorce. Where lies and forgeries did not succeed, Victorian prudery proved triumphant. Parnell fell from his political pinnacle and he was hounded to his death shortly afterwards at the early age of forty-five. When discussing Parnell's fate on one occasion Wilde remarked: 'There is something vulgar in all success. The greatest men fail – or seem to the world to have failed.'[45] He believed that the private lives of men and women should not become the subject of public scrutiny.

Wilde once described himself as 'a most recalcitrant patriot' in a letter in which he avowed his Home Rule sympathies.[46] He objected to any suggestion of Irish inferiority and he ascribed such an opinion to 'the insolence with which the English have always treated us' and to the fact that 'the Irish among the English-language races was the Celtic race, the race which had not accepted the Reformation'.[47] He shrank from fanatical patriotism, however, which he described privately as the 'most insincere form of self-conceit'.[48] On another occasion he spoke of patriotism as 'a virtue of the vicious'.[48] On the subject of Irish politics, as on other subjects, Wilde managed to adopt a number of positions, often apparently contradictory, as can be seen in the following answer which he gave to a reporter in America when questioned about his politics:

I do not wish to see the empire dismembered, but only to see the Irish people free, and Ireland still as a willing and integral part of the British empire. To dismember a great empire in this age of vast armies and overweening ambition on the part of other nations, is to consign the peoples of the broken country to weak and insignificant places in the panorama of nations; but people must have freedom and autonomy before they are capable of their greatest result in the cause of progress.[49]

The poet Theodore Wratislaw spent a weekend with Wilde in Goring-on-Thames in a house named The Cottage. In a short memoir of the visit, Wratislaw described how he gained an unexpected insight into the political philosophy of the Wilde household. It was a philosophy that did not have Wratislaw's sympathy. He had returned to the house for lunch following a short boat trip on the river Thames with Wilde and his son Cyril, during which Wilde had rowed them both in the sculling-boat:

> During lunch an amusing incident occurred, which I have remembered though I have forgotten so much. It is possible that I overlooked at the moment the Irish ancestry of Oscar and made some slighting remark about Home Rule . . . . The small boy flushed with anger, and violently demanded whether I was not a Home Ruler? I was both astonished and amused and was trying to think of some reply suitable for the juvenile politician when Oscar interposed, throwing peace on troubled waters.
>
> 'Ah!' said he, 'My own idea is that Ireland should rule England.'[50]

In his memoirs, *Return to Yesterday*, the English writer Ford Madox Ford recalled Wilde's frequent visits to his grandfather's home: 'He would sit beside the high fireplace and talk very quietly – mostly about public matters: Home Rule for Ireland and the like. My grandfather was a rather down-to-the-ground sort of person, so that Wilde to him talked very much like anyone else and seemed glad to be in a quiet room beside a fireplace.'[51] However, even in politics the Wilde family's contempt for 'trade' coloured Oscar's views. When Joseph Biggar, a pork-butcher from Belfast, was gaining power and influence within the Irish Parliamentary Party, Wilde was heard to remark: 'I can *never* consent to be led by – a bacon merchant!'[52]

In the mid 1880s Anglo-Irish affairs were going through a very difficult phase. Gladstone began to indicate his support for limited Home Rule for Ireland, and with this purpose in mind he introduced a Home Rule Bill at Westminster in 1886. It was very limited in scope, as the parliament in London would retain control over defence, foreign policy, trade and coinage. Despite its limited nature, the bill raised a storm of vituperation in England. There was a deep-seated belief among many English intellectuals at the time that the Irish or 'Celts', being an emotional and unstable race, were fundamentally unsuited for self-government. In contrast, the Anglo-Saxons, who were at that time managing an empire, were sober and steady and therefore ideal rulers. Gladstone's bill collapsed and he resigned as prime minister. He was replaced by Lord Salisbury at the head of a Tory government that was determined to restore 'law and order' in Ireland. Arthur Balfour was appointed chief secretary for Ireland and he introduced a ruthless policy of coercion.[53] Around this time Balfour met Edward Carson, who was already making an impression as a barrister. Balfour made Carson his crown prosecutor and the latter performed his task with such effectiveness that he became known as 'Coercion Carson'.

One of those who became a victim of the programme of coercion was the English poet Wilfrid Scawen Blunt. Blunt, who was also a wealthy English landlord, had become very involved in the struggle of the Irish Land League on behalf of Irish tenants, and he became a founder member of the British Home Rule Association. He travelled to Ireland on a number of occasions to campaign against evictions and he sent letters to the *Pall Mall Gazette* describing the scenes he witnessed. In 1887 Blunt was arrested for speaking to a meeting at Woodford near Loughrea, County Galway, which had been banned by the authorities. He was sentenced to two months' imprisonment by a magistrates court, but he appealed to Portumna Quarter Sessions and he was released on bail. The authorities decided to use the Blunt case to show that they were determined to suppress the tenant campaign. A senior legal team was sent to support the prosecution, and it included the new crown prosecutor, Edward Carson. The case lasted five days. The judge dismissed the appeal and confirmed the sentence. Blunt denounced his trial as a travesty of justice and in his book *The Land War in Ireland* he recalled Carson's role:

> The case against me was conducted by Atkinson and Carson, two of the Castle bloodhounds, who for high pay did the evil agrarian work in those days for the Government by hunting down the unfortunate peasantry when, in connexion with the eviction campaigns, they came within reach of the law. It was a gloomy role they played, especially Carson's, and I used to feel almost pity for the man when I saw him, as I several times did, thus engaged in the West of Ireland Courts.[54]

The establishment was jubilant over Blunt's imprisonment. Lord Salisbury wrote to Arthur Balfour telling him of his delight that Blunt had been 'run in'. Salisbury thought it would go down well with the electors: 'The great heart of the people always chuckles when a gentleman gets into the clutches of the law.'[55]

Blunt spent the first weeks of his prison sentence in Galway Gaol, before being transferred to complete the sentence in Kilmainham Gaol in Dublin. Whilst in prison he wrote a number of poems on the fly-leaf of his prayerbook, and it was these poems that formed the basis of a collection which he published under the title *In Vinculis*. The book bore the following dedication: 'To the priests and peasantry of Ireland who for three hundred years have preserved the tradition of a righteous war for faith and freedom.' In the preface Blunt wrote:

> Imprisonment is a reality of discipline most useful to the modern soul, lapped as it is in physical sloth and self-indulgence. Like a sickness or a spiritual retreat it purifies and ennobles; and the soul emerges from it stronger and more self contained.[56]

Many of Blunt's friends and contemporaries felt he had betrayed his side and had given comfort to the enemies of English rule in Ireland. A short time before his imprisonment, Blunt had met Arthur Balfour at the house of a friend and both men had discussed Ireland. Balfour told Blunt that he intended to suppress the Land League movement by subjecting the parliamentary leaders, some of whom were in poor health, to long terms of imprisonment with hard labour. Blunt was shocked by Balfour's cold blooded approach to Irish politics, and the following day the men had a bitter argument as they played tennis. Following his release from prison Blunt published details of this conversation with Balfour, an action that made him even more unpopular with the British establishment. It is against this background that the significance of Oscar Wilde's decision to write an enthusiastic review of *In Vinculis* in the *Pall Mall Gazette* must be assessed. It is a review that did not pull any punches and that certainly did not ingratiate Wilde with Arthur Balfour or with his protégé Edward Carson, both of whom had been determined to make 'an example' of the English poet.

> The opening sonnets, composed in the bleak cell of Galway Gaol, and written down on the fly-leaves of the prisoner's prayer-book, are full of things nobly conceived and nobly uttered, and show that though Mr Balfour may enforce 'plain living' by his prison regulations, he cannot prevent 'high thinking' or in any way limit or constrain the freedom of a man's soul . . . . Literature is not much indebted to Mr Balfour for his sophistical *Defence of Philosophic Doubt*, which is one of the dullest books we know, but it must be admitted that by sending Mr Blunt to gaol he has converted a clever rhymer into an earnest and deep-thinking poet. The narrow confines of a prison cell seem to suit the 'sonnet's scanty plot of ground', and an unjust imprisonment for a noble cause strengthens as well as deepens the nature.[57]

When Wilde was in prison eight years later, he expressed his feelings in a prose elegy rather than in a series of sonnets, but it is significant that he suggested that the work should be entitled *Epistola: In Carcere et Vinculis*. Robert Ross changed the title to *De Profundis*.

Wilde also reviewed a book by the historian J A Froude in the *Pall Mall Gazette* in 1889. Froude was well known for his unionist sympathies. In this review, Wilde removed any lingering doubts the establishment may have had about his political leanings. He described the history of English rule in Ireland as one of the great tragedies of modern Europe, before going on to observe that Froude 'like most penmen' overrated the power of the sword:

> Where England has had to struggle she has been wise. Where physical strength has been on her side, as in Ireland, she has been made unwieldy by that strength. Her own strong hands have blinded her. She has had force, but no direction.
>
> There are some who will welcome with delight the idea of solving the Irish question by doing away with the Irish people. There are others who will remember that Ireland has extended her boundaries, and that we have now to reckon with her not merely in the Old World but in the New.[58]

In a review of a book on Confucius, which was published in *The Speaker* in February 1890, Wilde observed that if the Chinese philosopher were to come back to earth, he 'might have something to say to Mr Balfour about his coercion and active misgovernment in Ireland'.[59] Wilde's contemporaries must have been surprised by such direct and open criticism, as it was often claimed that the playwright was reluctant to face reality or to speak bluntly. His friend Vincent O'Sullivan described this as an Irish characteristic: 'He prefers to teach by apology, by parable. Incidentally, it shows how Irish he was. One of the most charming traits of the Irish . . . is to say unpleasant things as pleasantly as possible . . . .'[60]

Parnell's fall from power in 1890 seemed to bury all Irish hopes of justice from England through constitutional means. Wilde, who thought highly of Parnell, was greatly disillusioned by these developments, and this disillusionment is reflected in his writings. Throughout his career he rarely lost an opportunity to satirise establishment values, but now his criticism became more direct and his comments more incisive. *The Critic As Artist* and *The Picture of Dorian Gray* were both written in this period, and both contain passages which, although they would not have matched the nationalist fury of the young Speranza, would certainly have gained her approval. In *The Critic As Artist* Ernest claimed that the English public was most at ease with mediocrity, and in *The Picture of Dorian Gray* Lord Henry Wotton declared that it was always rash to put forward an idea to a true Englishman. Dorian Gray visited the home of Lady Narborough, where he met her son-in-law Mr Chapman 'a red-cheeked, white-whiskered creature, who, like so many of his class, was under the impression that inordinate joviality can atone for an entire lack of ideas'.[61] Mr Chapman began to discuss the situation in the House of Commons in a loud voice:

> He guffawed at his adversaries. The word *doctrinaire* – word full of terror to the British mind – reappeared from time to time between his explosions. An alliterative prefix served as an ornament of oratory. He hoisted the Union Jack on the pinnacles of Thought. The inherited stupidity of the race – sound English common-sense he jovially termed it – was shown to be the proper bulwark for Society.[61]

Later in the novel, Wilde used a member of the aristocracy, Lord Henry Wotton, to express more blatant anti-establishment and subversive ideas in a passage of quick-moving dialogue:

> 'Beer, the Bible, and the seven deadly virtues have made our England what she is.'
> 'You don't like your own country, then?' she asked.
> 'I live in it.'
> 'That you may censure it the better.'
> 'Would you have me take the verdict of Europe on it?' he inquired.
> 'What do they say of us?'
> 'That Tartuffe has emigrated to England and opened a shop.'
> 'Is that yours, Harry?'
> 'I give it to you.'
> 'I could not use it. It is too true.'
> 'You need not be afraid. Our countrymen never recognise a description.'
> 'They are practical.'
> 'They are more cunning than practical. When they make up their ledger, they balance stupidity by wealth, and vice by hypocrisy.'
> 'Still, we have done great things.'
> 'Great things have been thrust on us, Gladys.'

'We have carried their burden.'
'Only as far as the Stock Exchange.'
She shook her head. 'I believe in the race,' she cried.
'It represents the survival of the pushing.'[62]

The use of an establishment figure to criticise the establishment was a technique familiar to Wilde from his knowledge of Greek literature. Aristophanes used the technique in *The Frogs* to berate Athenian politicians at a time when the city was in danger of defeat, and this underlying seriousness in the famous comedy has been identified as an important factor in its greatness.

The condemnation of *The Picture of Dorian Gray* in the English press was virtually unanimous. Wilde was accused of writing a dangerous and immoral book. The real reason for the onslaught, however, was his exposure of the hypocrisy and double standards of Victorian England. On this occasion his readers had realised that the joker was in earnest.

CHAPTER 14

Beyond pathos

Would you like to know the great drama of my life? It is that I have put my genius into my life — I have put only my talent into my works.[1]

Oscar Wilde

Of what value to the world are the petty details of their weaknesses and failings? We want to know simply what great thoughts a man has added to the world's treasures, what great impulses he gave to the world's progress . . . . Let us gather the eternal treasures, but leave the rest to the waters of oblivion.[2]

Speranza

WILDE PUBLISHED *THE HAPPY PRINCE AND OTHER TALES,* with illustrations by Walter Crane, in 1889. This was followed by six years of phenomenal productivity. Between 1889 and 1891 he published most of his essays and fiction, and the years 1892 to 1895 saw the publication of his great plays. Success followed success, he became one of the most talked about men in London, and hostesses competed to have him at their social functions.

Wilde enjoyed the social recognition and literary acclaim, both of which he had wanted for many years. His sense of achievement, however, was dampened by the growing realisation that he was no longer young. Youth eventually became 'the one thing worth having', and it was a recurrent theme in his writing. According to the wit and poet Oliver St John Gogarty:

This longing for youth, this dislike of old age is pre-eminently an Irish trait. Blind Raftery, the poet, who was born in Mayo but spent his days in Galway town, his face to the wall [i.e. blind], playing his music 'to empty pockets' says, in the last line of his famous poem, 'The County of Mayo', 'Old age would never find me and I'd be young again.' And in the twentieth century, Yeats in his 'Seven Woods' tells how the squirrels rejoiced 'As if they had been hidden in green boughs where old age cannot find them.' The ancient Irish had no Valhalla in the heavens. They had their Land of Youth in their own country, under the earth and under the waves.[3]

Charles Maturin's *Melmoth the Wanderer* and Wilde's *The Picture of Dorian Gray* have both been influenced by the ancient Irish story of Oisín who returned from the Land of Youth, where he had lived for many years without ageing. When he accidentally fell from his horse and touched Irish soil, the enchantment was broken and he suddenly aged. In one of the key passages of *Dorian Gray*, Lord Henry Wotton extols the importance of youth and its transitory nature:

> You have only a few years in which to live really, perfectly and fully. When your youth goes, your beauty will go with it, and then you will suddenly discover that there are no triumphs left for you, or have to content yourself with those mean triumphs that the memory of your past will make more bitter than defeats . . . . The common hill-flowers wither, but they blossom again . . . . But we never get back our youth. The pulse of joy that beats in us at twenty becomes sluggish. Our limbs fail, our senses rot. We degenerate into hideous puppets, haunted by the memory of the passions of which we were too much afraid, and the exquisite temptations that we had not the courage to yield to. Youth! Youth! There is absolutely nothing in this world but youth![4]

Lord Illingworth reminds Gerard in *A Woman of No Importance* that he has youth, 'the most wonderful thing in the world', on his side:

> There is nothing like youth. The middle-aged are mortgaged to Life. The old are in life's lumber-room. But youth is the Lord of Life. Youth has a kingdom waiting for it. Every one is born a king, and most people die in exile, like most kings. To win back

my youth, Gerald, there is nothing I wouldn't do – except take exercise, get up early, or be a useful member of the community.[5]

In *De Profundis* Wilde wrote: 'All homage is delightful to an artist and doubly sweet when youth brings it. Laurel and bay leaf wither when aged hands pluck them. Only youth has a right to crown an artist.'[6] Lord Alfred Douglas epitomised the beauty of youth for Wilde. The playwright's obsession with the young handsome aristocrat, sixteen years his junior, developed to an intensity that was both irrational and ominous. It was ironical that when at last Wilde was beginning to reap the rewards of endeavour, he had also begun to sow the seeds of his own destruction.

In July 1892 Trinity College Dublin was celebrating the tercentenary of its foundation, and the ubiquitous Mahaffy was responsible for organising the elaborate festivities. As former students flocked back to their Alma Mater from all over the world to join the celebrations, Oscar Wilde was travelling in the opposite direction. He was on his way to Bad Homburg in Germany for his first trip abroad with Alfred Douglas. At the time, Wilde was recovering from the banning of *Salomé* in London by the Lord Chamberlain because it depicted biblical characters on stage. *Salomé* was banned by evoking an archaic law which was enacted originally for the purpose of suppressing Catholic mystery plays. When interviewed by the press on the subject, Wilde gave vent to his fury and threatened to become a naturalised French subject, adding: 'I will not consent to call myself a citizen of a country that shows such narrowness in artistic judgement. I am not English. I am Irish which is quite another thing.'[7] George Bernard Shaw was one of the few writers who publicly condemned the banning of *Salomé*. Wilde wrote to Shaw to thank him for his support: 'England is the land of intellectual fogs but you have done much to clear the air. We are both Celtic, and I like to think that we are friends.'[8]

The success of *Lady Windermere's Fan,* which received its first performance on 20 February 1892, must have consoled Wilde to some extent during his difficulties with *Salomé*. When he returned from Bad Homburg with Douglas he began work immediately on *A*

Woman of No Importance. The anti-establishment epigrams of his previous work had been stimulated by the ill-treatment of Charles Stewart Parnell and by the anti–Home Rule bias of many English politicians. After the banning of *Salomé*, Wilde's motivation became more personal. Although *A Woman of No Importance* is not one of his best plays, it contains some of Wilde's most pointed social epigrams, such as 'The English country gentleman galloping after a fox – the unspeakable in full pursuit of the uneatable'.[9] He uses the American, Hester Worsley, to deliver a scathing attack on the English upper classes: 'You love the beauty that you can see and touch and handle, the beauty that you can destroy, and do destroy, but of the unseen beauty of life, of the unseen beauty of a higher life, you know nothing. You have lost life's secret. Oh, your English society seems to me shallow, selfish, foolish.'[9] Leading politicians including Arthur Balfour and Joseph Chamberlain attended the opening night of *A Woman of No Importance*. During the curtain-calls, the actors received enthusiastic applause, but when the author was called there were boos. Richard Ellmann suggests that the audience may have been irritated by Hester's declaration that England 'lies like a leper in purple'.[9] Wilde appears to have realised that he had gone too far, as the line was subsequently removed from the script. However, he returned to the attack in his next play *An Ideal Husband,* which is a satire on political corruption. Here again, Wilde uses epigrams most effectively to castigate the establishment. 'My dear father', Lord Goring remarks, 'Only people who look dull ever get into the House of Commons, and only people who are dull ever succeed there.'[10]

During this period Wilde and Douglas were constantly in each other's company. Douglas knew several male prostitutes and he introduced Oscar to their world. Wilde romanticised this activity by referring to it as 'feasting with panthers', a technique he had used years before at Portora when he knocked down an elderly man and transformed him subsequently into an 'angry giant'. Beautiful imagery or an appropriate phrase could conceal unsavoury realities; but not indefinitely. As rumours spread, Wilde ignored advice to moderate his behaviour. His response was very much like that of Dorian Gray who, on hearing from Basil Hallward that things were being said about him in London, explained: 'I don't wish to know anything about them. I love scandals about other people, but scandals about myself don't interest me. They have not got the charm of novelty.'[11] Wilde continued to live lavishly and to spend recklessly. He excused his extravagance on the basis that 'the virtues of prudence and thrift were not in my own nature or my own race'.[12] However, the expenses generated by the lavish lifestyle demanded by Alfred Douglas eventually created financial difficulties for Wilde, even though he was earning a considerable amount at the time. When Douglas began to indulge in temper tantrums and ugly scenes, Wilde cited his 'own proverbial good nature and Celtic laziness' as reasons why he did not end the relationship.[13]

Wilde allowed himself to be drawn into a feud between Douglas and his father, the Earl of Queensberry. In 1895 he embarked on an injudicious libel action against Queensberry, which collapsed when evidence of Wilde's homosexual activities was produced in court. Edward Carson defended Queensberry, and this may have lulled Wilde into a false sense of security, as Carson had lagged behind him academically when they were both at Trinity College. Wilde is said to have remarked when he heard that he was going to be cross-examined by Carson: 'No doubt he will perform his task with the added bitterness of an old friend.'[14] Carson was born in 1854, the same year as Oscar Wilde, and so when Wilde wrongly gave the court the impression that he was under forty, Carson made an immediate note. Carson always placed great emphasis on the importance of the opening question, and he used Wilde's statement about his age to begin the cross-examination. In this way he was able to undermine the playwright's credibility from the outset: 'You stated that your age was thirty-nine,' he said, 'I think you are over forty.'[15]

Later Carson read from one of Wilde's letters to Lord Alfred Douglas 'Your skin gilt soul walks between passion and poetry'. He then read it a second time, leaving the jury in no doubt as to what he thought of it. 'Is that a beautiful phrase?' he asked Wilde, to which the playwright retorted, 'Not as you read it, Mr Carson. You read it very badly.'[16] Carson found it difficult to control his temper during the verbal confrontation. His biographer A T Q Stewart has pointed out that: 'Some of these cuts were deeper than the audience could divine; old sensitivities were being irritated. The court gradually came to realise the deadly nature of the duel between these two.'[17] Carson had been apprehensive before the trial that he would come off the worse in any verbal exchange with his former classmate and he had hesitated to take the case until he was informed of the strong evidence that had been gathered against Wilde. Yet it was Wilde who eventually lost his confidence under Carson's gruelling cross-examination: 'You sting me and insult me and try to unnerve me, and at times one says things flippantly when one ought to speak more seriously. I admit it.'[18] After Queensbury's acquittal, Carson was congratulated by the judge on his searching cross-examination.[19] However, Carson was not elated after his victory and he felt uneasy about the part he had played in his old classmate's downfall.[20] He believed Wilde had suffered enough and that no further legal action should be taken, but his advice was ignored. In later years Carson denied that he was influenced by any 'Alma Mater sentimentality' for Wilde, but said that he felt sorry for him purely as 'a fellow-creature who had fallen so low. . . .'[21]

Wilde was arrested on 5 April 1895 on a charge of committing indecent acts. At the first trial the jury was unable to agree on a verdict. A fresh trial was ordered and Wilde was granted bail on 7 May. Like Parnell's fall five years earlier, Wilde's fall had been sudden and very public. After the first revelations, his name had been removed from the theatre hoardings in London, where his plays *An Ideal Husband* and *The Importance of Being Earnest* were playing to full houses. Soon the plays themselves would be taken off the stage. Parnell had made a desperate attempt to fight back after his fall, involving himself in a punishing series of engagements that ultimately cost him his life. His friend Michael J Horgan has left a vivid description of Parnell during this traumatic period: 'He looked like a hunted hind; his hair was dishevelled, his beard unkempt, his eyes were wild and restless.'[22] Wilde was literally hunted after his release on bail by a bunch of thugs hired by Queensberry. He found to his distress that no hotel would accept him. In desperation he headed at midnight to the house of his brother, to whom he had not spoken for eighteen months. 'Willie, give me shelter', he pleaded, 'or I shall die in the streets.' Willie said later that Oscar 'fell down on my threshold like a wounded stag'.[23]

Well-meaning friends advised that Oscar should leave the country, but his brother Willie rejected such counsel: 'Oscar will not run away', he said, 'he is an Irish gentleman, and he will stay and face the music.'[24] Between the first and second trial, W B Yeats collected letters of encouragement from many leading Irish literary figures, but Wilde was now in the grip of a system that had little regard for men of letters. He was preparing himself for his last great role in life, that of the outcast. Around this time Wilde read *The Crucifixion of the Outcast*, a short story by W B Yeats, and was very impressed by it. Before long he would transform some of Yeats' imagery of the noble malefactor into reality. It was a situation where life would imitate art. Wilde praised the story when he met Yeats for the last time: 'Your story in the *National Observer*, *The Crucifixion of the Outcast*, is sublime, wonderful, wonderful.'[25] Yeats reflected later 'if he would have chosen those precise compliments, or spoken so extravagantly, but for the turn his thoughts had taken'.[25]

Wilde was convicted at the second trial and sentenced to two years' hard labour on Saturday 25 May 1895. There were cries of 'shame' from the body of the court as the sentence was read out, but these were ignored, as were subsequent pleas for clemency. He served his sentence in conditions of dreadful physical and mental deprivation. At one point he was so weak that he collapsed in the prison chapel, injuring his ear when his head hit the ground, an incident that left him with a chronic ear condition. During his imprisonment his mother's health deteriorated. Disillusioned and in despair, she asked if Oscar could be brought to her so that she could see him before her death, but permission was refused. She died on 4 February 1896, and Constance travelled from the Continent to break the news to Oscar.

After his release from prison in 1897, Wilde spent three and a half years moving about the Continent under the name of Sebastian Melmoth. He explained the name in a letter to a friend:

For the moment I have, to avoid the prying eye and the foolish tongue, taken a curious name – M. Sebastian Melmoth – so, should you care to send me a line ever to tell me of your work, pray address me by my new title. Perhaps it sounds stranger to you than it does even to me. Melmoth is the name of that curious novel of my grand-uncle – Maturin – which thrilled Goethe, and les jeunes romantiques, and to which Balzac wrote a fascinating epilogue years ago. The book is now an extinct volcano, but I come from it like Empedocles, I hope, if the gods prove kind to one who denied them.[26]

It has been suggested that some of the fatality that appeared to motivate Wilde can be traced to the influence that *Melmoth The Wanderer* had on his young mind:

Undoubtedly the strongest imaginative influence on his boyhood was that of Maturin and his haunting novel, and one may suggest that the part of his mind which was always preoccupied with romances and romantic heroes and destinies may well have absorbed the book and the fate of its hero to such an extent that it influenced his life as well as his only novel.[27]

He had written his famous letter, *De Profundis*, to Lord Alfred Douglas while in prison. He wrote only one other great work, 'The Ballad of Reading Gaol', which he composed after his release. Wilde, the storyteller and conversationalist, needed a large and attentive audience before he could produce his best, and this was denied to him during his last years in exile. When he poured out his personal pain and anguish in 'The Ballad of Reading Gaol', he chose a metre that had been used by the Young Ireland poet Denis Florence McCarthy to express the pain and anguish of the Irish nation in 'A New Year's Song'. In his poem, which is six verses in length, McCarthy exhorts Irishmen to be prepared to die for their country should this prove necessary. The following lines are from the penultimate and last verses of 'A New Year's Song':

There's not a man of all our land
Our country now can spare,
The strong man with his sinewy hand,
The weak man with his prayer! . . . .

And wheresoe'er that duty lead,
There, there your post should be;
The coward slave is never freed,
The brave alone are free! . . . .[28]

The link between the two poems can be seen particularly well in one of the best-known stanzas of 'The Ballad of Reading Gaol', and it is also apparent that the two poems share more than the metre:

And all men kill the thing they love,
By all let this be heard,
Some do it with a bitter look,
Some with a flattering word,
The coward does it with a kiss,
The brave man with a sword.[29]

As in his other works, Wilde drew on several sources for his inspiration, either consciously or subconsciously, when writing 'The Ballad of Reading Gaol'. Many of these, such as Coleridge's 'Rhyme of the Ancient Mariner' and A E Housman's 'The Shropshire Lad', have been identified by scholars, but the influence of McCarthy's poem has been missed in the critical literature on the subject.

Denis Florence McCarthy was a friend of Thomas Davis and he wrote for *The Nation* under the pseudonym 'Desmond'. He was the author and editor of a number of volumes of poetry and a 'Life' of Shelley, but he was best known for his translations of the work of the Spanish dramatist Calderon. Speranza admired McCarthy's poetry and said that he wrote patriotic verse 'that clashed like cymbals'.[30] Wilde thought highly of McCarthy's work, but the admiration was mutual, as McCarthy also praised Oscar Wilde in a letter to Sir John Gilbert in 1877 for possessing 'so much amiable enthusiasm about everything that is beautiful and good'.[31] Wilde singled out McCarthy for special praise when he gave his lecture on the Irish poets of '48 in San Francisco in April 1882. He told his audience that Denis F McCarthy was a name 'of which we are all proud' and that his poem 'Pillar Towers of Ireland' was 'a better art article than all the dreary disquisitions of the antiquarians'.[32] McCarthy died in Dublin on Friday, 7 April 1882, just two days after Wilde's lecture in San

Francisco. 'A New Year's Song' was first published in *The Nation* in 1844, but it was also included in the revised edition of *The Spirit of the Nation*, which was published in the following year. It was this edition that had impressed Speranza so deeply when she was a young woman, converting her to the nationalist cause, and it was almost certainly one of the books from which she read to her children at bedtime in Merrion Square.

Propaganda poetry, such as that written by McCarthy and his fellow poets of *The Nation,* rarely achieves immortality. 'The Ballad of Reading Gaol' is also a propaganda poem, in which Wilde sublimates his own pain and suffering into a powerful plea against a cruel prison system and against the death penalty. The poem has been described as one of the few permanently successful propaganda poems in the English language. It is a direct appeal from the heart against man's inhumanity to man. The link between McCarthy's poem 'A New Year's Song' and 'The Ballad of Reading Gaol' suggests that Wilde was associating himself with the poets of '48 when he wrote his most famous poem. When introducing a reading of 'The Ballad of Reading Gaol' on Irish radio in 1992, the poet Seamus Heaney touched on Wilde's marginalised and victimised position in Victorian England as a result of his homosexuality and, to a lesser but significant extent, his Irishness:

> . . . at this distance in that particular light there is indeed a way of seeing Oscar Wilde as another felon of our land, another prisoner in an English jail so that the ballad then becomes the link in a chain including John Mitchell's *Jail Journal* and Brendan Behan's *The Quare Fellow*, prison literature. This poem written by the son of Speranza, . . . may be devoid of Irish nationalist political intent but it is full of subversive anti-Establishment sentiment. It has about it a kind of high banshee lament, the voice of one crying in the wilderness. So in that way it is not just a self elegy, not just a cry of a soul in pain, it is more a universal keen, an outcry not so much against power as against necessity and fate and it is this deep registering of an affront to human spirit which gives the poem its fevered majesty and carries it beyond pathos towards the tragic.[33]

When the second edition of 'The Ballad of Reading Gaol' was being prepared for publication in 1898, Wilde considered asking Michael Davitt, the Irish nationalist and socialist, to write a preface. Davitt, who was elected several times to Westminster, had spent long periods in prison because of his involvement with the Fenians and the Land League, and in 1885 he published *Leaves from a Prison Diary*. Wilde had communicated with him in 1897 about the treatment of prisoners: 'No one knows better than yourself how terrible life in an English prison is and what cruelties result from the stupidity of officialism, and the immobile ignorance of centralisation. You suffered for what was done by someone else. I, in that respect more unfortunate, for a life of senseless pleasure and hard materialism and a mode of existence unworthy of an artist, and still more unworthy of my mother's son.'[34]

Wilde had plans to write further works, but both muse and motivation seemed to have deserted him. In 1897 he wrote: 'I keep on building castles of fairy gold in the air: we Celts always do.'[35] Misunderstandings and errors of judgement kept him apart from his family and he found the enforced separation from his children extremely difficult to bear. Constance, acting on the advice of relatives, had changed the family name to Holland. Depressed and lonely, Wilde renewed his friendship with Alfred Douglas in 1897, and they spent the last three months of the year together in Naples, until financial exigencies forced them apart once again. During a period of despair, Wilde told Vincent O'Sullivan that he had contemplated suicide, but his superstitious nature had inhibited his resolve:

> 'There is here at Naples', he said one evening, 'a garden where those who have determined to kill themselves go. A short time ago, after Bosie had gone away, I was so cast down by the boredom of leaving the villa at Posilipo, and by the annoyance that some absurd friends in England were giving me, that I felt I could bear no more. Really, I came to wish that I was back in my prisoner's cell picking oakum. I thought of suicide . . . . But one night when there were no stars I went down to the garden. As I sat there absolutely alone in the darkness, I heard a rustling

noise, and sighing; and misty cloud-like things came round me. And I realized that they were the little souls of those who had killed themselves in that place, condemned to linger there ever after. They had killed themselves in vain. And when I thought that such would be the fate of my soul too, the temptation to kill myself left me and has not come back.[36]

During this period Wilde's conversation often dwelt on Irish themes. Vincent O'Sullivan recalled 'that he had a fund of stories perhaps gathered from his mother, of the older Irish poets like Mangan'.[37] Wilde may have had a special empathy with Mangan, the most brilliant of *The Nation* poets, whose life was ruined by his addiction to opium. Shortly before he died at the age of forty-six in 1849, Mangan wrote an apologia in which he described his sufferings. 'Often would I wander out into the fields', he wrote, 'And groan to GOD for help. "De Profundis clamo!" was my continual cry.'[38] Mangan is regarded as one of the most tragic figures in Irish literary history and it is not difficult to understand Wilde's interest in him during the troubled closing years of his own life.

Constance Wilde died following a spinal operation in April 1898 and she was buried in Genoa. After her death, Wilde was still not allowed to see his children. He continued to move from place to place on the Continent, constantly dogged by financial insecurity. He was a rather sad and pathetic figure, although at times he appeared to recover his old sparkle in conversation. He still spoke about Catholicism and he visited Rome again, twenty-three years after his first visit. Catholicism, according to his friend William Ward, 'haunted him from early days with a persistent spell'.[39] Chris Healy, a journalist who knew Wilde in Paris, recalled seeing him towards the end of his life: 'The last time I saw Wilde he was kneeling in the Church of Nôtre Dame. The sun streamed through the windows, the organ was pealing a majestic chant, and his head was bowed . . . when I left him he was still kneeling before the altar, his face hidden by his hands.'[40] Three weeks before he died, Wilde discussed religion during an interview with John Clifford Millage, Paris correspondent of the *Daily Chronicle*. He spoke of 'the artistic side of the Church' and 'the fragrance of its teaching' and he announced his intention to be received 'before long'.[41] Wilde had suspected for some time that he did not have long to live. 'If another century began, and I was still alive', he remarked about three months before his death, 'it would really be more than the English could stand.'[42]

Wilde did live to see the new century, but in October 1900 he developed meningitis or a brain abscess following an ear infection.[43] He was received into the Catholic Church on his deathbed at the Hotel d'Alsace in Paris by an Irish priest who was doing parochial work in the city at the time. It was his third baptism. At times during his final days he was drowsy and confused. At one stage he began to talk about the *Munster*, one of the passenger ships which crossed the Irish sea between Hollyhead and Kingstown. It was a journey he would never make again. He died on 30 November 1900 and he was buried three days later in Paris.

Epilogue

In 1954, the centenary of Wilde's birth, Trinity College Dublin held an exhibition of his work in its magnificent library. On 16 October a plaque designed by the actor Micheál Mac Liammóir was unveiled on the wall of the house where Wilde was born, 21 Westland Row. A small group gathered in front of the house for the unveiling ceremony, which was performed by the playwright Lennox Robinson. He spoke about Wilde's parents, his life and his work. He concluded:

> This morning, in London, in Chelsea, a plaque is being unveiled by Sir Compton Mackenzie on a house in which Oscar Wilde and his wife and family lived for many years. And this is very fitting, for all Wilde's brilliant comedies are of the world of fashionable London. And it is fitting that there is a plaque in Paris on the house in which he died, and that there is a noble memorial by Jacob Epstein over his tomb in Père Lachaise. But it is thrice fitting that we here, in Westland Row, standing in front of the modest house in which he was born, should emphatically claim him this morning as a great Irish writer.[1]

Appendix

HEART'S YEARNINGS[1]

Surely to me the world is all too drear,
To shape my sorrow to a tuneful strain,
It is enough for wearied ears to hear
The Passion–Music of a fevered brain,
Or low complainings of a heart's pain.

My saddened soul is out of tune with time,
Nor have I care to set the crooked straight,
Or win green laurels for some pleasant rhyme,
Only tired eyes I sit and wait,
Until the opening of the Future's Mystic Gate.

I am so tired of all the busy throng
That chirp and chatter in the noisy street,
That I would sit alone and sing no song
But listen for the coming of Love's feet.
Love is a pleasant messenger to greet.

O Love come close before the hateful day,
And tarry not until the night is dead,
O Love come quickly, for although one pray,
What has God ever given in thy stead
But dust and ashes for the head?

Strain, strain O longing eyes till Love is near,
O Heart be ready for his entering thee,
O Breaking Heart be free from doubt and fear,
For when Love comes he cometh gloriously,
And entering Love is very fair to see.

Peace, Peace O breaking heart, Love comes apace,
And surely great delight and gladness brings,
Now look at last upon his shining face,
And listen to the flying of his wings
And the sweet voice of Love that sings.

O pale moon shining fair and clear
Between the apple-blossoms white,
That cluster round my window here,
Why does Love tarry in his flight
And not come near for my heart's delight –

I only hear the sighing of the breeze
That makes complaint in a sweet undertune,
I only see the blossom-laden trees
Splintering the arrows of the golden moon,
That turn black night into the burnished noon.

Notes

Introduction (pp1-3)

1. Hyde, H M. 1977. *Oscar Wilde*. Methuen, London, p45.
2. Small, G. 1993. *Oscar Wilde Revalued*. ELT Press, Greensboro, p13.
3. Coakley, D. 1988. *The Irish School of Medicine*. Town House, Dublin. 1992. *Irish Masters of Medicine*. Town House, Dublin.
4. Sherard, R H. 1906. *The Life of Oscar Wilde*. Werner Laurie, New York, p86.
5. *Current Opinion* (New York, 1917). Vol lxiii, 119.

Chapter 1 (pp4-20)

1. Hart-Davis, R (Ed). 1962. *The Letters of Oscar Wilde*. Rupert Hart-Davis Ltd, London, p81.
2. Douglas, A. 1914. *Oscar Wilde and Myself*. John Long, London, p67.
3. Hart-Davis, R. 1962. *De Profundis. The Letters of Oscar Wilde*, p458.
4. Their fourth child, Jane, married Captain Robert McClure. The famous explorer of the north-west passage, Sir Robert John McClure, was the only child of this marriage.
5. Maturin, C R. 1812. *The Milesian Chief*. Colburn, London, vol 1, piv.
6. Jenkins, R G F and Simms, G O. 1985. *Pioneers and Partners: William Maturin and Henry Hogan*. Privately published, Dublin, p80.
7. Maturin died in 1824 at the age of forty-four, leaving Henrietta with four children in rather difficult circumstances. One of these children, Edward, became a professor of Greek in New York and he wrote a number of novels.
8. Maturin, C R. 1820. *Melmoth the Wanderer*. Archibald Constable, iv, p447.
9. *Ibid*, vol I, p30.
10. *Ibid*, vol I, p145.
11. Wilde, O. 1994. *The Picture of Dorian Gray*. Chapter XX. *Complete Works,* Harper Collins, p159.
12. O'Neill, M J. 1955. 'Irish poets of the nineteenth century' in *University Review*, Dublin, 1, 4, 29-33. Also Pepper, R D (Ed). 1972. *Irish Poets of the Nineteenth Century*. San Francisco, p33.
13. Yeats, W B. 1965. *Tribute to Thomas Davis*. Cork University Press, Cork, p17.
14. O'Sullivan, T. 1945. 'The Young Irelanders' in *The Kerryman*, Tralee, County Kerry, p107.
15. O'Reilly, J B. 1898. 'The poetry and song of Ireland' in *The Home University League*. New York, pCXIX.
16. Wilde, Lady. 19 March 1859. Letter to Lotten von Kraemer. National Library of Ireland.
17. Wilde, Lady. 1907. *Poems by Speranza*. Gill, Dublin.
18. De Breffny, B. 1973. 'The paternal ancestry of Oscar Wilde' in *The Irish Ancestor*, v, 96-9.

19. Wilde, W. 1844. *Narrative of A Voyage to Madeira, Teneriffe and Along the Shores of the Mediterranean*. Curry, Dublin, p339.
20. *Ibid*, pp353–4.
21. Wilde, O. 1994. *The Picture of Dorian Gray*. Chapter XI. *Complete Works*, p102.
22. Wilde, W. 1844. *Narrative of A Voyage to Madeira, Teneriffe and Along the Shores of the Mediterranean*. Curry, Dublin, pp252–4.
23. Spilett, G. 1979. 'An interview with Oscar Wilde' from *Gil Blas*, Paris, 22 November.
24. The identity of Henry Wilson's mother is unknown but it has been suggested that she was a well-known society lady named Mrs Crummels. (McAuliffe, Curtin. 1969. 'Henry Wilson' in *Irish Journal of Medical Science*.)
25. Wilde, O. 1994. *The Picture of Dorian Gray*. Chapter VI. *Complete Works*, p63.
26. Wilde, O. 1994. *A Woman of No Importance*. Act II. *Complete Works*, p489.
27. Wilde, O. 1994. *The Picture of Dorian Gray*. Chapter V. *Complete Works*, p61.
28. O'Cathaoir, B. 1990. *John Blake Dillon, Young Irelander*. Irish Academic Press, p125.
29. Froggatt, P. 1965. 'Sir William Wilde and the 1851 census of Ireland' in *Medical History*, 9, 302–27.
30. Wilde, Lady. 1880. *Memoir of Gabriel Beranger*. Bentley, London, p135.
31. The playwright Seán O'Casey attended the hospital as a child in the 1880s and he has recorded vivid recollections of his experiences in his autobiography *I Knock at the Door*. In 1897 St Mark's Hospital amalgamated with the smaller National Eye and Ear Infirmary to form the Royal Victoria Eye and Ear Hospital on Adelaide Road, Dublin. The original building of St Mark's still stands on Lincoln Place and now houses the genetics department of Trinity College Dublin.
32. Henry Wilson studied at the Royal College of Surgeons and Trinity College Dublin. He qualified in 1858, and subsequently studied in London, Heidelberg and Vienna. When he returned to Dublin he set up a practice at 29 Lower Baggot Street, and he joined his father at St Mark's. He was appointed professor of ophthalmics and aural surgery at the Royal College of Surgeons. He was also the first examiner in ophthalmic surgery at Trinity College.
33. Hart-Davis, R. 1962. *The Letters of Oscar Wilde*. Rupert Hart-Davis Ltd, London, p26.

Chapter 2 (pp21–25)
1. Hart-Davis, R. 1962. *The Letters of Oscar Wilde*. Rupert Hart-Davis Ltd, London, p512.
2. Blair, D H. 1939. *In Victorian Days and Other Papers*. Longmans, Green, London, p117.
3. Wilde, W. 1852. *Irish Popular Superstitions*. Facsimile edition. 1972. Irish University Press, p15.
4. Gilbert, R M. 1905. *Life of Sir John T Gilbert*. Longmans & Green, London, p20.
5. *Saunder's News-Letter*, 13 November 1851.
6. Wilde, Lady. Letters. University of Reading, acc 559, no 15.
7. *Ibid*, no 8.
8. The house is now owned by Trinity College Dublin, and the university in collaboration with the Trinity Oscar Wilde Society plans to develop it as a centre to commemorate the achievements of the Wilde family.

9. Wilde, Lady. 1925. *Ancient Legends, Mystic Charms and Superstitions of Ireland*. Chatto and Windus, London, p85.
10. Ferguson, S. 1865. *The Cromlech on Howth*. Day and Son, London, p3.
11. The king was given the name Oscar on the suggestion of Napoleon, another great enthusiast of Celtic mythology at a time when, according to Speranza, Napoleon 'was Ossian mad'. In the years before his rise to fame, Napoleon had courted Desiree Clary, the daughter of a Marseilles banker of Irish descent, but she rejected him and married an army officer named Bernadotte. When Desiree's first son was born, Napoleon suggested the name Oscar. Years later Bernadotte became one of Napoleon's marshals and eventually he was crowned King of Sweden. (Wilde, Lady. 1884. *Driftwood from Scandinavia*, p156.)
12. Sherard, R H. 1937. *Bernard Shaw. Frank Harris and Oscar Wilde*. Werner Laurie, London, p42.
13. Hopkins, R T. 1913. *Oscar Wilde. A Study of the Man and his Work*. Lynwood, London, p28.
14. Wilde, O. 1994. *The Picture of Dorian Gray*. Chapter XVII. *Complete Works*, p140.
15. Kernahan, C. 1917. *In Good Company: Some Personal Recollections*. John Lane, London, p208.

Chapter 3 (pp26–31)
1. Wilde, Lady. Letters. University of Reading, no 16.
2. *Ibid*, no 15.
3. *Ibid*, no 18.
4. *Ibid*, no 19.
5. Gilbert, R M. 1905. *Life of Sir John T Gilbert*. Longmans & Green, London, p40.
6. *Ibid*, p79.
7. *Ibid*, p81.
8. Colles, R. 1911. *In Castle and Court House*. Werner Laurie, London.
9. Edwards, O D. 1959. 'Oscar Wilde and Henry O'Neill' in *The Irish Book Lover*, 1, 1, 11–18.
10. Wilde, Lady. Letters. University of Reading. Acc 559, no 3.
11. *Daily Telegraph*, 4 April 1895.
12. Ferguson, Lady. 1846. *Sir Samuel Ferguson in The Ireland of His Day*. Blackwood, Edinburgh, p258.
13. *Ibid*, p273.
14. Hamilton Letters, National Library of Ireland, Ms 905.

Chapter 4 (pp32–47)
1. Gogarty, O St J. 1985. *Intimations*. Sphere Books, London, p30.
2. Merrion Square was a bastion of Anglo-Irish confidence, and there were few Catholics living on the square. On one occasion when Bernard Shaw wished to attack Oscar Wilde, he condemned what he described as his 'Merrion Square Protestant pretentiousness'.
3. Leinster House now contains the Irish houses of parliament.
4. A member of this family, Frances Pomeroy, Lady Harberton, wrote a controversial book in 1885 entitled *Reasons for Reform in Dress*. She was an active member of the

Rational Dress Society in London. Constance Wilde was also very involved in this society and both women worked closely together.

5. Gerard, F. 1898. *Picturesque Dublin*. Hutchinson, Dublin, p237.

6. *Ibid*, p243.

7. Gamble, J. 1811. *Sketches of History, Politics and Manners, taken in Dublin and the North of Ireland, in the Autumn of 1810*. London, pp26-7.

8. There is an oval plaque sculpted by Michael Biggs in Portland stone on the front of the house, which reads: 'Sir William Robert Wills Wilde, 1815-1876. Aural and ophthalmic surgeon; archaeologist; ethnologist; antiquarian; biographer; statistician; naturalist; topographer; historian; folklorist; lived in this house from 1855-1876.' It was unveiled by John Paul Lanigan, president of the Royal College of Surgeons, in 1971. The famous parliamentarian Henry Grattan would have visited 1 Merrion Square on several occasions in the eighteenth century, as the house was owned by one of his lifelong friends, Robert Day.

9. Warburton, J, Whitelaw, J, Walsh, R. 1818. *History of the City of Dublin*. Cadel and Davies, London, 1, p463.

10. Wilde, O. *The Importance of Being Earnest*. Act I. *Complete Works*, p368.

11. Shaw, G B. 1908. Letter to Frank Harris. Quoted in Ellmann's biography of Oscar Wilde, p274.

12. Ferguson, Lady. 1846. *Sir Samuel Ferguson in The Ireland of His Day*. Blackwood, Edinburgh, vol I, 268-69.

13. Gogarty, O St John. 1985. *Intimations*. Sphere Books, London, p31.

14. Webb, D A (Ed). 1951. *Of One Company*. Icarus, Dublin, p98.

15. Ferguson, Lady. 1846. *Sir Samuel Ferguson in The Ireland of His Day*. Blackwood, Edinburgh, vol I, 270.

16. Yeats, W B. 1955. *Autobiographies*. Macmillan, London, p135.

17. Speranza was also wont to compare the Irish to the Greeks: 'The Celts, on the contrary, with their Greek nature, love glory, and beauty, and distinction, everything that is free and splendid, but they hate toil and despise trade. They were made for warriors and orators, for a life of excitement and daring, lit by swift impulses, fast and fiery as electric flashes. They will do anything for love or fame.' (Wyndham, H, p221)

18. Yeats, W B. 1955. *Autobiographies*. Macmillan, London, p289.

19. Stanford, W B. 1984. *Ireland and the Classical Tradition*. Irish Academic Press, Dublin, p219.

20. Bystrom, Thorwaldsen and Hogan were all outstanding sculptors who spent a considerable period of their lives working in Rome before returning to their native countries. Bystrom designed a remarkable home in a Pompeian style, with marble steps, a sculptured frieze supported by pillars, and floors covered by mosaic.
During this visit to Scandinavia, Wilde received a degree, *honoris causa*, from Upsala University. Before he left the city his friend Baron de Kroemer, viceroy of Upsala, graciously presented him, as a memorial of the visit, with a drinking horn, mounted to simulate a raven, the claws, wings and head being of silver and bearing the inscription in Swedish: 'A healthful drink to him who has given so many a healing one.' The viceroy's daughter, Lotten de Kroemer, was a leading figure in Swedish literature, and like Speranza she ran a very influential salon. She was also greatly admired by Speranza for her advocacy of women's issues. (Wilde, Lady. 1884. *Driftwood from Scandinavia.*)

21. Wilde, Lady. 1884. *Driftwood from Scandinavia*. Bentley, London, p166.

22. *Driftwood from Scandinavia* was not published until 1884, and this was also the year that Oscar began work on his house in Tite Street.
23. Murphy, W M. 1978. 'Prodigal Father' in *The Life of John Butler Yeats*. Cornell University Press, Ithaca, p31.
24. Cameron, C A. 1913. *Reminiscences of Sir Charles A Cameron*. Hodges Figgis, Dublin, p48.
25. Lotten Von Kraemer, quoted by Richard Ellmann in *Oscar Wilde*, p17.
26. Anon. 1880. *Oscar Wilde, The Biograph*, IV, 130–35.
27. Atkinson, G T. 1929. 'Oscar Wilde at Oxford' in *The Cornhill Magazine*, lxvi, 559–64.
28. Glover, J. 1911. *Jimmy Glover His Book*. Methuen, London, p17.
29. Pearson, H. 1946. *The Life of Oscar Wilde*. Methuen, London, p17.
30. Sherard, R H. 1906. *The Life of Oscar Wilde*. Werner Laurie, New York, p89.
31. O'Neill, M J. 1955. 'Irish poets of the nineteenth century' in *University Review*, Dublin, 1, 4, 29–33.
32. See Catalogue of the Library of the Late T H Porter and of the Late Sir William Wilde. 1879. Trinity College Dublin. Over three hundred books are listed. It is of interest that William Wilde was adding to the collection right up to his death. One of his last acquisitions was Palliser's *China Collector's Guide* (1874), which he acquired around the time Oscar began to take an interest in blue china at Oxford.
33. Clarke, A. 1969. *The Celtic Twilight and the Nineties*. Dolmen Press, Dublin, p29.
34. Sherard, R H. 1906. *The Life of Oscar Wilde*. Werner Laurie, New York, p91.
35. Allingham, W. 1985. *William Allingham, A Diary, 1824-1889*. Penguin Books, Middlesex, p115.
36. Somerville, E, Ross, M. 1932. *An Incorruptible Irishman*. Nicholson and Watson, London, p220.
37. Lochart, J G. 1837. *Life of Sir Walter Scott*. Robert Cadell, Edinburgh, vi, p57.
38. Fallon, M. 1979. *Sketches of Erinensis*. Skilton and Shaw, London, p65.
39. Wilde, O. 1994. *The Picture of Dorian Gray*. Chapter XI. *Complete Works*, p99.
40. Wilde, O. 1994. *The Critic As Artist. Complete Works*, p1147.
41. Stokes, W. 1898. *William Stokes. His Life and Work*. Fisher Unwin, London, p84.
42. Mahaffy, J P. 1887. *The Principles of the Art of Conversation*. Macmillan, London, p78.
43. Mahaffy, J P. 1878. 'Dr William Stokes of Dublin' in *Macmillan's Magazine*, 37, 299–303.
44. Wilde, O. 1994. *The Decay of Lying. Complete Works*, p1073.
45. Wilde, O. 1994. *The Critic As Artist. Complete Works*, p1130.
46. Wilde, O. 1994. *The Picture of Dorian Gray. Complete Works*, p81.
47. Wilde, O. 1994. *The Picture of Dorian Gray*. Chapter I. *Complete Works*, p21.
48. O'Sullivan, V. 1938. *Aspects of Wilde*. Constable, London, p150.
49. Doyle, Sir A C. 1924. *Memories and Adventures*. Hodder and Stoughton, London, p80.
50. Wilde, O. 1994. *The Importance of Being Earnest*. Act I. *Complete Works*, p357.
51. Wilde, O. *Saturday Review*, 17 November 1894.
52. Wilde, O. 1994. *The Decay of Lying. Complete Works*, p1081.
53. Wilde, O. 1994. *The Critic As Artist. Complete Works*, p1114.
54. Sullivan, T D. 1876. *A Guide to Dublin*. A M Sullivan, Dublin, p82.

Chapter 5 (pp48–75)

1. Wilde, Lady. 1893. *Social Studies*. Ward and Downey, London, p74.
2. Wilde, O. 1994. *The Importance of Being Earnest*. Act I. *Complete Works*, p371.
3. No 1 Merrion Square has a Joycean connection, as Joyce waited outside the house for Nora Barnacle on the evening of 14 June 1904. It was their first date, and Nora did not turn up: 'I may be blind', he wrote to her that evening. 'I looked for a long time at a head of reddish-brown hair and decided it was not yours. I went home quite dejected.'
4. Wyndham, H. 1951. *Speranza. A Biography of Lady Wilde*. Boardman, London, p68.
5. Wilde, Lady. 1893. *Social Studies*. Ward and Downey, London, p70.
6. Wilde, O. 1994. *The Picture of Dorian Gray*. Chapter III. *Complete Works*, p43.
7. Croft-Cooke, R. 1972. *The Unrecorded Life of Oscar Wilde*. W H Allen, London, p105.
8. Wilde, Lady. 1893. *Social Studies*. Ward and Downey, London, pp111–18.
9. Gilbert, R M. 1905. *Life of Sir John T Gilbert*. Longmans & Green, London, p78.
10. The petition was sent to the provost of the university when the college was celebrating its tercentenary. It is now in the library of Trinity College. Constance Wilde was the second to sign the petition. Oscar Wilde was a supporter of the educational rights of women and when a woman won the Literature Scholarship at the Royal University of Ireland in 1888 he applauded the achievement in *The Woman's World* (vol 1, p85), observing that it 'shows how worthy women are of that higher culture and education which has been so tardily and, in some instances, so grudgingly granted to them'.
11. Wilde, Lady. 1893. *Social Studies*. Ward and Downey, London, pp18–19.
12. Wilde, Lady. 1891. *Notes on Men, Women and Books*. Ward and Downey, London, p112.
13. Olivecrona, R. 1863. Personal communication translated by W W Nelson in *Tidskrift for hemmet, tillegnad den svenska gvinnan*.
14. Wilson, T G. 1942. *Victorian Doctor*. Methuen, London, p307.
15. Mikhail, E H. 1979. *Oscar Wilde. Interviews and Recollections*. Macmillan, London, vol I, 167.
16. Cooper-Prichard, A H. 1931. *Conversation with Oscar Wilde*. Philip Allan, London, p7.
17. Wilde, O. 1994. *Lady Windermere's Fan*, Act IV. *Complete Works*, p460.
18. Registration of Deaths, Somerset House, London. (Personal communication from Merlin Holland.) Speranza died in February 1896 and in the register of deaths it was stated that she was seventy-six years old. This would mean that she was born in 1820 or early 1821. When she applied for a grant from the literary fund in 1888, she gave her date of birth as 27 December 1821. Oscar Wilde appeared to have had no idea of his mother's exact age. During his public bankruptcy examination on 12 November 1895, he was asked his mother's age and he replied, 'My mother's age is about 65 I should think.' She was in fact around seventy-five at the time. Manuscript B9/429, Public Record Office, London.
19. Wilde, O. 1994. *The Importance of Being Earnest*. Act III. *Complete Works*, p441.
20. Wilde, O. 1994. *A Woman of No Importance*. Act IV. *Complete Works*, p475.
21. Wilde, Lady. 1891. *Men, Women and Books*. Ward Downey, London, p144.
22. Gilbert, R M. 1905. *Life of Sir John T Gilbert*. Longmans & Green, London, p253.
23. Hamilton, C J. 1909. *Notable Irishwomen*. Sealy Bryers and Walker, Dublin, p187.

24. Wilde, O. 1994. *The Picture of Dorian Gray.* Chapter I. *Complete Works*, p22.
25. Wyndham, H. 1951. *Speranza. A Biography of Lady Wilde.* Boardman, London, p76.
26. Cooper-Prichard, A H. 1931. *Conversation with Oscar Wilde.* Philip Allan, London, p13.
27. Wyndham, H. 1951. *Speranza. A Biography of Lady Wilde.* Boardman, London, p70.
28. Wilde, O. 1994. *The Importance of Being Earnest.* Act IV. *Complete Works*, p412.
29. Wilde, O. 1994. *The Picture of Dorian Gray.* Chapter XI. *Complete Works*, p107.
30. Hart-Davis, R. 1962. *De Profundis. The Letters of Oscar Wilde*, p485.
31. Saltus, E. 1917. *Oscar Wilde. An Idler's Impression.* Brothers of the Book, Chicago, p15.
32. Ingleby, L C. 1912. *Oscar Wilde. Some Reminiscences.* Werner Laurie, London, p17.
33. Blair, D O H. 1938. 'Oscar Wilde as I knew him' in *Dublin Review,* cciii, 90-105. Reprinted in *In Victorian Days and Other Papers* (1939), Longmans Green, London, pp114-42.
34. Cooper-Prichard, A H. 1931. *Conversation with Oscar Wilde.* Philip Allan, London, p3.
35. Wilde, Lady. 1893. *Social Studies.* Ward and Downey, London, p45.
36. *Ibid*, pp46-7.
37. Ellmann, R. 1970. *The Artist as Critic: Critical Writings of Oscar Wilde.* Allen, London, p230.
38. Wilde, Lady. 1893. *Social Studies.* Ward and Downey, London, p47. Mr Charles Haughey as minister for finance introduced tax exemptions for artists and writers in Ireland in 1969. (Exemption of central earnings of writers, composers and artists, Section II, The Finance Act, 1969.)
39. Sherard, R H. 1906. *The Life of Oscar Wilde.* Werner Laurie, New York, p31.
40. Spencer, W T. 1923. *Forty Years in My Bookshop.* Constable, London, pp247-9.
41. Wilde, O. 1994. *Phrases and Philosophies for the Use of the Young. Complete Works*, p1245.
42. Gallienne, R L E. 1926. *The Romantic '90s.* Putnam, London, pp181-200.
43. Wilde, O. 1994. *The Importance of Being Earnest,* Act 1. *Complete Works*, p374.
44. Hamilton C J. 1909. *Notable Irishwomen.* Sealy Bryers and Walker, Dublin, p189.
45. Wilde, O. 1994. *The Picture of Dorian Gray. Complete Works*, p45.
46. Wilde, Lady, 1891. *Notes on Men, Women and Books.* Ward and Downey, London, p196.
47. O'Sullivan, T. 1945. 'The Young Irelanders' in *The Kerryman,* Tralee, p122.
48. Corkran, H. 1902. *Celebrities and I.* Hutchinson, London, p141.
49. Wilde, Lady. Letters. University of Reading, acc 559, no 2.
50. Yeats, W B. 1934. *Letters to the New Island.* Harvard University Press, Massachusetts, p77.
51. Ingleby, L C. 1912. *Oscar Wilde. Some Reminiscences.* Werner Laurie, London, p152.

Chapter 6 (pp76-85)

1. Redman, A. 1952. *The Wit and Humour of Oscar Wilde.* Dover Publications, New York, p159.
2. Wakeman, W F. 1870. *Lough Erne.* Mullany, Dublin, pp29-52.
3. Steele, W. 1861. *Examination held at The Royal School Portora.* McGlashan, Dublin, p11.

4. Purser, L C. 1932. Letter to A J A Symons. William Andrews Clark Library, University of California.
5. Nobody has been able to identify which of the lake's islands was named 'Grey Crow'.
6. Darlington, J. 1933. *The Dilemma of John Haughton Steele*. Burns Oates and Washbourne Ltd, Dublin, ppVII-VIII. John Sullivan was the son of Sir Edward Sullivan, lord chancellor of Ireland. After Portora he studied at Trinity College, and like Oscar Wilde he travelled in Greece with John Pentland Mahaffy. He gave up a career at the bar to join the Jesuit Order in 1900. He worked for most of his life at Clongowes Wood College, County Kildare. Portora and Clongowes are now 'twinned' schools, and amongst other joint activities, the two schools organise an annual literary competition called the Beckett/Joyce Award, named after famous respective former students. John Sullivan was a brother of Oscar Wilde's schoolfriend, Edward Sullivan, who became a leading authority on The Book of Kells.
7. Broad, L. 1954. *The Friendships and Follies of Oscar Wilde*. Hutchinson, London, p29.
8. Steele, W. 1891. *Portora Royal School*. Hely, Dublin, p10.
9. *Ibid*, p11.
10. *Ibid*, p12.
11. Hart-Davis, R. 1962. *The Letters of Oscar Wilde*. Rupert Hart-Davis, London, p3.
12. Harris, F. 1918. *Oscar Wilde*. Privately published, New York, vol i, p26.
13. *Ibid*, p25.
14. Wilde, Lady. 1850. Letters. University of Reading.
15. Steele, W. 1891. *Portora Royal School*. Hely, Dublin, p13.
16. Sherard, G F. 1906. *The Life of Oscar Wilde*. Werner Laurie, New York, p112.
17. O'Sullivan, V. 1938. *Aspects of Wilde*. Constable, London, p143.
18. Hart-Davis, R. 1962. *De Profundis. The Letters of Oscar Wilde*, p451.
19. Steele, W. 1891. *Portora Royal School*. Hely, Dublin, p14.

Chapter 7 (pp86-92)

1. Wilde, O. 1994. *A Woman of No Importance*. Act I. *Complete Works*, p477.
2. Wilde, O. 1994. *The Picture of Dorian Gray*. Chapter V. *Complete Works*, p59.
3. He was decorated with the Swedish Royal Order of the North Star by Carl Johann XV, son of King Oscar. It bore the appropriate motto 'Nescit Occasium' ('It knows no setting'). (Lady Wilde, *Driftwood from Scandinavia*, p157.)
4. Wilde, Lady. 1864. *Poems*. Duffy Dublin.
5. Wilde, W R W. 1864. *Ireland, Past and Present; The Land and the People*. McGlashan and Gill, Dublin, p50.
6. *Morning Post*, 16 December 1864.
7. There was a certain irony in Isaac Butt acting on behalf of Miss Travers as he was a noted philander. John Butler Yeats implied in one of his letters to his son William that Butt had been involved in a liaison with Jane Elgee before her marriage to William Wilde. Butt was leader of the Irish Parliamentary Party at Westminister before Parnell.
8. Wyndham, H. 1951. *Speranza. A Biography of Lady Wilde*. Boardman, London, p92.
9. 'Report of the evidence of Miss Mary Travers, given on the trial of the action brought by her against Sir William and Lady Wilde' in *Saunder's News-Letter*, 14 and 15 December 1864, p34. Trinity College Dublin.

Chapter 8 (pp93–105)

1. Hart-Davis, R. 1962. *The Letters of Oscar Wilde*. Rupert Hart-Davis Ltd, London, p25.
2. *Ibid*, p751.
3. National Library of Ireland, Ms 15281.
4. Robertson, N. 1960. *Crowned Harp*. Allen Figgis, Dublin, p73.
5. Hart-Davis, R. 1962. *The Letters of Oscar Wilde*, p433.
6. Wilde, Lady. 1880. *Memoir of Gabriel Beranger*. Bentley, London, p141.
7. Wilde, W. 1867. *Lough Corrib, Its Shores and Islands with Notices of Lough Mask*. McGlashan & Gill, Dublin, p1.
8. Gilbert, R M. 1905. *Life of Sir John T Gilbert*. Longmans & Green, London, p71.
9. Hart-Davis. 1989. *Selected Letters of Oscar Wilde*. Oxford University Press, Oxford, p258.
10. Wilde, O. 1906. *Impressions of America*. (Ed) S Mason. Keystone Press, Sunderland, p30. The story relates to a notorious *Irish* absentee landlord, the Marquess of Clanricarde, who had an estate of 56,000 acres in County Galway.
11. Wilde, O. 1879. Letter to A H Sayce, 28 May (Bodleian Library, Oxford), quoted in Ellmann's *Oscar Wilde*, p101.
12. Wilde, W. 1867. *Lough Corrib, Its Shores and Islands with Notices of Lough Mask*. McGlashan & Gill, Dublin, p257.
13. White, T de V. 1967. *The Parents of Oscar Wilde*. Hodder & Stoughton, London, p220.
14. Frewin, L. 1987. *The Importance of Being Oscar*. W H Allen, London, pp118–19.
15. Griffin, Gerald. 1938. *Oscar Wilde, The Wilde Geese: Pen Portraits of Famous Irish Exiles*. Jarrolds, London, p23.
16. *The Irish Monthly*, vi, 65, 610.
17. Ingleby, L C. 1912. *Oscar Wilde. Some Reminiscences*. Werner Laurie, London, p160.
18. O'Sullivan, V. 1938. *Aspects of Wilde*, Constable, London, p32.
19. Pater, W H. 1891. 'A Novel by Mr. Oscar Wilde' (review) in *The Bookman*, 1, 59–61.
20. Ingleby, L C. 1912. *Oscar Wilde. Some Reminiscences*. Werner Laurie, London, p56.
21. Shaw, G B. 1928. 'Memories of Oscar Wilde' in *Oscar Wilde* by F Harris. Privately published, New York, vol II, p12.
22. Mikhail, E H. 1979. *Oscar Wilde. Interviews and Recollections*. Macmillan, London, vol I, p165.
23. Upchurch, D A. 1992. *Wilde's Use of Irish Celtic Elements in 'The Picture of Dorian Gray'*. Peter Lang, New York.
24. Holland, V. 1987. *Son of Oscar Wilde*. Oxford University Press, London, 54.
25. Wilde, Lady. 1925. *Ancient Legends, Mystic Charms and Superstitions of Ireland*. Chatto and Windus, London, p20.
26. O'Sullivan, V. 1938. *Aspects of Wilde*. Constable, London, p64.
    When Oscar was staying at the villa at Posillipo in Naples with Lord Alfred Douglas, he was trying to finish 'The Ballad of Reading Gaol'. Their tranquillity was disturbed, however, as the seaside villa was infested by rats. The problem was eventually solved by a number of strategies, but Oscar insisted on giving most of the credit to a 'potent witch' who burned odours and muttered incantations in the house. Douglas also remembered that she told their fortunes and 'Oscar professed to

regard her as a wonderful and powerful sorceress'. (*The Autobiography of Lord Alfred Douglas*, p159.)

27. Hart-Davis, R. 1962. *The Letters of Oscar Wilde*. Rupert Hart-Davis Ltd, London, p349.
28. Yeats, W B. 1934. *Letters to the New Island*. Harvard University Press, Massachusetts, p78.
29. Yeats, W B. 1892. *Fairy and Folk Tales of Ireland*. Scott, London, pxv.
30. O'Sullivan, V. 1938. *Aspects of Wilde*. Constable, London, p35.
31. Hart-Davis, R. 1962. *The Letters of Oscar Wilde*. Rupert Hart-Davis Ltd, London, p389.
32. Wilde, O. 1994. *Lord Arthur Savile's Crime. Complete Works*, p160.
33. Wilde, Lady. 1925. *Ancient Legends, Mystic Charms and Superstitions of Ireland*. Chatto and Windus, London, p135.
34. O'Sullivan, V. 1938. *Aspects of Wilde*. Constable, London, p63.
35. Sherard, R H. 1906. *The Life of Oscar Wilde*. Werner Laurie, New York, p90.
36. Wilde, O. 1994. *Requiescat. Complete Works*, p748.
37. De Vere White, T. 1967. *The Parents of Oscar Wilde*. Hodder and Stoughton, London, p215.
38. Yeats, J B. 1946. *Letters to His Son. W B Yeats and Others*. Faber and Faber, London, p277.

Chapter 9 (pp106–117)
1. Wilde, O. 1994. *The Selfish Giant. Complete Works*, p283.
2. Dickinson, P L. 1929. *The Dublin of Yesterday*. Methuen, London, p1.
3. For a discussion of this subject see *Common Clothes and Clothing* by Anne O'Dowd (National Museum of Ireland, 1990) and 'Gléasadh buachaillí i sciortaí' by S Mac Philib in *The Folklore Journal* (1982), no 4. On the Aran Islands in the west of Ireland, boys wore skirts until the age of twelve to fourteen, well into the twentieth century.
4. Chandler, E and Walsh, P. 1989. *Through The Brass Lidded Eye*. Guinness Museum, Dublin, p8.
5. Kearney, R. 1992. *Master European Paintings*. National Gallery of Ireland, Dublin.
6. Benedetti. 1991. *Caravaggio and his Followers*. National Gallery of Ireland, Dublin, pp58-9.
7. Somerville-Large, P. 1979. *Dublin*. Hamish Hamilton, London, p251.
8. Willis, T. 1845. *Social and Sanitary Conditions of the Working Classes in the City of Dublin*. O'Gorman, Dublin, p43.
9. Somerville-Large, P. 1979. *Dublin*. Hamish Hamilton, London, p197.
10. Wilde, O. 1994. *The Happy Prince. Complete Works*, p272.
11. Wilde, O. 1994. *The Selfish Giant. Complete Works*, p283.
12. Hart-Davis, R. 1962. *De Profundis. The Letters of Oscar Wilde*, p475.
13. Bowen, E. 1943. *Seven Winters*. Longmans Green, London, p29.
14. Wilde, Lady. 1850. 'John Hogan' in *Dublin University Magazine*, xxxv; lvii, 72.
15. Fox, L C P. 1905. 'People I have met' in *Donahoe's Magazine*, LIII, 4, 397.
16. Wilde, O. *The Importance of Being Earnest*, Act II.
17. Wilde, Lady. *Letters*. Reading University, no 2.

18. Wakeman, W F. 1853. *Dublin: What's To Be Seen, And How To See It*. Hodges and Smith, Dublin, pvii.
19. Wilde, O. 20 Jan 1888. '*Pictures in the Fire* by George Dabziel' (review) in *Pall Mall Gazette*.

Chapter 10 (pp135–154)
1. Holland, V. 1987. *Son of Oscar Wilde*. Oxford University Press, Oxford, p26.
2. Wilde, O. 1994. *Phrases and Philosophies. Complete Works*, p1245.
3. Mahaffy, J P. 1871. 'Life in Trinity College, Dublin' in *The Dark Blue*, i, 487–93.
4. Mason, S. 1914. *Bibliography of Oscar Wilde*. Werner Laurie, London, p99.
5. Stanford, W B. 1941. *Classical Scholarship in Trinity College*. Hodges Figgis, Dublin, p236.
6. Wilde, O. Trinity College Notebooks. William Andrews Clark Memorial Library, Los Angeles.
7. Sherard, R H. 1906. *The Life of Oscar Wilde*. Werner Laurie, New York, p96.
8. Harris, F. 1918. *Oscar Wilde*. Privately published, New York, pp37–8.
9. Hinkson, H A. 1892. *Student Life in Trinity College Dublin*. Charles and Son, Dublin, p13.
10 *Ibid*, p26.
11. Wilde wrote this poem in a notebook belonging to his mother which is now in the Henry W and Albert A Berg Collection in New York Public Library.
12. I am grateful to Professor Maurice O'Connell for giving me this family anecdote.
13. Lewis, L and Smith, H J. 1936. *Oscar Wilde Discovers America*. Harcourt, New York, p8.
14. Wilson, T G. 1954. 'Oscar Wilde at Trinity College Dublin' in *The Practitioner*, 173, 473–80.
15. Griffin, Gerald. 1938. *Oscar Wilde, The Wilde Geese: Pen Portraits of Famous Irish Exiles*. Jarrolds, London, p68.
16. Harris, F. 1918. *Oscar Wilde*. Privately published, New York, vol I, p40.
17. Mahaffy, J P. 1859. An address delivered before the Undergraduate Philosophical Society of the University of Dublin. Browne and Nolan, Dublin, p18.
18. O'Connor, U. 1981. *Oliver St John Gogarty*. Granada, London, p18.
19. Stanford, W B & Mc Dowell, R B. 1971. *Mahaffy*. Routledge & Kegan Paul, London, p128.
20. *Ibid*, p28.
21. *Ibid*, p94.
22. Sayce, A H. 1923. *Reminiscences*. Macmillan, London, p128.
23. O'Connor, U. 1981. *Oliver St John Gogarty*. Granada, London, p31.
24. Webb, D A (Ed). 1951. *Of One Company*. Icarus, Dublin, p97.
25. Wilde, O. 1994. *The Importance of Being Earnest*. Act II.*Complete Works*, p375.
26. Gwynn, S. 1929. *Saints and Scholars*. Thornton Butterworth, London, p124.
27. Stanford, W B & Mc Dowell, R B. 1971. *Mahaffy*. Routledge & Kegan Paul, London, p60.
28. Mahaffy, J P. 1887. *The Principles of the Art of Conversation*. Macmillan, London, p1.
29. Stanford, W B & Mc Dowell, R B. 1971. *Mahaffy*. Routledge & Kegan Paul, London, p79.
30. *Ibid*, p75.

31. Hinkson, H A. 1892. *Student Life in Trinity College Dublin*. Charles and Son, Dublin, p39.
32. Stanford, W B. 1941. *Classical Scholarship in Trinity College*. Hodges Figgis, Dublin, p128.
33. Gogarty, O St J. 1985. *Imitations*. Sphere Books, London, p33.
34. Gogarty, O St J. 1983. *It Isn't This Time of Year At All!* Sphere Books, London, p49.
35. Gwynn, S. 1929. *Saints and Scholars*. Thornton Butterworth, London, p142.
36. Harris, F. 1918. *Oscar Wilde*. Privately published, New York, vol 11, p354.
37. Stanford, W B, Mc Dowell, R.B. 1971. *Mahaffy*. Routledge & Kegan Paul, London, p87.
38. Griffin, Gerald. 1938. *Oscar Wilde, The Wilde Geese: Pen Portraits of Famous Irish Exiles*. Jarrolds, London, p68.
39. Purser, L C. 1932. Letter to A J A Symons. William Andrews Clark Library, Los Angeles.
40. Tyrrell, R Y and Sullivan, E. 1906. *Echoes from Kottabos*. Grant Richards, London, p24.
41. Wyndham, H. 1951. *Speranza. A Biography of Lady Wilde*. Boardman, London, p175.
42. Stanford, W B. & Mc Dowell, R B. 1971. *Mahaffy*. Routledge & Kegan Paul, London, p156.
43. McParland, E. 1976. 'Trinity College III' in *Country Life*, 4138, pp9–12.
44. Hunt, J D. 1982. *The Wider Sea. A Life of John Ruskin*. Dent, London, p281.
45. Ruskin, J. 1869. 'The mystery of life and its arts' in *The Afternoon Lectures on Literature and Art*. McGee, Dublin, p98.
46. Philosophical Society 1874. Suggestion Book. Trinity College Dublin.
47. Ellmann, R. 1987. *Oscar Wilde*. Hamish Hamilton, London, p30.
48. Gilbert, R M. 1905. *Life of Sir John T Gilbert*. Longmans & Green, London, p201.
49. Robert Ross found a pawn ticket for the medal among Oscar's belongings after his death in Paris.

Chapter 11 (pp155–167)

1. Stanford, W B & Mc Dowell, R. B. 1971. *Mahaffy*. Routledge & Kegan Paul, London, p39.
2. Blair, D H. 1938. 'Oscar Wilde as I knew him' in *Dublin Review*, CCIII, 90–105. Reprinted in *In Victorian Days and Other Papers*. Longmans, Green, London, pp114–42.
3. Mahaffy, J P. 1874. *Social Life in Greece from Homer to Menander*. Macmillan, London, pVIII.
4. Stanford, W B & Mc Dowell, R. B. 1971. *Mahaffy*. Routledge & Kegan Paul, London, p85.
5. Mahaffy, J P. 1874. *Social Life in Greece from Homer to Menander*. Macmillan, London, p118.
6. *Ibid*, p119.
7. Wilde, O. 1994. *The Picture of Dorian Gray*. Chapter IX. *Complete Works*, p92.
8. Hyde, H M. 1982. *Oscar Wilde*. Methuen, London, p329.
9. Mahaffy, J P. 1874. *Social Life in Greece from Homer to Menander*. Macmillan, London, p305.
10. *Ibid*, p308.

11. *Ibid*, p312.
12. Stanford, W B & Mc Dowell, R B. 1971. *Mahaffy*. Routledge & Kegan Paul, London, p157.
13. *Ibid*, p390.
14. Cartledge, P. 1989. 'The Importance of being Dorian: an onomastic gloss on the Hellenism of Oscar Wilde' in *Hermathena,* cxlvii, 7-15.
15. Smith, P E and Helfand, M S. 1989. *Oscar Wilde's Oxford Notebooks*. Oxford University Press, Oxford. pvii.
16. Hart-Davis, R. 1962. *De Profundis. The Letters of Oscar Wilde*, p478.
17. Blair, D H. 1939. 'Oscar Wilde as I knew him' in *In Victorian Days and Other Papers*. Longmans, Green, London, pp114-42.
18. Schuchard, K. Personal communication. William Wilde was Worshipful Master of the Shakespeare Lodge in Dublin in 1841-2.
19. Hart-Davis, R. 1962. *The Letters of Oscar Wilde*. Rupert Hart-Davis Ltd, London, p11.
20. Wilde, O. 1876. 'Graffiti D'Italia' in *The Month*, ix, 33, 77-78. Reprinted in *Poems 1881* as 'Rome Unvisited'.
21. Wilde, O. 1994. *The Picture of Dorian Gray*. Chapter XI. *Complete Works*, p101.
22. Larcom correspondence. National Library of Ireland.
23. Wilson, T G. 1942. *Victorian Doctor*. Methuen, London, p315.
24. White, T de V. 1967. *The Parents of Oscar Wilde*. Hodder and Stoughton, London, p216.
25. 'Dear Wilde, the deeps close o'er thee; and no more
    Greet we or mingle on the hither shore,
    Where other footsteps now must print the sand,
    And other waiters by the margin stand.
    Gone; and alas! too late it wrings my breast,
    The word unspoken, and the hand unpressed;
    Yet will affection follow, and believe
    The sentient spirit may the thought receive,
    Though neither eye to eye the soul impart,
    Nor answering hand confess the unburthened heart.' [*Lady Ferguson*, ii, 309]
22. Larcom correspondence. National Library of Ireland.
26. Hart-Davis, R. 1962. *De Profundis. The Letters of Oscar Wilde*, p472.
27. Wilde, O. 1994. *The Importance of Being Earnest*. Act I. *Complete Works*, p368.
28. White, T de V. 1967. *The Parents of Oscar Wilde*. Hodder and Stoughton, London, p236.
29. Hart-Davis, R (Ed). 1962. *The Letters of Oscar Wilde*. Rupert Hart-Davis Ltd, London, p15.
30. *Ibid*, p20.
31. The biography is of great importance, as much of the information recorded by Wilde would otherwise have been lost. Beranger was born in Rotterdam in 1729 and came to Dublin in 1750, where he ran a small print shop. His sketches of Irish buildings two hundred years ago are of particular interest, as many of the structures have since disappeared. Wilde's own work in this regard is also worthy of mention. He made great efforts to preserve antiquities around Ireland and he paid particular attention to the monastic ruins at Glendalough. One of the churches there, Trinity Church, actually collapsed and fortunately it was restored from drawings that were

made for Wilde when he was in the area. See *Beranger's Views of Ireland*. (Ed) P Harbison. 1991. Royal Irish Academy, Dublin.

32. Wilde, W R. 1880. *Memoir of Gabriel Beranger*. Gill & Son, Dublin, p131.

33. Hart-Davis, R. 1962. *The Letters of Oscar Wilde*. Rupert Hart-Davis Ltd, London, p21.

34. Harris, F. 1918. *Oscar Wilde*. Privately published, New York, vol 1, p52.

35. Hart-Davis, R. 1962. *The Letters of Oscar Wilde*. Rupert Hart-Davis Ltd, London, p22.

36. *Ibid*, p24.

37. *Ibid*, p24.

38. *Ibid*, p25.

39. *The Month* and *Catholic Review* were published by the Jesuits of Farm Street in London. Wilde sought refuge there when he was released from prison, but he was refused.

Chapter 12 (pp168–179)

1. Hart-Davis, R. 1962. *The Letters of Oscar Wilde*. Rupert Hart-Davis Ltd, London, p34.

2. Hart-Davis, R. 1985. *More Letters of Oscar Wilde*. John Murray, London, p24.

3. Stanford W B & Mc Dowell, R B. 1971. *Mahaffy*. Routledge & Kegan Paul, London, p41.

4. Blair, D H. 1939. 'Oscar Wilde as I knew him' in *In Victorian Days and Other Papers*. Longmans, Green, London, p136.

5. Gogarty, O St J. 1968. *As I was Going Down Sackville Street*. Sphere Books, London, p318.

6. Hart-Davis, R. 1962. *The Letters of Oscar Wilde*. Rupert Hart-Davis Ltd, London, p36.

7. *Ibid*, p37.

8. Hart-Davis, R. 1962. *The Letters of Oscar Wilde*. Rupert Hart-Davis Ltd, London, p39. The Grosvenor Gallery was established by wealthy banker Sir Coutts Lindsay, for the exhibition of contemporary paintings.

9. Wilde published a number of poems in *The Irish Monthly* between 1876 and 1878. The magazine was founded in 1873 by the Jesuit Mathew Russell, and edited by him until his death in 1912.

10. White, T de V. 1967. *The Parents of Oscar Wilde*. Hodder and Stoughton, London, p241.

11. Hart-Davis, R. 1962. *The Letters of Oscar Wilde*. Rupert Hart-Davis Ltd, London, p43.

12. 'St Mark's Ophthalmic Hospital' in *British Medical Journal* (1877), 1, 825.

13. Hart-Davis, R. 1962. *The Letters of Oscar Wilde*. Rupert Hart-Davis Ltd, London, p48.

14. *Ibid*, p47.

15. Benson, E G. 1930. *As We Were: A Victorian Peep Show*. Longmans, London, p246.

16. Edwards, O D. 1959. 'Oscar Wilde and Henry O'Neill' in *Irish Book*, 1, 1, 11–18.

17. Hart-Davis, R. 1962. *The Letters of Oscar Wilde*. Rupert Hart-Davis Ltd, London, p512.

18. Wilde, Lady. Letter. William Andrews Clark Library, Los Angeles.

19. Nelson, W W. 1987. *Oscar Wilde From Ravenna to Salomé*. Dublin University Press, Dublin, p23.
20. Hart-Davis, R. 1962. *The Letters of Oscar Wilde*. Rupert Hart-Davis Ltd, London, p52.
21. *Ibid*, p53.
22. *Ibid*, p54.
23. *Ibid*, p55.
24. Cooper-Prichard, A H. 1931. *Conversation with Oscar Wilde*. Philip Allan, London, p13.
25. Hart-Davis, R. 1989. *Selected Letters of Oscar Wilde*. Oxford University Press, Oxford, p28.
26. Wilde, Lady. National Library of Ireland, Ms 15281.

Chapter 13 (pp180–202)
1. Mikhail, E H. 1979. *Oscar Wilde. Interviews and Recollections*. Macmillan, London, p63.
2. Wilde, O. 1994. *The Picture of Dorian Gray*. Preface. *Complete Works*, p17.
3. Wilde, O. 1887. 'Aristotle at Afternoon Tea' in *Pall Mall Gazette*. 16 December.
4. Stanford, W B and Mc Dowell, R B. 1971. *Mahaffy*. Routledge & Kegan Paul, London, p85.
5. Wilde, O. 1994. *The Decay of Lying. Complete Works*, p1091.
6. Wilde, O. 1994. *The Critic As Artist. Complete Works*, p1154.
7. Berg Collection. New York Public Library, quoted in *Oscar Wilde* by Richard Ellmann, p9.
8. Hart-Davis, R. 1962. *The Letters of Oscar Wilde*. Rupert Hart-Davis Ltd, London, p40.
9. Wilde, Lady. Letters. University of Reading, no 10.
10. Wilde, O. 1994. *Vera*. Act III. *Complete Works*, p714.
11. Wilde, Lady. Letters. William Andrews Clark Libary, University of California, Los Angeles. This letter was probably written in 1876 or 1877.
12. Wyndham, H. 1951. *Speranza*. Boardman, London, p204.
13. *Irish Nation*, New York, 14 January 1882.
14. *The Atlantic Constitution*. 5 July 1882. 'Oscar Wilde - Arrival of the Great Esthete.'
15. Hart-Davis, R. 1985. *More Letters of Oscar Wilde*. John Murray, London, p48.
16. Hart-Davis, R. 1962. *The Letters of Oscar Wilde*. Rupert Hart-Davis Limited, London, p92.
17. Fitz-Simon, C. 1983. *The Irish Theatre*. Thames and Hudson, London, p112.
18. Wilde, O. 1994. *The Critic As Artist. Complete Works*, p1119.
19. Holland, V. 1979. *Oscar Wilde and his World*. Thames & Hudson, London, pp82–4.
20. Kernahan. 1917. *In Good Company; Some Personal Recollections*. John Lane, London, pp189–235.
21. Small, G. 1993. *Oscar Wilde Revalued*. ELT Press, Greensboro, p99.
22. *Dublin Evening Mail*, 23 November 1883, p3.
23. Wilde, Lady. 1883. Letter to Oscar Wilde. William Andrews Clark Library.
24. Ryan, W P. 1894. *The Irish Literary*. Privately published, London, p28.
25. *Ibid*, p119.
26. Hart-Davis, R. 1962. *De Profundis. The Letters of Oscar Wilde*, p477.

27. Anon. 1880. *Oscar Wilde. The Biograph*, iv, 130–35.
28. Hart-Davis, R. 1962. *The Letters of Oscar Wilde*. Rupert Hart-Davies Ltd, London, p112.
29. *Ibid*, p287.
30. O'Sullivan, V. 1938. *Aspects of Wilde*. Constable, London, p80.
31. Kiberd, D. 1980. 'The fall of the stage Irishman' in *The Genres of the Irish Literary Revival*. (Ed) R Schleifer. Wolfhound Press, Dublin, pp39–60.
32. Sherard, R H. 1906. *The Life of Oscar Wilde*. Werner Laurie, London, p447.
33. *Ibid*, p442.
34. Nelson, W W. 1987. *Oscar Wilde From Ravenna to Salomé*. Dublin, p20.
35. *Dublin University Review*, vol I, 1, 15. 1885.
36. Hart-Davis, R. 1962. *The Letters of Oscar Wilde*. Rupert Hart-Davis Ltd, London, p194.
37. Hart-Davis, R. 1962. *The Letters of Oscar Wilde*. Rupert Hart-Davis Ltd, London, p233.
38. Wilde, Oscar (ed). 1887–89. *The Woman's World*. Cassell, London, Feb 1889.
39. Wilde, Oscar (ed). 1887–89. *The Woman's World*. Cassell, London, March 1889.
40. Wilde, O. *Pall Mall Gazette*, 16 December 1887.
41. Wilde, O. *Pall Mall Gazette*, 9 November 1887.
42. Wilde, O. *Pall Mall Gazette*, 17 December 1887.
43. Stokes, W. 1898. *William Stokes, His Life and Work*. Fisher Unwin, London, p85.
44. Hart-Davis, R. 1989. *Selected Letters of Oscar Wilde*. Oxford University Press, Oxford, p111.
45. O'Sullivan, V. 1938. *Aspects of Wilde*. Constable, London, p222.
46. Hart-Davis, R. 1962. *The Letters of Oscar Wilde*. Rupert Hart-Davis Ltd, London, p232.
47. O'Sullivan, V. 1938. *Aspects of Wilde*. Constable, London, p79.
48. Cooper-Prichard, A H. 1931. *Conversation with Oscar Wilde*. Philip Allan, London, p20.
49. Mikhail, E H. 1979. *Oscar Wilde. Interviews and Recollections*. Macmillan, London, vol 1, p92.
50. Wratislaw, T. 1979. *Oscar Wilde: A Memoir*. The Eighteen Nineties Society, London, p13.
51. Ford, M F. 1931. *Return to Yesterday*. Victor Gollancz, London, pp40–45.
52. Dixon, E H. 1930. *As I Knew Them; Sketches of People I Have Met on the Way*. Hutchinson, London, p34.
53. Lyons, F S L. 1985. *Ireland Since the Famine*. Fontana Press, p189.
54. Blunt, W S. 1912. *The Land War in Ireland*. Swift, London, p365.
55. Hyde, H M. 1953. *Carson*. Heinemann, London, p80.
56. Blunt, W S. 1888. *In Vinculis*. Kegan, Paul and Trench, London, pp vii–viii.
57. Wilde, O. 1889. 'Poetry and Prison: Mr Wilfrid Blunt's In Vinculis' in *Pall Mall Gazette*, xlix, 7425, 3 Jan, p3.
58. Wilde, O. 1889. Review of *The Two Chiefs of Dunboyne*. *Pall Mall Gazette* (13 April 1889), xlix, p3.
59. Wilde, O. 1890. Review of *Chuang Tsu*, translated from the Chinese by Herbert A Giles in *The Speaker*, 1; 6, 144–6.
60. *Current Opinion* (New York, 1917). 'The Celtic Quintessence of Oscar Wilde's genius.' Vol lxiii, p119.

61. Wilde, O. 1994. *The Picture of Dorian Gray*. Chapter XV. *Complete Works*, pp128–31.
62. Wilde, O. 1994. *The Picture of Dorian Gray*. Chapter XVII. *Complete Works*, pp140–41.

Chapter 14 (pp203–215)
1. Mason, S. 1905. *Oscar Wilde. A Study*. Holywell Press, Oxford, p49.
2. Hamilton, C J. 1909. *Notable Irishwomen*. Sealy Bryers and Walker, Dublin, p174.
3. Gogarty, O St John. 1983. *It Isn't This Time of Year At All!* Sphere Books, London, p244.
4. Wilde, O. 1994. *The Picture of Dorian Gray*. Chapter 11. *Complete Works*, p31.
5. Wilde, O. 1994. *A Woman of No Importance*. Act III. *Complete Works*, p492.
6. Hart-Davis, R (Ed). 1962. *De Profundis. The Letters of Oscar Wilde*, p459.
7. Ellmann, R. 1987. *Oscar Wilde*. Hamish Hamilton, London, p352.
8. Hart-Davis, R. 1962. *The Letters of Oscar Wilde*. Rupert Hart-Davis Ltd, London, p332.
9. Wilde, O. 1994. *A Woman of No Importance*. Act I. *Complete Works*, p465–83.
10. Wilde, O. 1994. *An Ideal Husband*. Act IV. *Complete Works*, p570.
11. Wilde, O. 1994. *The Picture of Dorian Gray*. Chapter XII. *Complete Works*, p111.
12. Hart-Davis, R. 1962. *De Profundis. The Letters of Oscar Wilde*, p427.
13. *Ibid,* p429.
14. Marjoribanks, E and Colvin, I. 1932-6. *The Life of Lord Carson*. Gollanz, London, p202.
15. Hyde, H M. 1953. *Carson*. Heinemann, London, p134.
16. *Ibid*, p135.
17. Stewart, A T Q. 1981. *Edward Carson*. Gill & Macmillan, Dublin, p49.
18. *Ibid*, p50.
19. The judge, R Henn Collins, was also a graduate of Trinity College Dublin. He later became Lord Collins of Kensington.
20. After the collapse of the first prosecution against Wilde, Carson went to the solicitor-general to plead that he should not be tried again as he had 'suffered a great deal'. The Establishment was relentless, however, and Wilde was placed on trial for a second time. As one of Wilde's biographers, Hesketh Pearson, has pointed out, 'the prosecution had become a persecution'.
21. Griffin, Gerald. 1938. *Oscar Wilde, The Wilde Geese: Pen Portraits of Famous Irish Exiles*. Jarrolds, London, p75.
22. O'Brien, R B. 1898. *The Life of Charles Stewart Parnell*. Smith Elder, London, ii, p298.
23. Sherard, R H. 1906. *The Life of Oscar Wilde*. Werner Laurie, New York, p358.
24. Sherard, R H. 1902. *Oscar Wilde: The Story of an Unhappy Friendship*. Hermes Press, London, p169.
25. Yeats, W B. 1955. *Autobiographies*. Macmillan, London, p287.
26. Hart-Davis, R. 1985. *More Letters of Oscar Wilde*. John Murray, London, p158.
27. Woodcock, G. 1949. *The Paradox of Oscar Wilde*. Boardman, London, p41.
28. Davis, T. 1846. *The Spirit of the Nation*. Duffy, Dublin, p190. The link in metre between the two poems was identified by the Trinity academic A J Levanthal, a friend of Samuel Beckett. See *Thomas Davis and Young Ireland 1945*, edited by M J McManus.
29. Wilde, O. 1994. 'The Ballad of Reading Gaol.' *Complete Works*, pp883–99.

30. Wilde, Lady. 1893. *Social Studies*. Ward and Downey, London.
   Speranza was dismayed when McCarthy began to develop antiquarian interests. When he read a paper entitled 'An essay on the collation of certain ancient Spanish manuscripts', Speranza wrote a poem entitled 'A Remonstrance', which began with the lines:

   > Stand on the heights, O Poet! nor come down
   > Amid the wise old serpents, coiled around
   > The Tree of Knowledge in Academies.

31. Gilbert, R M. 1905. *Life of Sir John T Gilbert*. Longmans & Green, London, p262.
32. O'Neill, M J. 1955. 'Irish poets of the nineteenth century' in *University Review*, Dublin, 1, 4, 29-33.
33. Heaney, S. 1992. Introduction to a reading of 'The Ballad of Reading Gaol'. RTE, Dublin.
34. Hart-Davis, R. 1962. *The Letters of Oscar Wilde*. Rupert Hart-Davis Ltd, London, p586.
35. *Ibid*, p666.
36. O'Sullivan, V. 1938. *Aspects of Wilde*. Constable, London, pp69-70.
37. Anon. 1917. 'The Celtic quintessence of Oscar Wilde's genius' in *Current Opinion* (New York), lxiii, 119.
38. Kilroy, J (Ed). 1968. *The Autobiography of James Clarence Mangan*. Dolmen, Dublin, p23. James Clarence Mangan (1803-49) was one of the more remarkable Irish poets of the nineteenth century. 'Dark Rosaleen' is one of his best known works. His autobiographical fragment was first published in the *Irish Monthly* in 1882. It was subsequently included in the third edition of Mangan's *Poets and Poetry of Munster* (Ed C P Meehan), which was published in 1883.
39. Holland, V. 1987. *Son of Oscar Wilde*. Oxford University Press, Oxford, p252.
40. Healy, C. 1904. *Confessions of a Journalist*. Chatto and Windus, London, p137.
41. Burke, E. 1961. 'Oscar Wilde: the final scene' in *London Magazine*, 1, 2, 37-43.
42. Ellmann, R. 1987. *Oscar Wilde*. Hamish Hamilton, London, p137.
43. Richard Ellmann gave neurosyphilis as the cause of Oscar's death. However, the distinguished medical historian Professor J B Lyons has examined all the available evidence and concluded that there is no convincing evidence that Oscar had tertiary syphilis, and that his death was due to pyogenic meningitis following an infection of the right ear. (Lyons. 1991. *What Did I Die Of?* Lilliput Press, Dublin.)

Epilogue (p216)
1. Robinson, L. 1956. *I Sometimes Think*. Talbot Press, Dublin, p108.

Appendix (p217)
1. From *The Poetry of Oscar Wilde: A Critical Edition*. PhD dissertation by Bobby Fong, University of California, Los Angeles, 1978.

Bibliography

Almy, P W H. 1894. 'New views of Mr Oscar Wilde' in *The Theatre* (London), xxiii, 119-27.

Amor, A C. 1983. *Mrs Oscar Wilde*. Sidgwick and Jackson, London.

Anon. 1880. 'Oscar Wilde' in *The Biograph*, iv, 130-35.

Bailey, K C. 1947. *History of Trinity College*. Hodges Figgis, Dublin.

Beckson, K. 1970. *Oscar Wilde. The Critical Heritage*. Routledge and Kegan Paul, London.

Birnbaum, M. 1914. *Oscar Wilde Fragments & Memories*. Elkin Mathews, London.

Blair, H D. 1938. 'Oscar Wilde as I Knew Him' in *Dublin Review*, cclll, 90-105. Reprinted in *In Victorian Days and Other Papers* (1939). Longmans, Green, London.

Blunt, W S. 1888. *In Vinculis*. Kegan Paul and Trench, London.

1932. *My Diaries*. Martin Secker, London.

Braybrooke, P. 1930. *Oscar Wilde. A Study*. Studies Publications, London.

Broad, L. 1954. *The Friendships and Follies of Oscar Wilde*. Hutchinson, London.

Brooke, S A and Rolleston, T W. 1905. *A Treasury of Irish Poetry*. Smith, Elder and Co, London.

Burke, E. 1961. 'Oscar Wilde: the final scene' in *London Magazine*, 1, 2, 37-43.

Byrne, P. 1953. *The Wildes of Merrion Square*. Staples Press, Dublin.

Cameron, C A. 1913. *Reminiscences of Sir Charles A Cameron*. Hodges Figgis, Dublin.

Cartledge, P. 1989. 'The Importance of Being Dorian: an onomastic gloss on the Hellenism of Oscar Wilde' in *Hermathena*, cxlvii, 7-15.

Catalogue of the Library of the Late Rev T H Porter with addition for account of the Executors of the Late Sir William Wilde. Dublin 1879.

Chamberlain, J E. 1977. *Ripe Was the Drowsy Hour. The Age of Oscar Wilde*. Seabury Press, New York.

Chandler, E and Walsh, P. 1989. *Through The Brass Lidded Eye. Photography in Ireland (1839-1900)*. Guinness Museum, Dublin.

Coleman, J. 1932. 'Bibliography of Lady Wilde' in *Irish Book Lover*, vol 20, no 3, p60.

Comyn, J. 1981. *Irish At Law*. Secker and Warburg, London.

Cooper-Prichard, A H. 1931. *Conversation with Oscar Wilde*. Philip Allan, London.

Corkran, H. 1902. *Celebrities and I*. Hutchinson, London.

Cowell, J. 1980. *Where They Lived in Dublin*. O'Brien Press, Dublin.

Cox, M. 1988. *The Illustrated J S Le Fanu*. Equation, Northampton.

Craig, M. 1980. *Dublin 1660-1860*. Figgis, Dublin.

Croft-Cooke, R. 1972. *The Unrecorded Life of Oscar Wilde*. W H Allen, London.

1974. 'Oscar Wilde discoveries' in *Books and Bookmen*, xix, 40-43.

Curtin, J Mc A. 1969. 'Henry Wilson' in *Irish Journal of Medical Science*, 2, 8, 369-79.

Darlington, J. 1933. *The Dilemna of John Haughton Steele*. Burns Oates and Washbourne Ltd, Dublin.

De Breffny, B. 1972. 'Speranza's ancestry' in *The Irish Ancestor*, iv, 2, 94-103.

1972. 'The paternal ancestry of Oscar Wilde' in *The Irish Ancestor*, v, 2, 96-9.

De Burca, S. 1973. 'The Queen's Royal Theatre 1829-1966' in *Dublin History Record*, 27, 1, 10-26.

Dickinson, P L. 1929. *The Dublin of Yesterday*. Methuen, London.

Douglas, A. 1914. *Oscar Wilde and Myself*. John Long, London.

1940. *Oscar Wilde. A Summing-Up*. Richard Press, London.

1970. *The Autobiography of Lord Alfred Douglas*. Libraries Press, New York.

Doyle, A C. 1924. *Memories and Adventures*. Hodder and Stoughton, London.

Edwards, O W. 1989. *The Fireworks of Oscar Wilde*. Barrie and Jenkins, London.

Ellmann, R. 1987. *Oscar Wilde*. Hamish Hamilton, London.

1988. *Four Dubliners*. Cardinal, London.

Ervine, St John. 1951. *Oscar Wilde: A Present Time Appraisal*. Allen University, London.

Fawkes, R. 1979. *Dion Boucicault*. Quartet Books, London.

Ferguson, Lady. 1846. *Sir Samuel Ferguson in The Ireland of His Day*. Blackwood, Edinburgh.

Fido, M. 1973. *Oscar Wilde*. Hamlyn, London.

Finch, E. 1938. *Wilfrid Scawen Blunt*. Jonathan Cape, London.

Finger, C J. 1923. *The Tragic Story of Oscar Wilde's Life*. Haldeman-Julius, Kansas.

Finneran, R J. 1976. *Anglo-Irish Literature*. The Modern Language Association of America, New York.

Fitz-Simon, C. 1983. *The Irish Theatre*. Thames and Hudson, London.

Ford, F M. 1931. *Return to Yesterday*. Gollancz, London.

Fox, L C P. 1905. 'People I have met' in *Donahoe's Magazine*, 53, 4, 397.

Frewin, L. 1987. The *Importance of Being Oscar*. W H Allen, London.

Froggatt, P. 1977. 'Sir William Wilde' in *Proceedings of the Royal Irish Academy*, 77, 10, 261-78.

Gerard, F. 1898. *Picturesque Dublin*. Hutchinson, Dublin.

Gide, André. 1905. *Oscar Wilde*. (Ed) Stuart Mason. Holywell Press, Oxford.

Gilbert, R M. 1905. *Life of Sir John T Gilbert*. Longmans & Green, London.

Gogarty, O St J. 1968. *As I was Going Down Sackville Street*. Sphere Books, London.

1982. *Tumbling In The Hay*. Sphere Books, London.

1983. *It Isn't This Time of Year At All!* Sphere Books, London.

1985. *Intimations*. Sphere Books, London.

Going, W. 1958. 'Oscar Wilde and Wilfrid Blunt' in *Victorian Magazine*, xii, 27-9.

Goodman, J. 1988. *The Oscar Wilde File*. Allen, London.

Graves, R P. 1889. *Life of Sir William Rowan Hamilton*. Hodges Figgis, Dublin.

Griffin, G. 1938. *Pen Portraits of Famous Irish Exiles*. Jarrolds, London.

Gwynn, S. 1929. *Saints and Scholars*. Thornton Butterworth, London.

1938. *Dublin Old and New*. Browne & Nolan, Dublin.

Hamilton, C J. 1909. *Notable Irishwomen*. Sealy Bryers and Walker, Dublin.

Harris, F. 1918. *Oscar Wilde*, vols I & II. Privately published, New York.

1947. *Frank Harris. His Life and Adventures*. Richard Press, London.

Hart-Davis, R (Ed). 1962. *The Letters of Oscar Wilde*. Rupert Hart-Davis Ltd, London.

1985. *More Letters of Oscar Wilde*. John Murray, London.

1989. *Selected Letters of Oscar Wilde*. Oxford University Press, Oxford.

Hayward, R. 1943. *The Corrib Country*. Tempest, Dublin.

Healy, C. 1904. *Confessions of a Journalist*. Chatto and Windus, London.

Henebry, R. 1909. 'Whitley Stokes' in *The Celtic Review*, vi, 21, 65–84.

Hinkson, H A. 1892. *Student Life in Trinity College Dublin*. Charles and Son, Dublin.

Hogan, R. 1979. *Macmillan Dictionary of Irish Literature*. Macmillan, London.

Holland, V. 1966. *Time Remembered*. Victor Gollanz, London.

1979. *Oscar Wilde and his World*. Thames & Hudson, London.

1987. *Son of Oscar Wilde*. Oxford University Press, Oxford.

Holland, C F. 1991. *Trinity College Dublin and the Idea of A University*. Trinity College Dublin Press, Dublin.

Hone, J (Ed). 1954. *J B Yeats. Letters to his Son*. Faber & Faber, London.

Hopkins, R T. 1913. *Oscar Wilde. A Study of the Man and his Work*. Lynwood, London.

Hunt, J D. 1982. *The Wider Sea. A Life of John Ruskin*. Dent, London.

Hutchinson, H. 1920. *Portraits of the Eighties*. Fisher Unwin, London.

Hyde, H M. 1970. *Their Good Names*. Hamish Hamilton, London.

1982. *Oscar Wilde*. Methuen, London.

Ingleby, L C. 1912. *Oscar Wilde. Some Reminiscences*. Werner Laurie, London.

Jackson, J W (Ed). 1991. 'Aristotle at afternoon tea' in *The Rare Oscar Wilde*. Fourth Estate, London.

Jenkins, R G F and Simms, G O. 1985. *Pioneers and Partners: William Maturin and Henry Hogan*. Privately published, Dublin.

Jullian, P. 1986. *Oscar Wilde*. Paladin, London.

Kavanagh, P. 1946. *The Irish Theatre*. The Kerryman, Tralee.

Kavanagh, R. 1992. 'Sir William Wilde. His contributions to Irish archaeology' in *Roscommon Historical and Archaeological Society Journal*, 4, 1–12.

Kennedy, T. 1980. *Victorian Dublin*. Albertine Kennedy Publishing, Dublin.

Kiberd, D. 1980. 'The fall of the stage Irishman' in *The Genres of the Irish Literary Revival*. (Ed) R Schleifer. Wolfhound Press, Dublin.

Kingsmill, H. 1987. *Frank Harris*. Biographia, London.

Kramer, D. 1973. *Charles Robert Maturin*. Twayne Publishers, New York.

Kronenberger, L. 1976. *Oscar Wilde*. Little Brown, Boston.

Lambert, E. 1967. *Mad with Mad Heart. A Life of the Parents of Oscar Wilde*. Muller, London.

Laver, J. 1954. *Oscar Wilde*. Longmans, London.

Leslie, S. 1962. 'Oscar Wilde and Catholicism' in *The Month*, xxviii, 234–7.

Lewis, L and Smith, H J. 1936. *Oscar Wilde Discovers America*. Harcourt, New York.

Little, F J. 1943/4. 'A glimpse at Victorian Dublin' in *Dublin Historical Record*, vi, 8–24.

Luce, J V. 1992. *Trinity College Dublin. The First 400 Years*. Trinity College Dublin Press, Dublin.

Ludlam, H. 1962. *A Biography of Dracula*. Fireside Press, London.

Lyons, F S L. 1973. *Ireland Since the Famine*. Fontana, London.

Lyons, J B. 1991. *What Did I Die Of?* Lilliput Press, Dublin.

Mac Giolla Phádraig, B. 1966. 'Dublin one hundred years ago' in *Dublin Historical Record*, xxii, 56–71.

MacLiammóir, M. 1968. *An Oscar of No Importance*. Heinemann, London.

MacManus, M J. 1945. *Thomas Davis and Young Ireland*. Stationary Office, Dublin.

Mahaffy, J P. 1859. *An Address Delivered before the Undergraduate Philosophical Society of the*

University of Dublin. Browne and Nolan, Dublin.
1869. 'Trinity College Dublin' in *Macmillan's Magazine*, xx, 463-72.
1871. 'Life in Trinity College Dublin' in *The Dark Blue*, i, 487-93.
1872. *Kant's Critical Philosophy. The Aesthetic and Analytic*. Longmans and Green, London.
1874. *Social Life in Greece from Homer to Menander*. Macmillan, London.
1882. *The Decay of Modern Preaching*. Macmillan, London.
1887. *The Principles of the Art of Conversation*. Macmillan, London.
1900. *Rambles and Studies in Greece*. Coates, Philadelphia.
Marlow, L. 1953. *Seven Friends*. Richards Press, London.
Martin, R B. 1985. *With Friends Possessed, A Life of Edward Fitzgerald*. Faber and Faber, London.
Mason, S. 1905. *Oscar Wilde. A Study*. Holywell Press, Oxford.
Maunsell, W P. 1850. *The Idler In College or The Student's Guide*. McGlashan, Dublin.
McCarthy, D F. 1850. *Ballads, Poems, and Lyrics*. Original and translated. McGlashan, Dublin.
McGrath, F. 1945. *Father John Sullivan*. Longman, London.
Meenan, F O C. 1968. 'The Victorian doctors of Dublin – a social and political portrait' in *Irish Journal of Medical Science*, 1, 7, 311-20.
Melville, J. 1994. *Mother of Oscar*. John Murray, London.
Mikhail, E H. 1979. *Oscar Wilde. Interviews and Recollections*. Macmillan, London.
Miller, R K. 1984. *Oscar Wilde*. Frederick Ungar, New York.
Murphy, W. 1978. *Prodigal Father. The Life of John Butler Yeats*. Cornell, Ithaca and London.
National Gallery of Ireland, 1981. *Illustrated Summary Catalogue of Paintings*. Gill and Macmillan, Dublin.
Nelson, W W. 1987. *Oscar Wilde from Ravenna to Salomé*. Dublin University Press, Dublin.
O'Brien, E. 1984. *A J Levanthal*. The Con Levanthal Scholarship Committee, Dublin.
O'Brien, K. 1982. *Oscar Wilde in Canada*. Personal Library, Toronto.
O'Brien, R B. 1898. *The Life of Charles Stewart Parnell*. Smith Elder, London.
O'Casey, S. 1949. *I knock at the Door*. Macmillan, New York.
O'Connor, U. 1981. *Oliver St John Gogarty*. Granada, London.
O'Shea, J G. 1990. 'Unsullied Wilde' in *Journal of the Royal College of Physicians of London*, 24, 3, 242-3.
O'Sullivan, T. 1945. *The Young Irelanders*. The Kerryman, Tralee.
O'Sullivan, V. 1938. *Aspects of Wilde*. Constable, London.
Packenham, T & V. 1988. *Dublin, A Traveller's Companion*. Constable, London.
Page, N. 1991. *An Oscar Wilde Chronology*. Macmillan, London.
Pater, W. 1891. 'A Novel of Mr Oscar Wilde' in *The Bookman*, London, i, 59-61.
Pearl, C. 1979. *The Three Lives of Gavan Duffy*. New South Wales University Press, Kensington, Australia.
Pearson, H. 1946. *The Life of Oscar Wilde*. Methuen, London.
Pepper, R D (Ed). 1972. *Irish Poets and Poetry of the Nineteenth Century*. (Wilde's lecture in San Francisco.) Book Club of California, San Francisco.
Peter, A. 1925. *Dublin Fragments Social and Historic*. Hodges Figgis & Co, Dublin; John

Murray, London.

Pine, R. 1983. *Oscar Wilde*. Gill & Macmillan, Dublin.

Queensberry, Marquess of. 1949. *Oscar Wilde and the Black Douglas*. Hutchinson, London.

Raby, P. 1988. *Oscar Wilde*. Cambridge University Press, Cambridge.

Ransome, A. 1915. *Oscar Wilde. A Critical Study*. Methuen, London.

Raymond, J P and Ricketts, C. 1932. *Oscar Wilde*. Nonesuch Press, London.

Redman, A. 1952. *The Wit and Humour of Oscar Wilde*. Dover Publications, New York.

Renier, G J. 1938. *Oscar Wilde*. Nelson, London.

Robertson, N. 1960. *Crowned Harp*. Allen Figgis, Dublin.

Robinson, L. 1956. *I Sometimes Think*. Talbot Press, Dublin.

Ruskin, J. 1869. 'The mystery of life and its arts' in *The Afternoon Lectures on Literature and Art*. McGee, Dublin.

Saltus, E. 1917. *Oscar Wilde: An Idler's Impression*. Brothers of the Book, Chicago.

Schwab, M. 1863. *The First Temptation*. Cautley Newby, London.

Shaw, H. 1850. *New City Pictorial Directory*. Henry Shaw, Dublin.

Sheehy, J. 1980. *The Rediscovery of Ireland's Past: the Celtic Revival (1830-1930)*. Thames and Hudson, London.

Sherard, R H. 1902. *Oscar Wilde: The Story of an Unhappy Friendship*. Hermes Press, London.

1906. *The Life of Oscar Wilde*. Werner Laurie, New York.

1915. *The Real Oscar Wilde*. Werner Laurie, New York.

1937. *Bernard Shaw, Frank Harris and Oscar Wilde*. Werner Laurie, London.

Small, G. 1993. *Oscar Wilde Revalued*. ELT Press, Greensboro.

Sommerville-Large, L B. 1964. 'Dublin eye hospitals in the 19th century' in *Dublin Historical Record*, xx, 1, 19-28.

Somerville-Large, P. 1979. *Dublin*. Hamish Hamilton, London.

Spencer, W T. 1923. *Forty Years in My Bookshop*. Constable, London.

Stanford, W B. 1941. *Classical Scholarship in Trinity College*. Hodges Figgis, Dublin.

1980. *Enemies of Poetry*. Routledge and Kegan Paul, London.

1984. *Ireland and the Classical Tradition*. Irish Academic Press, Dublin.

Stanford, W B & McDowell, R B. 1971. *Mahaffy*. Routledge & Kegan Paul, London.

Starkie, W. 1963. *Scholars and Gypsies*. Murray, London.

Stewart, A T Q. 1981. *Edward Carson*. Gill & Macmillan, Dublin.

Sullivan, T D. 1876. *A Guide to Dublin*. A M Sullivan, Dublin.

'The Censure and *Salomé*' in *The Pall Mall Budget* (1892). London, xl, 947.

Travers, M. 1863. *Florence Boyle Price or, A Warning by Speranza*. Privately published, Dublin.

Tremayne, P. 1979. *Irish Masters of Fantasy*. Wolfhound Press, Dublin.

Turpin, J. 1982. *John Hogan*. Irish Academic Press, Dublin.

Tyrrell, R Y and Sullivan, E. 1906. *Echoes from Kottabos*. Grant Richards, London.

Upchurch, D. 1992. 'Wilde's use of Irish Celtic elements' in *The Picture of Dorian Gray*. Peter Lang, New York.

Wakeman, W. 1853. *Dublin: What's To Be Seen, And How To See It*. Hodges and Smith, Grafton Street.

Walsh, C. 1982. *The Homes of Irish Writers*. Anvil Books, Dublin.

Webb, D A (Ed). 1951. *Of One Company*. Icarus, Dublin.

White, Terence de V. 1967. *The Parents of Oscar Wilde*. Hodder and Stoughton, London.

Wilde, Lady. 1850. 'John Hogan: our portrait gallery' in *Dublin University Magazine*, xxxv; lvii, 72.

1862. *Poems*. Duffy, Dublin.

1880. *Memoir of Gabriel Beranger*. Bentley, London.

1884. *Driftwood from Scandinavia*. Bentley, London.

1891. *Notes on Men, Women and Books*. Ward and Downey, London.

1893. *Social Studies*. Ward and Downey, London.

1925. *Ancient Legends, Mystic Charms and Superstitions of Ireland*. Chatto and Windus, London.

Wilde, O. 1909. *A Critic In Pall Mall*. Methuen, London.

1949. *De Profundis. The Complete Text*. (Ed) Vyvyan Holland. Methuen, London.

1979. *Hellenism*. Tragura Press, Edinburgh.

1994. *Complete Works of Oscar Wilde*. Harper Collins, London.

Wilde, O (Ed). 1887-9. *The Woman's World*. Cassell, London.

Wilde, W R. 1844. *Narrative of A Voyage to Madeira, Teneriffe, and Along the Shores of the Mediterranean*. 2nd ed. Curry, Dublin.

1849. *The Beauties of the Boyne*. James McGlashan, Dublin.

1849. *The Closing Years of Dean Swift's Life; with Remarks on Stella*. Hodges and Smith, Dublin.

1857. *A Descriptive Catalogue of The Antiquities in the Museum of the Royal Irish Academy, Dublin*. Gill, Dublin.

1864. *Ireland. Past and Present; The Land and the People*. McGlashan and Gill, Dublin.

1867. *Lough Corrib, Its Shores and Islands with Notices of Lough Mask*. McGlashan & Gill, Dublin.

1880. *Memoir of Gabriel Beranger*. Gill & Son, Dublin.

1979. *Irish Popular Superstitions*. Irish Academic Press, Dublin.

Wills, F. 1898. *W G Wills*. Longmans, London.

Wilson, T G. 1942. *Victorian Doctor*. Methuen, London.

Winwar, F. 1940. *Oscar Wilde and the Yellow 'Nineties*. Harper, London.

Woodcock, G. 1949. *The Paradox of Oscar Wilde*. Boardman, London.

Wratislaw, T. 1979. *Oscar Wilde: A Memoir*. The Eighteen 'Nineties Society, London.

Wyndham, H. 1951. *Speranza. A Biography of Lady Wilde*. Boardman, London.

Yeats, W B. 1891. 'Oscar Wilde's last book' in *United Ireland*. 26 September, p5.

1934. *Letters to the New Island*. Harvard University Press, Massachusetts.

1955. *Autobiographies*. Macmillan, London.

1965. *Tribute to Thomas Davis*. Cork University Press, Cork.

1979. *Fairy and Folk Tales of Ireland*. Picador, London.

Index

Index